ISBN 978-1-331-17157-7
PIBN 10153709

1 MONTH OF
FREE
READING

at

www.ForgottenBooks.com

By purchasing this book you are eligible for one month membership to ForgottenBooks.com, giving you unlimited access to our entire collection of over 700,000 titles via our web site and mobile apps.

To claim your free month visit:
www.forgottenbooks.com/free153709

LITERARY FRIVOLITIES

FANCIES

FOLLIES AND FROLICS

By WILLIAM T. DOBSON

In hoc est hoax
Et quiz et joax
With gravity for graver folks

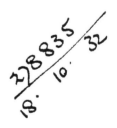

London
CHATTO AND WINDUS, PICCADILLY
1880

NOTE.

WHERE the authorship of any of the extracts given in this book is not acknowledged, it is not without search having been made for their source. The gathering together of the materials incorporated has been the labour of years, and it is hoped that the work may not be without a certain degree of interest as well as amusement.

C O N T E N T S.

	PAGE
INTRODUCTION	9
ALLITERATION	17
LIPOGRAMS	58
BOUTS RIMÉS	69
MACARONICS	87
CHRONOGRAMS	116
ECHO VERSES	122
JESUITICAL VERSES	143
MONOSYLLABIC VERSE	150
NONSENSE VERSE, ETC.	158
CENTONES OR MOSAICS	176
ANAGRAMS	192
THE PALINDROME	215
LITERARY MISFORTUNES	228
FIGURATE OR SHAPED POEMS	258
PROSE POEMS	271
INDEX	285

LITERARY FRIVOLITIES.

INTRODUCTION.

TILITY is not always the chief object of literary labour, neither is "value received" always its aim and end; for in this kind of work, as in some others, difficulty and expected applause are frequently great incentives. With many writers, more particulârly in former times, various curious styles of composition were much in favour — one, for instance, would have a predilection for composing verses with the omission in each stanza of a particular letter; others, again, would write verses in such a way as to enable their compositions to be read from the end to the beginning of the line, or *vice versâ*, as the reader chose; while a third vexed himself in the composition of alliterative, or, perhaps, monosyllabic poetry. Some old writers also amused themselves in devising combinations of

Latin words, which might be changed in their order and recombined, so as to form new sentences. Of one example of this species of literary trifling, a verse in honour of the Virgin Mary, it was asserted by its author that it would admit of twelve hundred changes, without suffering in sense or grammar. The verse was—

"Tot tibi sunt dotes, virgo, quot sidera cœli ;"

which·means—

"Virgin, thy virtues are as numerous as the stars of the heavens."

The wonder is, in regard to these, how their indefatigable concocters found out the number of changes the words would admit; for, as regards another example, its author states that it would take ninety-one years and forty-nine days to perform the changes, at the rate of twelve hundred daily—the total number of which the words are capable amounting to "thirty-nine million nine hundred and sixteen thousand eight hundred!" This wonderful verse is as follows:

"Lex, grex, rex, spes, res, jus, thus, sal, sol bona lux, laus!
Mars, mors, sors, fraus, faex, Styx, nox, crux, pus, mala vis, lis !"

·which may be rendered—

" Law, flocks, kings, hopes, riches, right, incense, salt, sun good
    torch, praise to you !
Mars, death, destiny, fraud, impurity, Styx, night, the cross, bad
    humours and evil power, may you be condemned ! "

Another class of literary triflers may be named
here—those who chose to display a kind of microscopic skill by writing so small that their work
appeared to the naked eye only as a mere wavy
line. Laborious ingenuity of these various kinds,
so far from being discouraged, was rather pleasur-
ably indulged in by some of our ancient writers,
of whom might have been expected other and
better things.

In relation to those who have chosen to exert
themselves in the way of microscopic writing, apart from authorship, as feats of this kind
hold no place in the following parts of this work,
it may not be out of place to say a little here.
The fact, as Pliny relates, that the " Iliad " of
Homer, containing 15,000 verses, had been written
in so small a compass as to be wholly enclosed in
a nutshell, has often been referred to as one of
those things which require to be seen to be
believed; and yet, however doubtful such a feat
may appear, it is certain that one Huet, who at
first thought it impossible, demonstrated by experi-

ment that it could be done. A piece of vellum
10 inches in length and 8 wide would hold 250
lines, each line containing 30 verses, and thus, filling
both sides of the vellum, 15,000, the whole number
of verses in the " Iliad," could be written upon it;
and this piece of vellum, folded compactly, would
go easily into the shell of a walnut. Another
ancient trifler of this kind is said to have written a
distich in golden letters, which he enclosed in the
rind of a grain of corn.

Of these microscopic writers, Peter Bales, an
eminent writing-master of his day, who kept a school
near the Old Bailey during the time of Elizabeth,
may be said to have been *facile princeps.* We are
told in the Harleian MS. 530, of "a rare piece of
work brought to pass" by him, this being the
"whole Bible contained in a large English walnut
no bigger than a hen's egg; the nut holdeth the
book; there are as many leaves in his book as the
great Bible, and he hath written as much in one of
his little leaves as a great leaf of the Bible." This
book, which certainly would be almost unreadable,
and of which the paper or other material on which
it was written must have been very thin, " was seen
by many thousands." Another feat performed by
Peter Bales was the writing of the Lord's Prayer, the

Creed, the Ten Commandments, two short Latin prayers, and his own name, motto, day of month and year of our Lord and reign of Queen Elizabeth, all within the circle of a penny, èncased in a ring of gold, the whole so clearly done as to be perfectly readable. This work he presented to the Queen at Hampton Court, and she very graciously accepted the offering. It is nothing unusual nowadays to find writing of almost if not quite as minute character as this, seeing that the Ten Commandments have been written in a compass small enough to be covered by a fourpenny piece!

An account is preserved in an old "Monthly Magazine" of a beautiful specimen of penmanship executed by a Mr. Beedell of Ottery St. Mary's. This piece of workmanship was surrounded by an elegant border,—itself the labour of six weeks, —containing tastefully arranged within it the following figures:—"Common hare, varying hare of the northern countries of Europe, pine martin, otter, wild cat; harrier (hunting piece); three foreign birds on a tree; a correct representation of Ottery St. Mary's Church, surrounded by a beautiful border; ruins of a castle, encompassed by a very neat and pretty border." At the bottom of all this Mr. Beedell also wrote, as another specimen of minute penmanship, the Lord's Prayer, Belief, and two verses of the third Psalm, in the circumference of a common-sized pea.

There is said to be a portrait of Queen Anne among the treasures of the British Museum on which appear a number of minute lines and scratches, which, when examined through a microscope, are discovered to be the entire contents of a small folio book in the library. A similar effort in the way of microscopic caligraphy was discovered some years ago by a gentleman who had bought at a sale a pen-and-ink portrait of Alexander Pope, surrounded by a design in scroll-work. Examining this through a glass, in order, if possible, to discover the artist's name, he was astonished to find that the fine lines in the surrounding scroll were nothing less that a Life of the poet, so minutely transcribed as only to be legible by the aid of a magnifier. This was believed to be an imitation of a similar effort in the way of portraiture which was at one time in the library of St. John's College at Oxford, where a head of Charles I. was drawn in minute characters, so fine as to resemble the lines of an engraving, but which, when closely examined, was found to be the Book of Psalms, the Creed, and the Lord's Prayer. One other instance of this kind of work has been recorded, that of a portrait of Richelieu, which appears on the title of a French book: the Cardinal's head is surrounded by a glory of forty rays, each ray containing the name of a French Academician. Of one person who was an adept at this kind of writing, the almost incredible feat is recorded of placing the Lord's Prayer, the Creed, seven of the Commandments, the 103d, 133d, and 144th Psalms, with name and date, within the circumference of a sixpence! while another is said to have written the whole Book of Malachi in a pyramid the size of a little finger.

Without here noticing further any of the various kinds of Literary Frivolities contained in the following pages,—and of which, in many cases, the examples have been greatly limited,—we cannot conclude this Introduction without adverting to one which, it is hoped, is quite unique, for nothing approaching it in absurdity or inutility has come under our notice, or that of any one else we trust, as it might fairly be taken as an indication that something was decidedly wrong with the mental condition of the person who could throw away his time and labour upon so frivolous a pursuit: it is given here on the authority of an article which appeared in the "Leisure Hour." The case referred to was that of an unfortunate genius who had discovered that there were 33,535 ways of spelling the word *scissors!* Imagine any sane person sitting down and laboriously following out the idea of writing any word, and this word in particular, 33,535 times! Imagine the frequent revisals necessary to ascertain the certainty of non-repetition—reminding one forcibly of the labours of Sisyphus, always pushing the stone up the hill, and then having immediately to descend and repeat the process when the stone had rolled down again! Yet this was actually done—done in a neat and handsome manuscript volume, containing about three hundred pages of three columns each. The most patient man that ever lived might have been beaten in a trial of this nature—the crank were nothing in comparison!

ALLITERATION.

HE curious phase of Literary Frivolity called Alliteration is the composition of sentences or lines of verse with words beginning with the same letter, and has been considered by some critics a "false ornament in poetry," by others has been looked upon as frivolous, while a third class have sanctioned its use as a worthy and impressive embellishment. It is a somewhat mechanical aid to the rhythm of verse, and in the reciting or reading of a long piece of poetry, the reciter or reader might find his organs of speech aided in some degree by the succession of similar sounds, and this might also have a pleasant cadence to those who listened. However, this could only apply for a short time, as alliteration too long continued would weary and become ridiculous, and suggest that a laborious effort had been made to keep up the alliterative strain, while the pleasure derived would only be as transitory as

B

that derived from witnessing the clever feats of an acrobat, with a corresponding sigh of relief when the performance was over.

> "'Tis not enough no harshness gives offence;
> The words must seem an echo of the sense."

Alliterative writing does not imply, however, that each word or syllable must commence with the same letter, it being sufficient that a repetition of similar or imitative sounds are produced, so as to give a certain degree of harmony and strength; and in the sense of having utility in this way, alliteration has been used by the whole range of poets. In the early ages such a feature in poetry might have been welcome, and in some degree necessary, when, as in Scandinavian, Old German, and Icelandic verse, "the harmony neither depended on the quantity of syllables, like that of the ancient Greeks and Romans, nor on the rhymes at the end, as in modern poetry, but consisted altogether in alliteration, or a certain artful repetition of the sounds in the middle of the verses. This was adjusted according to certain rules of their prosody, one of which was that every distich should contain at least three words beginning with the same letter or sound. Two of these correspondent sounds might be placed either in the first or second line of the distich, and one in the other; but all three were not regularly to be crowded into one line. This will be best understood by the following examples:

'*M*eire og *M*inne
*M*ogu heimdaller.

'*G*ab *G*inunga
Enn *G*ras huerge.'" *

The writers of the early Teutonic and Celtic tongues revelled with great effect in this trick of speech—not only in solemn legal formularies, in spells of horror, as well as in the flights of the poet, but also in ordinary descriptions and in their common proverbs—the Celtic especially readily lending itself to this device of jingling repetition. Several early English poems, written in this kind of alliterative metre, without rhyme, are extant, among which that entitled "Piers Plowman's Visions" (written about 1350) is the one most generally known; but few readers except those whose delight is in musty tomes, and who are deep in the mysteries of black-letter lore, are acquainted with more than the name of that poem.

* "Percy's Reliques."

When our more ancient poetry was, towards the end of last century, drawn forth from the oblivion to which it had been too long consigned, the public was seized with a kind of Gothic fever, and was so delighted with the novelty of the feast, that one and all declared everything was excellent— antiquity became a sufficient passport to praise, and much ingenuity was exercised in discovering fanciful beauties in even the most worthless productions. That excitement soon passed away, but it produced excellent effects; and, freeing the mind from the shackles of a prevalent artificial style, gave a liberty to appreciate and enjoy the truer poetry of nature. But it must be granted that the diction and style of many of our elder poets are so rude as to render the perusal of their works distasteful to modern readers. Few, we believe, except enthusiastic antiquaries, have had the courage to travel through " Piers Plowman," or would think their trouble repaid by the snatches of true poetry interspersed; and yet in this poem, and many others equally rugged, passages of great poetical power and beauty are to be found, which deserve to be rescued from oblivion.

The following lines are quoted by Dr. Percy from a manuscript supposed to be older than

" Piers Plowman," and are descriptive of a vision wherein the poet sees a combat between "our lady Dame Life" and "the ugly fiend Dame Death." The lines portray Dame Life, and are a good example of the old style of alliteration as used in place of modern rhyme :

"Shee was *b*righter of her *b*lee [colour]
　　Then was the *b*right sonn ;
Her *r*udd *r*edder than the *r*ose
　　That on the *r*ise [bough] hangeth ;
*M*eekly smiling with her *m*outh
　　And *m*erry in her lookes ;
Ever *l*aughing for *l*ove
　　As shee *l*ike would.
And as shee came *b*y the *b*ankes
　　The *b*oughes eche one
They *l*owted to that *l*adye
　　And *l*ayd forth their branches ;
*B*lossomes and *b*urgens [buds]
　　*B*reathed full sweete ;
*F*lowers *f*lourished in the *f*rith
　　Where shee *f*orth stepped ;
And the *g*rasse, that was *g*ray,
　　*G*reened belive [instantly]."

An old Scottish poem by Dunbar (1465–1530), " The Twa Maryit Wemen and the Wedo," so indelicate as to place it outside the pale of all

respectable homes, is remarkable for being composed in this alliterative blank verse, a style not
known to have been used in Scotland previously.

About the beginning of the sixteenth century
this kind of versification began to change its form,
and at length the old uncouth verse of the ancient
writers was unfavourably looked upon when lacking the ornament of rhyme. Yet when this latter
began to be superadded, all the niceties of alliteration were retained along with it, and the song of
"Little John Nobody" exhibits the union very
clearly. This old ballad will be found in " Percy's
Reliques," and is a witty satire on the Reformation
under King Edward VI. We give the first and
last verses, it being too long to quote in its
entirety :

"In December, when the dayes draw to be short,
    After November, when the nights wax noysome and
        long;
    As I past by a place privily at a port,
    I saw one sit by himself making a song ;
    His last talk of trifles, who told with his tongue
    That few were fast i' the faith. I freyned that freak
    Whether he wanted wit, or some had done him wrong.
        He said, he was little John Nobody, that durst not
            speake.

Thus in no place, this Nobody, in no time I met,
Where no man, ne nought was, nor nothing did
   appear ;
Through the sound of a synagogue for sorrow I swett,
That Aeolus through the eccho did cause me to hear.
Then I drew me down into a dale, whereas the dumb-
   deer
Did shiver for a shower ; but I shunted from a freyke :
For I would no wight in this world wist who I were,
   But little John Nobody, that dare not once speake."

By degrees the correspondence of final sounds engrossed the whole attention of the poet, and, fully satisfying the reader, the internal embellishment of alliteration was no longer studied exclusively, and has latterly been applied only to light and trivial subjects, to which it seems best adapted. The poet who sets himself sedulously nowadays to resuscitate this almost defunct limb of his art may behold his own probable fate in that of Rogers, a line of one of whose polished verses—

   "So up the tide of time I turn my sail,"

was at once unmercifully rendered by an irreverent critic into—

   "So up the tide of time I turn my tail."

Alliteration does, however, independently of its greater suitability to whatever is light and trivial, when sparingly and discreetly used, add to the beauty of a poetical sentiment, and may also aid the force and piquancy of a witty remark. For the one, take an example from Sydney Smith, who, when contrasting the position of curates and the higher dignitaries of the English Church, spoke of them as "the Right Reverend Dives in the palace, and Lazarus in orders at the gate, doctored by dogs and comforted with crumbs;" for the other, take Pope's line—

"Fields for ever fresh, and groves for ever green."

Thus when an alliterative phrase presents itself with some degree of spontaneity, it adds to the expressiveness of the sentiment, and Pope has acknowledged this in a line which is itself alliterative—

"Apt alliteration's artful aid."

Still, when this "aid" is hunted after and strained for, it is apt to become a deformity.

The best proof of the value in which alliteration was formerly held is found in the fact that it has been used more or less by all the poets, ancient and modern, sacred and profane. The odes of Anacreon abound in specimens of it, and it has

added grace and dignity to the lines of Homer and
Virgil, has feathered the poetic shafts of Shakespeare and Gay, shown itself in the volatile genius
of French poesy, and given emphasis and force
to the lines of Schlegel and Bürger—lending its
"artful aid" to the poetry of almost every clime,
and tinging the literature of almost every language.
One of the earliest examples is the celebrated line
of Virgil—

"Quadrupedumque putrem sonitu quatit ungula campum"—

a line which is admired by the best critics as
illustrating, in a happy manner, "the measured
gallop of the haughty war-horse." This line, as Sir
Walter Scott says, "expressing a cavalry charge,"
was criticised severely by Scott's Triptolemus
Yellowley, who "opined that the combatants, in
their inconsiderate ardour, galloped over a new-
manured ploughed field." The lines written by
Virgil on the folding doors of the amphitheatre
may serve as another example of his alliterative
powers. He had written, anonymously, a couplet
containing an elegant compliment to the Emperor
Augustus, the authorship of which was claimed by
one Bathyllus. Chagrined at this, Virgil re-wrote
the original lines, with the following addition:

" Hos ego versiculos feci, tulit alter honores
    Sic vos non vobis   .   .   .   .
    Sic vos non vobis   .   .   .   .
    Sic vos non vobis   .   .   .   .
    Sic vos non vobis   .   .   .   .

Various attempts were made, but without success, to fill up the lines, when Virgil completed it himself as follows:

" Sic vos non vobis nidificatis aves ;
Sic vos non vobis vellera fertis boves ;
Sic vos non vobis, mellificatis apes ;
Sic vos non vobis fertis aratra boves."

The old English and Scottish ballads abound in alliteration, and in Weber's " Ballad of Flodden Field "—a poetical romance of the sixteenth century—there are a number of good examples, and here follow some extracts from it:

" Most liver* lads in Lonsdale bred,
    With weapons of unwieldy weight ;
All such as Tatham Fells had fed,
    Went under Stanley's streamer bright.

From Bolland billmen bold were boun,
    With such as Bottom-Banks did hide ;
From Wharemore up to Whittington,
    And all to Wenning Water side.

       * Nimble, active.

From Silverdale to Kent-Sand side,
　　Whose soil is sown with cockle-shells;
From Cartmel eke and Conny-side,
　　With fellows fierce from Furney's fells.

All Lancashire for the most part
　　The lusty Stanley stout did lead;
A stock of striplings, strong of heart,
　　Brought up from babes with beef and bread.

From Warton unto Warrington,
　　From Wigan unto Wiresdale,
From Weddicar to Waddington,
　　From old Ribchester to Ratchdale.

From Poulton and Preston with pikes,
　　They with the Stanley stout forth went;
From Pemberton and Pilling Dikes,
　　For battle billmen bold were bent.

With fellows fresh and fierce in fight,
　　Which Horton Fields turned out in scores;
With lusty lads, liver and light,
　　From Blackburn and Bolton i' the Moors.

With children chosen from Cheshire,
　　In armour bold for battle drest;
And many a gentleman and squire
　　Were under Stanley's streamer prest.

Strike but three strokes with stomachs stout,
　　And shoot each man sharp arrows three,—

And you shall see without all doubt
The scoulding Scots begin to flee.

. . . . .

The master Scot did mark so right

That he with bullet brast his brain,
And hurled his heels his head above ;
Then piped he such a peel again,
The Scots he from their ordnance drave."

Amongst our early poets, no one gives a better example of alliteration than Quarles in one of his Emblems (Book II. Emblem 2). Quarles was a poet who did not need the aid of alliteration to "lend liquidity to his lines," and though often queer, quaint, and querulous, is never prosy, prolix, or puling. The lines are as follow :

" Oh, how our widened arms can over-stretch
Their own dimensions ! How our hands can reach
Beyond their distance ! How our yielding breast
Can shrink to be more full and full possest
Of this inferior orb ! How earth refined
Can cling to sordid earth ! How kind to kind !
We gape, we grasp, we gripe, add store to store ;
Enough requires too much ; too much craves more.

. . . .

The grave is sooner cloyed than men's desire :
We cross the seas, and midst her waves we burn,

Transporting lives, perchance that ne'er return;
We sack, we ransack to the utmost sands
Of native kingdoms, and of foreign lands;
We travel sea and soil, we pry, we prowl,
We progress, and we prog from pole to pole;
We spend our midday sweat, our midnight oil,
We tire the night in thought, the day in toil."

Spenser, Dryden, and Gray — the latter two professedly taking their style from the former—all dealt largely in alliteration. Gray especially gave particular heed to this embellishment, and in his odes almost every strophe begins with an alliterative line—thus:

" Ruin seize thee, ruthless king."
" Weave the warp, weave the woof."
" Eyes that glow, and fangs that grin."
" Thoughts that breathe, and words that burn."

Spenser gives some very good examples:

" In woods, in waves, in wars, she wonts to dwell—
And will be found with peril and with pain."

" They cheerly chaunt, and rhymes at random flung."

" Still, when she slept, he kept both watch and ward,
And when she waked, he waited diligent."

" He used to slug, to sleep, in slothful shade."

The early Scottish poets also used this feature —Gawain Douglas, Dunbar, and Alexander Scot especially. Dunbar's "Dance of the Seven Deadly Sins," a poem of animated picturesqueness not unlike Collins' "Ode to the Passions," contains the following :

> " Then Ire came in, with sturt and strife,
>   His hand was aye upon his knife,
>   He brandished like a bear ;
> Boasters, braggarts, and barganeris : *
> After him passit in pairs,
>   All bodin in feir of weir. †
>
> .   .   .   .   .
>
> Next in the dance followed Envy,
>   Filled full of feud and felony,
>   Hid malice and despite."

Alexander Scot, who has been called the Scottish Anacreon, sent "Ane New Year's Gift " to Queen Mary, which contains many alliterative lines, such as the following, when, speaking of the Reformers of his day, he says they go about—

" Rugging and ryving up kirk rents like rooks ;

and the Address concludes with a stanza beginning—

> " Fresh, fulgent, flourist, fragrant flower formose,
>   Lantern to love, of ladies lamp and lot,
>   Cherry maist chaste, chief carbuncle and chose," &c.

---

* Bullies.   † Arrayed in trappings of war.

Alexander Montgomery, another Scottish poet contemporary with Scot, wrote an allegorical poem entitled "The Cherry and the Slae," in which are some sweet and striking natural descriptions written in richly alliterative verse, of which we give two stanzas :

"The cushat croods, the corbie cries,
The cuckoo conks, the prattling pies
    To geck there they begin ;
The jargon of the jangling jays,
The cracking craws and keckling kays,
    They deav'd me with their din ;
The painted pawn, with Argus eyes,
    Can on his May-cock call,
The turtle wails on wither'd trees,
    And Echo answers all.
      Repeating, with greeting,
        How fair Narcissus fell,
      By lying and spying
        His shadow in the well.

The air was sober, saft, and sweet,
Nae misty vapours, wind, nor weet,
    But quiet, calm, and clear ;
To foster Flora's fragrant flowers,
Whereon Apollo's paramours
    Had trinkled mony a tear ;

The which, like silver shakers, shined,
Embroidering Beauty's bed,
Wherewith their heavy heads declined
In Mayè's colours clad ;
Some knopping, some dropping
Of balmy liquor sweet,
Excelling and smelling
Through Phœbus' wholesome heat."

Neither has Shakespeare omitted this feature, for, amid many others, we find this in "As You Like It :"—

"The churlish chiding of the winter's wind."

Again, in "Love's Labour's Lost," Master Holofernes says :—

" I will something affect the letter, for it argues facility—
The preyful princess pierced and pricked a pretty pleasing pricket."

Shakespeare has also this other example :—

" She sings so soft, so sweet, so soothing still,
That through the throat ten thousand tones there thrill."

The following couplet applies to the famous Cardinal Wolsey :—

" Begot by butchers, but by bishops bred,
How high his honour holds his haughty head ! "

Lord North, at the court of James I., wrote a set of sonnets each beginning with a letter of the alphabet in regular succession; and in the seventeenth century the device of alliteration was carried to the verge of absurdity, when, even in the pulpit, the preacher would address his flock as the "chickens of the Church, the sparrows of the Spirit, and the sweet swallows of salvation." The old divines give many curious specimens of this peculiarity of composition. For instance, in Trapp's Commentary on the Bible, concerning the passage in Proverbs iv. 16, containing the words, "For they sleep not," the quaint old author remarks: "As empty stomachs can hardly sleep, so neither can graceless persons, till gorged and glutted with sweetmeats of sin, with the murdering morsels of mischief." Again, on Jeremiah xxviii. 17, speaking of the death of the false prophet Hananiah, Trapp says: "Such a hoof is grown over some men's hearts, as neither ministry, nor misery, nor miracle, nor mercy, can possibly mollify." About the same time, also, books sometimes received curious alliterative titles, as "The Hiveful of Honey," "The Handful of Honeysuckles," "The Seven Sobs of a Sorrowful Soul for Sin," &c. Sir Thomas Browne gives another instance in the following sentence: " Even that vulgar and tavern music which makes one man merry, another mad, strikes in me a deep fit of devotion and a profound contemplation of the first composer," &c.

Pope gives the idea of labour in the following line by the very difficulty of pronouncing the same recurring sound:

" Up the high hill he heaves the huge round stone ; "

and by the alliteration in the following he connects three similar things, and shows the contrast of two others:

" Puffs, powders, patches, bibles, billet-doux."

Dean Peacock's " Life of Dr. Thomas Young " has this:

" Medical men, my mood mistaking,
  Most mawkish monstrous messes making,
  Molest me much ; more manfully
  My mind might meet my malady ;
  Medicine's mere mockery murders me."

Similar to the above are the following verses, which appeared some time ago in a volume of poems called " Songs of Singularity," by the London Hermit. They are supposed to be a Serenade in M flat, sung by Major Marmaduke

Muttinhead to Mademoiselle Madeline Mendosa Marriott:

"My Madeline! my Madeline!
　　Mark my melodious midnight moans;
　Much may my melting music mean,
　　My modulated monotones.

　My mandolin's mild minstrelsy,
　　My mental music magazine,
　My mouth, my mind, my memory,
　　Must mingling murmur 'Madeline.'

　Muster 'mid midnight masquerades,
　　Mark Moorish maidens', matrons' mien,
　'Mongst Murcia's most majestic maids
　　Match me my matchless Madeline.

　Mankind's malevolence may make
　　Much melancholy music mine;
　Many my motives may mistake,
　　My modest merits much malign.

　My Madeline's most mirthful mood
　　Much mollifies my mind's machine;
　My mournfulness' magnitude
　　Melts—makes me merry—Madeline!

　Match-making ma's may machinate,
　　Manœuvring misses me misween;
　Mere money may make many mate;
　　My magic motto's, 'Madeline!'"

> Melt, most mellifluous melody,
>   Midst Murcia's misty mounts marine,
>   Meet me 'mid moonlight—marry me,
>   Madonna mia !—my Madeline !"

The following is the 49th chapter of " Tusser's Husbandry" (1590), and is

> " A brief conclusion, where you may see
>   Each word in the verse begin with a T."

> "The thrifty that teacheth the thriving to thrive,
>   Teach timely to traverse the thing that thou 'trive [contrive],
>   Transferring thy toiling, to timeliness taught,
>   Thus teaching thee temp'rance to temper thy thought.
>   Take trusty (to trust to) that thinketh to thee,
>   That trustily thriftiness trowleth to thee.
>   Then temper thy travell to tarry the tide,
>   This teacheth thee thriftiness, twenty times try'd.
>   Take thankful thy talent, thank thankfully those
>   That thriftily teacheth thy time to transpose.
>   Troth twice to be teached, teach twenty times ten.
>   This trade thou that taketh, take thrift to thee then."

The song annexed is founded on the peculiarity known as the Newcastle *burr*, and first appeared in a provincial paper in December 1791 :

> " Rough rolled the roaring river's stream,
>   And rapid ran the rain,

When Robin Rutter dreamt a dream
　　Which racked his heart with pain.
He dreamt there was a raging bear
　　Rushed from the rugged rocks,
And strutting round with horrid stare
　　Breathed terror to the brocks.*

But Robin Rutter drew his sword,
　　And rushing forward right,
The horrid creature's throat he gored,
　　And barred his rueful spite.
Then, stretching forth his brawny arm
　　To drag him to the stream,
He grappled Grizzle, rough and warm,
　　Which roused him from his dream."

The subjoined advertisement appeared in a
Manchester paper in 1829:

SPANKER :
" The Property of O——D——.

" Saturday, the 16th September next, will be sold, or
set up for sale, at Skibbereen :

" A strong, staunch, steady, sound, stout, safe, sinewy,
serviceable, strapping, supple, swift, smart, sightly,
sprightly, spirited, sturdy, shining, sure-footed, sleek,
smooth, spunky, well-skinned, sized, and shaped sorrel
steed, of superlative symmetry, styled SPANKER; with
small star and snip, square-sided, slender-shouldered,

---

* Badgers.

sharp-sighted, and steps singularly stately; free from strain, spavin, spasms, stringhalt, staggers, strangles, surfeit, seams, strumous swellings, scratches, splint, squint, scurf, sores, scattering, shuffling, shambling-gait, or sickness of any sort.   He is neither stiff-mouthed, shabby-coated, sinew-shrunk, saddlebacked, shell-toothed, skin-scabbed, short-winded, splay-footed, or shoulder-slipped; and is sound in the sword-point and stifle-joint.   Has neither sick-spleen, sleeping-evil, snaggle-teeth, subcutaneous sores, or shattered hoofs; nor is he sour, sulky, surly, stubborn, or sullen in temper.   Neither shy nor skittish, slow, sluggish, or stupid.   He never slips, strips, strays, starts, stalks, stops, shakes, snivels, snaffles, snorts, stumbles, or stocks in his stall or stable, and scarcely or seldom sweats.   Has a showy, stylish switch-tail, or stern, and a safe set of shoes on; can feed on stubble, sainfoin, sheaf-oats, straw, sedge, or Scotch grass.   Carries sixteen stone with surprising speed in his stroke over a six-foot sod or a stone wall.   His sire was the Sly Sob-bersides, on a sister of Spindleshanks by Sampson, a sporting son of Sparkler, who won the sweepstakes and subscription plate last session at Sligo.   His selling price is sixty-seven pounds, sixteen shillings and sixpence sterling."

Our later poets have occasionally found a charm and aid in alliteration, and Coleridge in one of his poems gives a fine specimen :

" The fair breeze blew, the white foam flew,
    The furrow followed free."

And Burns terms Tam O' Shanter—

"A blethering, blustering, drunken blellum;"

while he calls the ploughman's collie, in the "Twa Dogs"—

A rhyming, ranting, roving billie."

Sir Walter Scott gives the following verse:

"St. Magnus control thee! that martyr of treason;
St. Ronan rebuke thee with rhyme and with reason!
By the mass of St. Martin, the might of St. Mary,
Begone, or thy weird shall be worse if thou tarry!
Begone to thy stone, for thy coffin is scant of thee;
The worm, thy playfellow, wails for the want of thee!
Phantom, fly hence, take the cross for a token!
Hence pass till Hallowmass! My spell is spoken!"

Lord Byron, in the opening stanzas of the "Curse of Minerva" gives this verse:

"Slow sinks, more lovely ere his race be run,
Along Morea's hills the setting sun;
Not, as in northern climes, obscurely bright,
But one unclouded blaze of living light;
O'er the hushed deep the yellow beam he throws,
Gilds the green wave that trembles as it glows.
On old Ægina's rock and Hydra's isle
The god of gladness sheds his parting smile;
O'er his own regions lingering loves to shine,
Though there his altars are no more divine.

Descending fast, the mountain-shadows kiss
Thy glorious gulf, unconquered Salamis !
Their azure arches through the long expanse,
More deeply purpled, meet his mellowing glance,
And tenderest tints, along their summits driven,
Mark his gay course and own the hues of heaven ;
Till darkly shaded from the land and deep,
Behind his Delphian rock he sinks to sleep."

A modern novel, * published lately, gives instances of how deftly similar sounds can be interwoven even in prose. Speaking of a certain bishop, the author says he has "the respect of rectors, the veneration of vicars, the admiration of archdeacons, and the cringing courtesy of curates." In another place, the bishop's wife says "there are regal rectors, vicious vicars, and captious curates."

Lithgow, the eccentric traveller, wrote a poem in which every word began with the same letter, of which the first two lines are here given :

" Glance, glorious Geneve, gospel-guiding gem,
    Great God, govern good Geneve's ghostly game."

The following lines are by a Mr. Dunbar, and are descriptive of the five handsome daughters of the late Scroope Colquitt, Esq., of Green Bank, Liverpool :

* " The Princess Clarice," by Mortimer Collins.

" Minerva-like, majestic Mary moves,
  Law, Latin, liberty, learned Lucy loves,
  Eliza's elegance each eye espies,
  Serenely silent Susan smiles surprise,
  From fops, fools, flattery, fairest Fanny flies."

The best of this class of poems, however, is said to be the following :

THE SIEGE OF BELGRADE.

" Ardentem aspicio atque arrectis auribus asto."— *Virgil.*

An Austrian army, awfully arrayed,
Boldly by battery besieged Belgrade ;
Cossack commanders cannonading come,
Dealing destruction's devastating doom ;
Every endeavour engineers essay
For fame, for fortune, forming furious fray ;
Gaunt gunners grapple, giving gashes good ;
Heaves high his head heroic hardihood ;
Ibrahim, Islam, Ismail, imps in ill,
Jostle John, Jarovlitz, Jem, Joe, Jack, Jill,
Kick kindling Kutosoff, kings' kingsmen kill ;
Labour low levels loftiest, longest lines ;
Men marched 'mid moles, 'mid mounds, 'mid mur-
  d'rous mines.
Now nightfall's near, now needful nature nods,
Opposed, opposing, overcoming odds.
Poor peasants, partly purchased, partly pressed,
Quite quaking, Quarter! quarter! quickly quest.

Reason returns, recalls redundant rage,
Saves sinking soldiers, softens seigniors sage.
Truce, Turkey, truce! truce, treach'rous Tartar train!
Unwise, unjust, unmerciful Ukraine,
Vanish, vile vengeance! vanish, victory vain!
Wisdom wails war—wails warring words.   What were
Xerxes, Xantippe, Ximenes, Xavier?
Yet Yassey's youth, ye yield your youthful yest,
Zealously, zanies, zealously, zeal's zest.

.

The foregoing has been variously imitated, and
here are a few specimens:

> Arthur asked Amy's affection;
>   Bet, being Benjamin's bride,
> Coolly cut Charlie's connection;
>   Deborah, Dicky denied.
> Eleanor's eye, efficacious,
>   Frederick's fatality feels;
> Giles gained Georgiana—good gracious!
>   Harry hates Helen's high heels.
> Isaac is Isabel's idol;
>   Jenny jeers Jonathan Jones;
> Katherine knows knock-knee'd Kit Kriedal;
>   Love's leering Lucy's long bones.
> Mary meets mortifications;
>   Nicholas Nancy neglects;
> Oliver's odd observations
>   Proves Peter poor Patty protects.

Quaker Quintilian's queer quibbles
    Red Rachel's reasons resist :
Soft Simon's sympathy scribbles
    Tales to tall Tabitha Twist.
Urs'la unthinking, undoing
    Volatile Valentine's vest ;
William's wild wickeder wooing
    'Xceeds youthful Zelica's zest.

An Artful and Amusing Attempt at Alphabetical Alliteration Addressing Aurora.

Awake Aurora ! and across all airs
By brilliant blazon banish boreal Bears,
Crossing cold Canope's celestial crown,
Deep darts descending dive delusive down.
Entranced each eve Europa's every eye
Firm fixed forever fastens faithfully,
Greets golden guerdon gloriously grand ;
How holy Heaven holds high His hollow hand !
Ignoble Ignorance, inapt indeed,
Jeers jestingly just Jupiter's jereed !
Knavish Khamschatkans, knightly Kurdsmen know
Long Labrador's light lustre looming low ;
'Midst myriad multitudes majestic might
No nature nobler numbers Neptune's night.
Opal of Oxus, or old Ophir's ores,
Pale Pyrrhic pyres prismatic purple pours—
Quiescent quivering, quickly, quaintly queer,
Rich, rosy, regal rays resplendent rear ;

Strange shooting streamers, streaking starry skies,
Trail their triumphant tresses—trembling ties.
Unseen, unhonoured Ursa—underneath,
Veiled, vanquished—vainly vying—vanisheth ·
Wild Woden, warning, watchful—whispers wan
Xanthitic Xeres, Xerxes, Xenophon,
Yet yielding yesternight, Yules yell yawns
Zenith's zebraic zigzag, Zodiac zones.

Exercise on the Alphabet.

Andrew Airpump asked his aunt her ailment.
Billy Button bought a buttered biscuit.
Captain Crackscull cracked a catchpoll's coxcomb.
Davy Doldrum dreamt he drove a dragon.
Enoch Elkrig eat an empty eggshell.
Francis Fripple flogged a Frenchman's filly.
Gaffer Gilpin got a goose and gander.
Humphrey Hunchback had a hundred hedgehogs.·
Inigo Impey itched for an Indian image.
Jumping Jackey jeered a jesting juggler.
Kimbo Kemble kicked his kinsman's kettle.
Lanky Lawrence lost his lass and lobster.
Matthew Mendlegs missed a mangled monkey.
Neddy Noodle nipped his neighbour's nutmegs.
Oliver Oglethorpe ogled an owl and oyster.
Peter Piper picked a peck of pepper.
Quixote Quixite quizzed a queerish quidbox.
Rawdy Rumpus rode a rawboned racer.
Sammy Smellie smelt a smell of small coal.

Tiptoe Tommy turned a Turk for twopence.
Uncle Usher urged an ugly urchin.
Villiam Veedy viped his vig and vaistcoat.
Walter Waddle won a walking wager.
X, Y, Z have made my brains to crack O—
X smokes, Y snuffs, Z chews too strong tobacco.
Though oft by X, Y, Z much lore is taught,
Still Peter Piper beats them all to naught.

The preceding is a literary folly indeed; and
though the following is not much better, it is at
least sensible:

ALLITERATIVE LOVE LETTER.

Adored and angelic Amelia, accept an ardent and
artless amourist's 'affection, alleviate an anguished
admirer's alarms, and answer an amorous applicant's
ardour. Ah, Amelia! all appears an awful aspect.
Ambition, avarice, and arrogance, alas! are attractive
allurements, and abuse an ardent attachment. Appease
an aching and affectionate adorer's alarms, and anon
acknowledge affianced Albert's alliance as acceptable
and agreeable. Anxiously awaiting an affectionate and
affirmative answer, accept an admirer's aching adieu.
Always angelic and adorable Amelia's affectionate
amourist, Albert.

XTRAVANGANZA XTRAORDINARY.

Charles X., x-king of France, was xtravagantly xtolled,
but is xceedingly xecrated. He xhibited xtraordinary

xcellence in xigency; he was xemplary in xternals, but xtrinsic on xamination; he was xtatic under xhortation, xtreme in xcitement, and xtraordinary in xtempore xpression. He was xpatriated for his xcesses; and, to xpiate his xtravagance, xisted and xpired in xile.

Here is another kind of alliterative versification:

To Mrs. Gee on her Marriage.

Sure, madam, by your choice your taste we see;
What's *g*ood, or *g*reat, or *g*rand, without a G?
A *g*odly *g*low must sure on G depend,
Or *oddly low* our righteous thoughts must end.
The want of G all *g*ratitude effaces;
And, without G, the Graces would run races!

The Latin language has also had its versifiers of this kind, for we find that one Hugbald, a monk, wrote an "Ecloga de Calvis," in which all the words begin with a *c*. So also in the "Nugæ Venales," there is a Latin poem of a hundred lines called "Pugna Porcorum, per Publium Porcium, poetam," in which all the words begin with a *p*. Subjoined are a few lines of this curious effusion:

"Propterea properans Proconsul, poplite prono,
Præcipitem Plebem, pro patrum pace proposeit.
Persta paulisper, pubes preciosa! precamur.
Pensa profectum parvum pugnæ peragendæ.
Plures plorabant, postquam præcelsa premetur

Prælatura patrum, porcelli percutientur
Passim, posteaquam pingues porci periere."

A Latin poem in praise of William III. commences thus:

"Agglomerata acies, addensans agminis alas,
Advolat auxiliis, arvoque effulget aperto:
Auriacusque ardens animis, animosior arte,
Auctoratus adest, arma aureus, aureus arma
Adfremit ; auratis armis accingitur armos."

Perhaps the most notable Latin example is a poem written by Christianus Pierius, called "Christus Cruxifixus," said to extend to nearly one thousand lines, each word of which begins with *c*—

"Consilebratulæ cunctorum carmine certum," &c.

Whatever beauty or utility may lie in alliteration, it is to be found largely in the proverbial expressions and common sayings of all countries. Thus, in our own, we frequently couple "hearts and hands," "hearths and homes," "life and limb," "great and good ;" whilst in proverbs we have "Better buy than borrow," "Wilful waste makes woful want," "Love me little, love me long," "Like master like man," "Money makes the mare to go," "A true tale never tines (loses) in the telling," &c., &c.

Our last instance of alliteration is one picked up in a provincial newspaper, containing an account of a local *fête*, and not only the words, but each syllable in the line, begins with the same letter:

"Let lovely lilies line Lee's lonely lane."

Alphabetic Curiosities—Single-Rhymed Alphabets.

As a fitting pendant to alliteration, though only in a slight degree connected with it, we give here some alphabetic curiosities.

Acrostic Verses on Writing (*circa* 1785).

All letters even at the head and feet must stand;
Bear light your pen and keep a steady hand;
Carefully mind to mend in every line—
Down strokes are black, but upper strokes are fine.
Enlarge your writing if it be too small;
Full in proportion make your letters all;
Game not in school-time, when you ought to write;
Hold in your elbow, sit fair to the light.
Join all your letters by a fine hair-stroke;
Keep free from blots your piece and writing-book.
Learn the command of hand by frequent use;
Much practice doth to penmanship conduce.

Never deny the lower boys assistance ;
Observe from word to word an equal distance.
Provide yourself of all things necessary ;
Quarrel not in school though others dare you.
Rule your lines straight and make them very fine ;
Set stems of letters fair above the line,
The tops above the stems—the tails below ;
Use pounce to paper if the ink goes through.
Veer well your piece, compare how much you've
    mended ;
Wipe clean your pen when all your task is ended.
Your spelling mind—write each word true and well ;
Zealously strive your fellows to excel.

LIFE'S ALPHABET.

Active in life's race we start,
Bounding on with joyous heart,
Counting neither cost nor pain,
Dazzled with the hopes of gain ;
Earthly pleasures, earthly joys,
Flock around us merry boys.

Gracefully we lead the van,
Honours wait the "coming man,"—
Indian wealth and Grecian fame
Join to raise an honoured name.
Kingdoms tremble at our tread,
Laurels wait to crown our head.

Measured next our steady pace—
Nothing wears so bright a face.

D

Oft we think our labours vain,
Pleasures linger on the wane;
Quickly from our eager grasp
Rush the phantoms of the past.

Stooping, then, amid the strife,
Tempest-tossed and tired of life,
Unadorned with laurels rare,
Vain the hope to do and dare;
Welcome now the lowly bed—
Youthful visions all are fled.

The following was originally published at the
time of the Crimean War, each line being accompanied by an appropriate illustration designed by
R. B. Brough:

THE TURKISH ALPHABET.

A was an Aberdeen wise in debates :
B was a Bear taught to dance on hot plates ;
C was a Czar who would whip round the world ;
D the Defiance that at him was hurled.
E was an Emperor struck with dismay ;
F was a Frenchman in Besika Bay.
G was the Greeks who for freedom would strike ;
H was a Hospodar warranted like.
I was an Insult that hurt the Porte's pride ;
J was a Jassy by friends occupied.
K was the Knife to which war was declared ;
L was a Lion, and how much *he* cared.
M was a Minister sniffing a row ;
N was a Newspaper, Turkey's friend now.

O was Own Correspondent so trusty ;
P was a Port[e], old and thin and turned crusty.
Q was a Question whose solving we all laugh at ;
R was a Rout of the Russians at Kâlafat ;
S was a Supplement telling it all ;
T was a Tradesman who'd sold for a fall.
U was an Urquhart for foresight well vaunted ;
V was the Vessels still ready if wanted.
W was a Westmoreland—teach kings he used to ;
X the 'Xtremities Russia's reduced to.
Y was a Yell for the friends of the Czar ; and
Z was the Zanies who're frightened at war.

The following is taken from an old "Scots Almanac," and is supposed to be one of the toasts popular among the Jacobites, being known as

LORD DUFF'S TOAST.

A B C . . A Blessed Change.
D E F . . Down every Foreigner.
G H J . . God Help James.
K L M . . Keep Lord Mar.
N O P . . Noble Ormond Preserve.
Q R S . . Quickly Resolve Stuart.
T U V W . Truss up Vile Whigs.
X Y Z . . 'Xert Your Zeal.

L E G ON THE DEATH OF L X AND R N S,
  SQUIRE OF THE COUN T OF S X.

In S X once there lived M N,
  Who was Xceeding Y Y ;

But with so much O B C T
　　It almost closed his I I.

When from his chair E would R I I,
　　U would have laughed to C
The awkwardness his fat did cause
　　To this old O D T.

But barring that E was so fat,
　　E was a right good fell O,
And had such horror of X S
　　U never saw him mell O.

N O O so red E did not like,
　　As that which wine will give,
So did S A to keep from drink
　　As long as E did live.

Two daughters fair this old man had,
　　Called Miss M A and L N,
Who, when the old chap took his E E,
　　Would try to T T the men.

Over the C C, these maids to please,
　　There came two gallants gay;
M A and L N ceased to T T,
　　And with them ran away.

These gallants did them so M U U,
　　And used such an M N C T
Of flattery, U must X Q Q
　　Their fugitive propensity.

The poor old man heaved many S I I,
　　For frail M A and L N;

E called each gallant gay a rogue,
    A rascal, and a villain.

And all with half an I might C
    His gradual D K,
Till M T was his old arm-chair,
    And E had passed away.

SINGLE-RHYMED ALPHABETS.

Some years ago a writer who signed himself
"Eighty-One" sent to "Notes and Queries" an
alphabet, single-rhymed, and challenged the Eng-
lish-speaking world to produce another. "Eighty-
One's" production was the following:

A was an Army to settle disputes;
B was a Bull, not the mildest of brutes;
C was a Cheque, duly drawn upon Coutts;
D was King David, with harps and with lutes;
E was an Emperor, hailed with salutes;
F was a Funeral, followed by mutes;
G was a Gallant in Wellington boots;
H was a Hermit, and lived upon roots;
I was Justinian his Institutes;
K was a Keeper, who commonly shoots;
L was a Lemon the sourest of fruits;
M was a Ministry—say Lord Bute's;
N was Nicholson, famous on flutes;
O was an Owl, that hisses and hoots;
P was a Pond, full of leeches and newts;

Q was a Quaker in whitey-brown suits ;
R was a Reason, which Paley refutes ;
S was a Sergeant with twenty recruits ;
T was Ten Tories of doubtful reputes ;
U was Uncommonly bad cheroots ;
V Vicious motives, which malice imputes ;
X an Ex-King driven out by emeutes ;
Y is a Yawn ; then, the last rhyme that suits,
Z is the Zuyder Zee, dwelt in by coots.

The challenge of " Eighty-One " was taken up,
and in a very short time a number of pieces were
sent in to the Editor, of which only a few were
selected and published. Mr. J. B. Workard sent
two, of which we take the first :

A 's the accusative ending in -*am ;*
B was a Butcher, who slaughtered a lamb ;
C was a candidate, "plucked " on exam—;
D was a Door that was shut with a slam ;
E was an Error in *Times* telegram ;
F was a foreigner come from Siam ;
G was Guava—a breadfruit or yam ;
H was a Hypocrite, Humbug, or sham ;
I was an Infidel, sneering at " flam ;"
J was a Jew—call him Āăbraham ;
K was King Cole, who was fond of a dram ;
L was a Lady, accosted as Ma'am ;
M was her Mother—we won't say her dam ;
N was a noodle, his prænomen Sam ;
O was an Omnibus slid on a tram ;

P were some Praises, so faint as to damn ;
Q was the Queen—*illa da gloriam ;*
R was a Rampant and Riotous Ram ;
S was a Sinner, as you are and I am ;
T was a Tort, or an action *qui Tam ;*
U was the Univ—, on the banks of the Cam ;
V was a Viscount—suppose we say Pam ;
W a Woman addicted to jam ;
X an exasperous letter to cram ;
Y was a Yankee digesting a clam ;
Z was a Zetlander curing a ham.

The next is by Mr. Mortimer Collins :

A is my Amy, so slender of waist ;
B 's little Bet, who my button replaced ;
C is good Charlotte, good maker of paste ;
D is Diana, the forest who traced;
E is plump Ellen, by Edward embraced ;
F is poor Fanny, by freckles defaced ;
G is Griselda, unfairly disgraced ;
H is the Helen who Ilion effaced ;
I is fair Ida, that princess strait-laced ;
J is the Judy Punch finds to his taste ;
K, Katty darling, by fond lovers chased ;
L is Laurette, in coquetry encased ;
M is pale Margaret, saintly and chaste ;
N is gay Norah, o'er hills who has raced ;
O is sweet Olive, a girl olive-faced ;
P 's pretty Patty, so daintily-paced ;
Q some fâir Querist, in blue stockings placed ;
R is frail Rose, from her true stem displaced ;

S   is brisk Sall, who a chicken can baste;
T   is Theresa, at love who grimaced;
U   is pure Una, that maid undebased;
V   is Victoria, an empire who graced;
W   is Winifred, time who will waste;
X   is Xantippe, for scolding well-braced;
Y   's Mrs. Yelverton: ending in haste,
Z   is Zenobia, in panoply cased.

The last we select bears the signature of
E. A. D.:

A   stands for Apple, most useful of trees;
B   for the busiest of creatures, the Bees;
C   for a Cold, that will cause you to wheeze;
D   for a Doctor, that will cure you for fees;
E   for an Earwig, your hearing to tease;
F   for a Fortune in lacs of rupees;
G   for a Goblet of wine with its lees;
H   for a Horse, but with two broken knees;
I   for an Iceberg, on which you will freeze;
J   for a Jumper, that hops like parched peas;
K   for a Kirtle, worn over chemise;
L   for a Lady, whose hand you may squeeze;
M   for the Mineral called Manganese;
N   for a Nun, among strict devotees;
O   for an Octave in musical glees;
P   for a Pope, with his crosses and keys;
Q   for a Quilt, that will harbour the fleas;
R   for Religion, where no one agrees;
S   stands for Snuff, that will cause you to sneeze;
T   for a Table of marriage degrees;

U for an Ulcer, a horrid disease ;
V stands for Virtue, that nobody sees ;
W for Welshman, fondest of cheese ;
X for Xenodochy,* strangers to ease ;
Y for a Yawl, just catching the breeze ;
Z stands for Zenith—or Zeal—which you please.

Xenodochy, "reception of strangers."

LIPOGRAMS.

IPOGRAM is the name applied to a species of verse in which a certain letter, either vowel or consonant, is altogether omitted —that is to say, the author in what he writes will avoid the use of one letter in particular; a kind of literary work involving an amount of labour and ingenuity altogether inadequate to the result achieved; and if to anything at all in this book the title of Literary Frivolity may be more specially applied, it is to this.

One of the earliest who tried this kind of verse was the Greek poet Lasus (538 B.C.), who wrote an ode upon the Centaurs and a hymn to Ceres without inserting the letter *s* in the composition; and it is recorded of another Greek, Tryphiodorus, also of the sixth century B.C., that he composed a poem on the destruction of Troy in twenty-four books, from each of which in succession was excluded one letter of the Greek alphabet: the first book had no *a,* the second no *β,* the third no *γ,* and so on throughout. The works of Pindar also contain an ode in which the letter *s* does not appear; so that if this kind of literary folly has little beauty, it has at least the sanction of antiquity.

Several French poets have written works after this fashion, and some of those of Lope de Vega— works now little heard of, and perhaps better so, since many of these were of unworthy character— are lipogrammatic. The Spanish poet wrote no less than fifteen hundred plays; and among De Vega's other writings are five tales, from each of which one of the five vowels was excluded—a conceit which must have cost their author considerable labour.

Gregorio Leti on one occasion wrote a discourse throughout which he omitted the letter *r;* and in the sixth century Fabius Fulgentius, a Christian monk, performed a similar feat to that of Tryphiodorus. This fashion seems also to have extended to the farther East, for Isaac Disraeli tells that "a Persian poet read to the celebrated Jami a 'gazel' of his own composition, which Jami did not like; but the writer replied it was notwithstanding a very curious sonnet, for *the letter Aliff* was not to be found in any one of the words! Jami sarcastically replied, 'You can do a better thing yet : take away *all the letters* from every word you have written ! ' "

The following example of a lipogrammatic song does not contain the letter *s :*

COME, LOVE, COME.

Oh ! come to-night : for naught can charm
    The weary time when thou'rt away.
Oh ! come ; the gentle moon hath thrown
    O'er bower and hall her quivering ray.
The heather-bell hath mildly flung
    From off her fairy leaf the bright
And diamond dewdrop that had hung
    Upon that leaf—a gem of light.
                Then come, love, come.

To-night the liquid wave hath not—
    Illumined by the moonlit beam
Playing upon the lake beneath,
    Like frolic in an autumn dream—
The liquid wave hath not, to-night,
    In all her moonlit pride, a fair
Gift like to them that on thy lip
    Do breathe and laugh, and home it there.
                Then come, love, come.

To-night ! to-night ! my gentle one,
    The flower-bearing Amra tree
Doth long, with fragrant moan, to meet
    The love-lip of the honey-bee.

But not the Amra tree can long
  To greet the bee, at evening light,
With half the deep, fond love I long
  To meet my Nama here to-night.
                Then come, love, come.

Akin to this lipogrammatic trifling was the fashion of making all the lines of a piece of poetry begin or end with the same letter. Under Alliteration reference has already been made to the set of sonnets written by Lord North, each of which began with a successive letter of the alphabet. Of the kind which makes each line end with the same letter is " The Moral Proverbs of Christine of Pisa," one of our earliest printed English works, having been translated into English by Earl Rivers, brother of the Lady Grey who married Edward IV. This work must have been one of considerable labour, but as these literary eccentricities were looked upon with much favour in those times, no doubt the noble author had his reward. The poem concludes with ::

  " Of these sayings Christine was the authoresse,
  Which in making had such intelligence
  That thereof she was mirrour and mistresse;
  Her works testifie the experience.
  In French language was written this sentence;
  And thus Englished, does it rehearse
  Antoin Woodvylle, Earl of Ryverse."

This curious work was printed in Westminster Abbey about 1477 by William Caxton, who added the following lines to the book:

> "Go now, thou little quire, and recommend me
> Unto the special grace of my good lorde,
> Th' Earl Ryvers, for I have imprinted thee,
> At his commandment, following every worde
> His copy, as his secretary can recorde,
> At Westminster of Februarie the XX daye,
> And of Kyng Edwarde the XVII yere vraye."

It will be seen that neither the noble Earl nor his printer felt themselves in any way trammelled or hindered by the ordinary rules of spelling, and added the vowel when it suited them.

There is little difficulty in finding specimens amongst our early poets of this peculiarity. Opening the "Faerie Queen" at random, we find the following stanza in Canto iv.:

> "Her life was nigh unto death's dore yplaste;
> And thredbare cote, and cobled shoes, hee ware;
> Ne scarse good morsell all his life did taste;
> But both backe and belly still did spare,
> To fill his bags, and richesse to compare:
> Yet childe ne kinsman living had he none
> To leave them to; but thorough daily care
> To get, and nightly feare to lose his owne,
> He led a wretched life, unto himself unknowne."

Again, in the works of Gascoigne (died 1578),

who is said by Warton to be the author of the first comedy written in English prose, the "Comedie of Supposes," from which, it is said by another literary historian, Shakespeare borrowed part of the plot and of the phraseology for his "Taming of the Shrew," we learn that "Alexander Neuile deliured him this theame, *Sat cito si sat bene*, wherevpon hee compiled these seuen Sonets in sequence," of which we give Sonnets iv. and v.:

"To prinke me vp and make me higher plaste,
　All came to late that taryed any time,
　Pilles of prouision pleased not my taste,
　They made my heeles to heauie for to climbe:
　Mee thought it best that boughes of boystrous oake,
　Should first be shreade to make my feathers gaye.
　Tyll at the last a deadly dynting stroke,
　Brought downe the bulke with edgetooles of decaye:
　Of every farme I then let flye a lease,
　To feede the purse that payde for peeuishnesse,
　Till rente and all were falne in such disease,
　As scarse coulde serue to mayntayne cleanlynesse:
　They bought, the bodie, fine, ferme, lease, and lande,
　All were to little for the merchauntes haunde.

All were to little for the merchauntes haunde,
　And yet my brauerye bigger than his booke:
　But when this hotte accompte was coldly scande,
　I thought highe time about me for to looke:
　With heauie cheare I caste my heade abacke,
　To see the fountaine of my furious race.

Comparde my loss, my liuing, and my lacke,
In equall balance with my iolye grace.
And sawe expences grating on the grounde
Like lumps of lead to presse my purse full ofte,
When light rewarde and recompence were founde,
Fleeting like feathers in the winde alofte :
These thus comparde, I left the Courte at large,
For why ? the gaines doth seldome quitte the charge."

Churchyard literature furnishes another specimen
of this species of versification, as found on a tomb-
stone at Hadleigh in Suffolk:

" The charnel mounted on the wall
   Lets to be seen in funeral
   A matron plain domesticall,
   In pain and care continual.
· Not slow, nor gay, nor prodigal,
   Yet neighbourly and hospital.
   Her children yet living all,
   Her sixty-seventh year home did call
   To rest her body natural
   In hope to rise spiritual."

Another fashion allied to this is the resolute
adoption of only one vowel throughout—univocalic
trifling. This, however, is a very difficult matter,
for the English language does not lend itself readily
to univocalics, and few examples are to be had.
Perhaps the following is among the best, in which
the vowel *e* is the only one used :

"Persevere, ye perfect men,
Ever keep the precepts ten."

An ingenious writer in "Notes and Queries" some years ago made an attempt at a series of verses, each of which contained only one vowel. The following was the result:

THE RUSSO-TURKISH WAR.

War harms all ranks, all arts, all crafts appal;
At Mars' harsh blast, arch, rampart, altar fall!
Ah! hard as adamant a braggart Czar
Arms vassal-swarms, and fans a fatal war!
Rampant at that bad call, a Vandal band
Harass, and harm, and ransack Wallach-land.
A Tartar phalanx Balkan's scarp hath past,
And Allah's standard falls, alas! at last.

THE FALL OF EVE.

Eve, Eden's empress, needs defended be;
The Serpent greets her when she seeks the tree.
Serene she sees the speckled tempter creep;
Gentle he seems—perverted schemer deep—
Yet endless pretexts, ever fresh, prefers,
Perverts her senses, revels when she errs,
Sneers when she weeps, regrets, repents she fell,
Then, deep-revenged, reseeks the nether Hell!

THE APPROACH OF EVENING.

Idling I sit in this mild twilight dim,
Whilst birds, in wild swift vigils, circling skim.

E

Light wings in sighing sink, till, rising bright,
Night's Virgin Pilgrim swims in vivid light.

INCONTROVERTIBLE FACTS.

No monk too good to rob, or cog, or plot,
No fool so gross to bolt Scotch collops hot.
From Donjon tops no Oronooko rolls.
Logwood, not lotos, floods Oporto's bowls.
Troops of old tosspots oft to sot consort.
Box tops our schoolboys, too, do flog for sport.
No cool monsoons blow oft on Oxford dons,
Orthodox, jog-trot, book-worm Solomons !
Bold Ostrogoths of ghosts no horror show.
On London shop-fronts no hop-blossoms grow.
To crocks of gold no Dodo looks for food.
On soft cloth footstools no old fox doth brood.
Long storm-tost sloops forlorn do work to port.
Rooks do not roost on spoons, nor woodcocks snort.
Nor dog on snowdrop or on coltsfoot rolls,
Nor common frog concocts long protocols.

The same subject continued.

Dull humdrum murmurs lull, but hubbub stuns.
Lucullus snuffs up musk, mundungus shuns.
Puss purs, buds burst, bucks butt, luck turns up
    trumps ;
But full cups, hurtful, spur up unjust thumps.

This playing upon vowels is in a manner ri-
valled by the following ingenious verses, in which
a single word is held to throughout. They were
written by Allain Chartier, a French poet of the

sixteenth century, and are descriptive of a rope-maker:

> " Quand un cordier cordant
> Veut corder une corde,
> Trois cordons accordant
> A sa corde il accorde.
>
> Si l'un des trois cordons
> De la corde décorde,
> Le cordon decordant
> Fait décorder la corde."

Dr. Wallis put these lines into English, and, by adding two or three relative words, gave four additional lines:

> "When a twiner a twisting will twist him a twist,
> For the twining his twist he three twines doth entwist;
> But if one of the twines of the twist do untwist,
> The twine that untwisteth, untwisteth the twist.
>
> Untwirling the twine that untwisteth between,
> He twists with his twister the two in a twine;
> Then twice having twisted the twines of the twine,
> He twisteth the twines he had twisted in vain.
>
> The twain that, in twisting before in the twine,
> As twines were entwisted, he now doth untwine,
> 'Twixt the twain intertwisting a twine more between,
> He, twisting his twister, makes a twist of the twine."

Cuthbert Bolton (1603) in a similar manner thus plays upon one word in one of his poems:

" Fortune is sweet, Fortune is sour,
Fortune will laugh, Fortune will lower ;
The fading fruit of Fortune's flower
Doth ripe and rot, both in an hour.
Fortune can give, Fortune can take,
Fortune can mar, Fortune can make ;
When others sleep, poor I do wake,
And all for unkind Fortune's sake.
Fortune sets up, Fortune pulls down,
Fortune soon loves, but hates as soon.
Fortune, less constant than the moon,
She'll give a groat and take a crown."

BOUTS RIMÉS.

OUTS RIMÉS, or rhyming terminations, are verses of a light and trifling
character, and, as their name shows, are of
French origin, amongst which people for a genera-
tion they were great favourites, and that at a time
when wit and learning greatly flourished. They
are words which rhyme to one another, and being
given as a playful task for the purpose of amusement at an evening-party, are generally composed
into verse in an offhand manner—the verse being
a kind of doggerel, catching up the rhyming words
in the order given. The more uncommon the
rhyming words, the more the amusement derived
and the ingenuity displayed. Suppose the words
to be—*grant, ask, shan't, task,* one of the party
would produce:

"If from good-nature you begin to grant
 Whatever favours folk may please to ask,
'Twill grow more difficult to say I shan't,
 And courtesy will be a ·weary task."

While another would give—

> "Sweet one, I pant for what you can grant.
>   What is it? dost thou ask.
> 'Tis a kiss that I want; so don't say I shan't,
>   When assent is an easier task."

The first who brought Bouts Rimés into anything like notoriety was one Dulot, a French poetaster, who had a custom of preparing lists of rhyming words in this fashion, to be filled up with lines at leisure. On one occasion, having been robbed of his papers, Dulot was heard regretting the loss of several hundred sonnets; this loss somewhat astonished his friends, who were condoling with him on his misfortune, when he said, "They were blank sonnets," and explained the mystery by describing his Bouts Rimés. This curious habit of Dulot's appeared so entertaining to his friends, that not long after it became quite a fashionable amusement, and a favourite task of French ladies to their lovers.

Much entertainment must evidently attend such an intellectual competition, where a company is gathered together capable in any degree of carrying it out, and some sharpening of the wits must be the consequence. On one such occasion the words given were *brook, why, crook, I,* and the following was the result, given by Horace Walpole, who was present:

> " I sit with my toes in a brook ;
>   If any one asks me for why,—
> I hits them a rap with my crook ;
>   'Tis sentiment kills me, says I."

But to better show the difference in composition which may result and the amusement to be derived from Bouts Rimés, take the following lines written against the words *wave, lie, brave, die:*

> " Dark are the secrets of the gulfing wave,
>   Where, wrapped in death, so many heroes lie ;
> Yet glorious death's the guerdon of the brave,
>   And those who bravely live can bravely die."

> " Whenever I sail on the wave,
>   O'ercome with sea-sickness I lie !
> I can *sing* of the sea, and look brave,
>   When I *feel* it, I feel like to die !"

> " High o'er the ship came on the 'whelming wave—
>   One crash ! and on her beam I saw her lie !
> Shrieked high the craven, silent stood the brave,
>   But hope from all had fled,—'twas only left to die."

Soon after the introduction of Bouts Rimés into France they became fashionable in England also. Sir John and Lady Miller of Batheaston when on a tour in Italy procured an antique vase at Frascati, and this vase they brought home and placed in their villa, which they on occasion turned into a temple of Apollo, Lady Miller being the high-priestess and the vase the shrine of the deity. General invitations were sent to all the fashion of Bath every Thursday. One week a series of Bouts Rimés were given out, to be filled up and returned on the next day of meeting. As the company arrived they were ushered into a room where they found the old vase decorated with laurel, and as each lady or gentleman passed they deposited within it their version of the Rimés given out the preceding Thursday. Having thus all contributed their offering to Apollo, a lady was selected to draw them out one by one and hand them to a gentleman to read aloud. After this a committee was appointed to award the prizes to the four best productions, whose authors were presented by the high-priestess with a fillet of myrtle, and crowned amidst the plaudits of the company. Only one of the prize-verses on these occasions, written by the then Duchess of Northumberland, has been preserved, and it is given as a sample of the literary spirit which pervaded the upper classes towards the end of last century. The words given were *brandish, standish, patten, satin, olio, folio, puffing, muffin, feast on, Batheaston.*

"The pen which I now take and brandish,
  Has long lain useless in my standish.
  Know every maid, from her in patten
  To her who shines in glossy satin,
  That could they now prepare an olio,
  From best receipt of book in folio,
  Ever so fine, for all their puffing,
  I should prefer a buttered muffin :
  A muffin Jove himself might feast on,
  If eat with Miller at Batheaston."

In the "Correspondence of Mrs. Delany," the editor, Lady Llanover, refers to this amusement, and gives a specimen written by Mrs. Delany in reply to words which had been sent her—these being, *bless, less, find, mind, grove, love.*

"When friendship such as yours our hours bless,
  It soothes our cares, and makes affliction less ;
  Oppressed by woes, from you I'm sure to find
  A sovereign cure for my distempered mind ;
  At court or play, in field or shady grove,
  No place can yield delight without your love."

Not content with this, however, Mrs. Delany gave a second verse on the same words :

"When me with your commands you bless,
  My time is yours; nor can I offer less ;
  There so much truth and love I find,
  That with content it fills my mind ;
  Happy to live in unfrequented grove,
  Assured of faithful Nanny's love."

The following words were given out one evening at an entertainment :

Dark, around, hark, sound, shrill, still,
Where, strife, drear, life, bright, night—

which produced the subjoined verses :

" 'Tis Night—the mourning vest of Nature—dark
And gloomy is the starless sky ; around
A melancholy stillness reigns ; but hark !
'Tis but the hooting owl.   A sound
Again breaks on the silence ; 'tis a shrill
Cry from some churchyard—all again is still.

Where now the grandeur of creation ?   Where
The crowds that mingle in the busy strife ?
All's now a dismal chaos, lone and drear,
Rayless and black.   And thus it is with life—
Awhile the scene is beautiful and bright ;
Then comes one deep, and dark, and cheerless night."

On another occasion the words *prove, why, love, calamity,* gave birth to these :

" Of Baxter I cannot ap-prove,
    And the reason is obvious why ;
  For the Church he'd nor favour nor love
    So him I'd with Calamy-tie."

" In life we mingled joys and sorrows prove,
    Confused, and none can give a reason why ;
  Hate quickly treads upon the heels of love,
    And morning's bliss quells night's calamity."

The words *doth, river, both, deliver*, produced the next couple:

> "The Brahmin of the East, who doth
>   Wash in the Ganges river,
> Thinks he doth soul and body both
>   From future pains deliver."

> "Oh wretched is the man that doth
>   Fall in a rocky river;
> For why? he's drowned and murdered both—
>   No aid can him deliver."

Other tasks produced the annexed verses:

> " Few things appear more sad
>   Than to see an old man weep;
> And few make the mind more glad
>   Than a crying child asleep!"

> "What is life?
>   What is death?
> Continued strife—
>   The want of breath!"

So prevalent did this amusement eventually become, that societies were formed to follow it up, and we extract here an account of a meeting of one of these which appeared in the columns of the *Edinburgh Evening Courant* in September 1815—

"ANSTRUTHER MUSOMANIK SOCIETY.

"On Friday last, the 29th September, was celebrated in the Hall of Apollo the second anniversary of the institution of the Musomanik Society of Anstruther. The votaries of that jolly and rejoicing deity rushed in to catch a glimpse of his golden countenance, and to partake, not only of those good things which the influence of his inspiration had generated in heads and in brains, but of those better things which the influence of his beams had produced in valleys and on hills. Every blast blew in a bard; every bard brought with him joy and good-humour. Their hall was profusely decorated with all the ornaments suitable to the occasion; its walls were hung round as usual with prints of all the celebrated poets, adorned with sprigs of laurel. Scott seemed to look down from his elevation near the roof with complacency; Lord Byron appeared to lower, no longer a misanthrope, on the merriment; and the manly eye of Burns seemed to kindle on the wall, and start into the scene, with its fiery and commanding flash. So richly were the roof and sides covered with flower and foliage, that the chamber was like one of those shady recesses of Tempe, into which the Muses were wont to retire to converse with Cupid and the Graces; nor were forgotten the accustomed symbols and emblematic dishes, expressive of the number, the poverty, the vanity, the irritability, the frivolity, and light-headedness of poets. The cod-roe which last year so finely typified the 'numbers without number' of the irritable genus, was somehow strangely forgotten; but its place was supplied by a plateful of mushrooms, to denote the sudden appearance and rapid and total evanishment of our fungous, short-lived tribe. On the centre of the table a Parnassus of paste heaved up its baken mass, on whose top stood the god of the festival, holding in his hand the scroll of sanction, and shining in all his pride of pastry and glory of leaf-gold. The sides of the mountain appeared so horribly steep, rugged, and perpendicular, that not even a hobbler of paste could establish his feet upon them. Its base seemed to be strewed over with the broken limbs of pastry bards, that had rolled down in ruin from the insuperable ascent; an evil omen for the brethren, and which might have excited in their breasts thoughts of dire foreboding, had not their natural unconquerable propensity to laughter been of use to them in converting the melancholic into the mirthful. But it would be tedious to relate all the pomp and preparation, and solemnity and jocundity of the festival; all the toasts, songs, and jokes that enlivened and prolonged the entertainment. Suffice it to say, that good-humour was never more conspicuous than in the hearts and faces of the brethren; that innocent and self-delighted vanity, that mighty mother of all poems and all books, was never more harmlessly gratified; and that the sour and hemlock visage of contumelious criticism herself would have gladly sweetened into joy, and shared, if not abetted, the festivity of the evening."

These Fifeshire associated rhymesters ventured to publish a thin volume entitled " Bouts Rimés; or, Poetical Pastimes of a few Hobblers round the base of Parnassus," dedicated to the lovers of

Rhyme, Fun, and Good-Fellowship throughout the British Empire. We give a few specimens from that book, and our readers will bear in mind that at every meeting of the Club, rhymes were given to each member which he was required to fill up at once. One evening the words given were—*pen, scuffle, men, ruffle,* and in a short time a number of verses were returned, of which three are here given :

> "One would suppose a silly pen
>   A shabby weapon in a scuffle ;
> But yet the pen of critic men
>   A very hero's soul would ruffle."

> " I grant that some by tongue or pen
>   Are daily, hourly in a scuffle ;
> But then we philosophic men
>   Have placid tempers naught can ruffle.'

> "Last night I left my desk and pen,
>   For in the street I heard a scuffle,
> And there, torn off by drunken men,
>   I left my coat-tails and shirt-ruffle."

Again, the following rhymes were given—*bubble, jig, stubble, whirligig,* which were thus answered :

> " My heated brain begins to bubble,
>   With joy I dance the airy jig ;
> My hair lies flat, once stiff as stubble,
>   While round I fly—a whirligig ! "

" What is this life ? a smoke, a bubble,
    In this gay world, a foolish jig,
A joyless field of barren stubble,
    And what is man ?—a whirligig."

For the annual meeting of the Society, however, a somewhat different method was observed. About eight days previous the president gave out rhymes for an ode or poem of the length of twenty or thirty lines, leaving each rhymester to choose his own subject; and at the festival, when from fifteen to twenty pieces were read after dinner, each piece closing with the same rhymes, it was amusing to note the different subjects, styles, and ideas chosen by the writers, and the productions afforded no small amount of pleasantry to the Society. A few specimens are here given:

THE GOLDEN AGE.

Aid me, O Muse! to laud in rhyme
The golden and primeval time,
            Old Saturn's happy day,
When Virtue over every clime
Danced with young Pleasure in her prime,
And chased, with joyful shoutings, crime
            And sorrow far away.

Then free and happy, sinless man
Exulting o'er earth's valleys ran,
            Whilst in the starry frame

His meditative eye began
The finger of his God to scan,
As, musing on the Almighty's plan,
   He felt devotion's flame.

It seemed as if his sacred train
Of thoughts, pure issue of the brain,
   To Virtue's lyre did chime;
It seemed as if, in lieu of rain,
The skies dropped honey on each plain,
Whilst grateful earth sent up again
   Hymns holy and sublime. .

ADDRESS TO ONE OF THE BRETHREN.

Dear Fowler, plague upon all rhyme !
'Tis nothing but a waste of time,
   And life's an April day,
In this our peevish, plashy climè.
Then let's improve our manhood's prime,
No more commit the poet's crime,
   But throw the pen away.

Thus said I—poor deluded man !
To court staid Prudence off I ran,
   And all at once to frame
My ways with wisdom I began,
Looked round with interested scan ; .
But lo ! the Muses marred the plan,
   Apollo fed the flame.

Then, Phœbus, come with all thy train,
And ope the portals of my brain,
   Give thoughts for every chime ;

And as the clouds' soft dropping rain
Cheers and revives the sterile plain,
Fecundate this dull head again
   To reach the true sublime.

The Last Day.

How dread, methinks, how awfully sublime,
When the last trump shall stop the march of time !
What shall avail on that tremendous day
The hero's laurel or the poet's bay ?
Methinks I see the rosy-fingered dawn ;
Shed her last ray o'er every hill and lawn;
Never to rise hath sunk the fulgent moon ;
The sun may rise, but never reach his noon.
From earth—from heaven, with ripened force entire,
Bursts the wild sweep of all-devouring fire ;
From heaven's high arch to the infernal lake,
Shall all creation to her centre shake ;
Its fearful flight the trembling soul shall wing,
And to its God each vice and virtue bring.
Oh, may there then on earth be found but few
Not well prepared to bid the world adieu.

Morning on Arthur's Seat.

On Arthur's lofty top sublime,
Seamed by the iron hand of Time,
I sit and view the coming day,
Smiling from Portobello Bay.
On Abercorn the ruddy dawn
Tinges each tower, and tree, and lawn ;
On high the waning pale-faced moon
Is lost ere she attains her noon.

F

´But see, with radiant orb entire,
Beaming, appears the god of fire !
O'er Duddingstone's enchanting lake,
While scarce a leaf the breeze doth shake ;
The wild duck skirrs on rattling wing,
Condolence to its mate to bring.
Few are thy charms, Edina ! oh, how few !
With scenes like these content, I'd bid thee long
    adieu !

JOHNNIE DOWIE'S.*

Though far from low, yet not sublime,
Here we pass our joyous time ;
Excluded from the light of day,
Here sit the children of the bay.
What care we for the orient dawn?
What care we for the dewy lawn?
What care we for the pale-faced moon?
What care we for the sun at noon?
Here sparkling foams Bell's best "entire ; "
Here blazing burns John Dowie's fire.
What care we for the breezy lake?
What care we though the mountain shake?
Fancy, begone on eagle wing ;
Come, Meg, another bottle bring.
Come, bring us bottles not a few ;
A dozen yet we'll drink ere bidding John adieu !

* An old-fashioned tavern, situated in a dark alley in Edinburgh ;
only one room had a window, all the rest being lighted during the
day by candles. It was a favourite haunt of Burns. Some years
ago the march of city improvement swept this Bacchanalian temple
away, and a roadway now passes over its site.

LOVE.

O Love, 'twas thou that didst first insp-ire,
   And bade my numbers softly roll,
Set all this youthful heart on fire,
   And tuned to harmony my soul.

When Catherine did her charms dis-play,
   (The Loves and Graces in her train),
Could I unconsious turn away,
   Nor feel love's poignant pleasing pain?

Her charms unlocked a precious store
   The hard of heart can never find:
Earth seemed a sweet enchanted shore,
   Such pleasing dreams possessed my mind.

Soft were my strains—Love bade them flow,
   While Hymen's torch began to burn;
No note e'er breathed the wail of woe,
   For "sweet's the love that meets re-turn."

O woman! Nature's fairest flower,
   Sweeter than rosebuds in the spring,
May Care ne'er cloud thy passing hour,
   Nor pluck the down from Pleasure's wing.

When called to blissful scenes above,
   Where joys in endless prospect rise,
May virtue, innocence, and love,
   Attend thee to thy native skies.

ADDRESS TO THE SOCIETY.

Dear Junta of Bards, whom I love and adm-ire,
  Whose hearts are so true, and whose heads are so d-roll,
Now awake ye your glory, and, free in your fire,
  To-day let us skim off the cream of the soul.

To-day, 'tis the season of jest and of play,
  When Phœbus, with grâce and with mirth in his train,
Hops down from Olympus to whistle away
  All mists from our heads—from our bosoms all pain. ,

He comes—and his quiver is rattling with store
  Of arrows that burn to fly forth uncon-fin'd ;
He comes—and the towns that engirdle our shore
  Gleam forth and rejoice in the splendour of mind.

He hath shot at my heart, and my blood in its flow
  Bounds brisk with ideas that blaze and that burn ;
Away, empty world ! with thy wealth and thy woe,
  And ne'er to disturb my dear dreamings re-turn.

I dream that I walk among odour and flower,
  In the gardens of song where our amaranths spring,
Where the leaves of the trees whisper verse, and each hour
  Waves the fragrance of joy from his fanciful wing.

Now in vision I mount with the Muses above,
  Heaven's turrets shine brighter in gold as I rise,
While safe in the passport of song, wit, and love,
  I walk amid angels and skim through the skies.

We conclude this notice of Bouts Rimés with
an anecdote of a young American poet named

Bogart, who had an extraordinary facility for composing impromptu verses, so much so, that he was believed by some persons to prepare them beforehand. To test this, on one occasion at a literary party in New York, it was proposed to write down the letters forming the name of a beautiful lady called Lydia Kane, and as the letters afforded as many lines as a stanza in "Childe Harold," that book was to be opened at random, and the concluding words of the stanza were to form the Bouts Rimés of an acrostic of Lydia Kane. To this singular proposition Bogart at once assented, saying that he should perform his task in ten minutes. The stanza in "Childe Harold" chanced to be the following:

"And must they fall? the young, the proud, the brave,
  To swell one bloated chief's unwholesome reign?
  No step between submission and a grave?
  The rise of rapine and the fall of Spain?
  And doth the Power that man adores ordain
  Their doom, nor heed the suppliant's appeal?
  Is all that desperate valour acts in vain?
  And counsel sage, and patriotic zeal,
The veteran's skill, youth's fire, and manhood's heart of
      steel?"

Bogart cleverly performed his task by producing the following verse within the stated time:

"*L*ovely and loved, o'er the unconquered brave
*Y*our charms resistless, matchless girl, shall reign,
*D*ear as the mother holds her infant's grave,
*I*n Love's warm regions, warm, romantic Spain.
*A*nd should your fate to courts your steps ordain,
*K*ings would in vain to regal pomp appeal,
*A*nd lordly bishops kneel to you in vain,
*N*or Valour's fire, Love's power, nor Churchman's zeal
*E*ndure 'gainst Love's (*time's up*) untarnished steel."

MACARONICS.

F all the curious kinds of literary composition, the most difficult and the most
humorous is that termed Macaronic, in
which, along with Latin, words of other languages
are introduced with Latin inflections, although the
name has also been applied to verses which are
merely a mixture of Latin and English, and it is
thought that the idea of *poetry* of this nature was
first suggested by the barbarous Monkish Latin.
Teofilo Folengo, a learned and witty Benedictine,
who was born at Mantua in 1484 and died in 1544,
has been supposed by some to be the inventor of
this style of verse ; other authorities, however,
contend that he was only the first to apply the
name, which he is said to have selected with
reference to the mixture of ingredients in the
dish called Macaroni. Octavius Gilchrist, in mentioning Teofilo Folengo of Mantua as the supposed inventor, says, in his "Opus Macaronicum"

(first printed in 1517), "He was preceded by the laureate Skelton, whose works were printed in 1512, who was himself anticipated by the great genius of Scotland, Dunbar, in his 'Testament of Andro Kennedy,' * and the last must be considered as the reviver or introducer of macaronic or burlesque poetry." Folengo, under the name of Merlinus Cocaius, published a long satiric poem called "Libriculum ludicrum et curiosum, partim latino, partim italiano sermone compositum." Since then he has had many imitators, but the art cannot be said to have been extensively culti-vated, although specimens are to be found in almost all European languages. In 1829, Genthe (Halle) gave to the literary world of Germany an excellent history of macaronic poetry, together with a collection of the principal works of this nature. In this country he has been followed by Mr. Sandys, who published in 1831 an interesting work entitled " Specimens of Macaronic Poetry ; " † but the most agreeable and amusing book of this

---

* First printed in 1508.

† This little work contains only three or four macaronic poems, all of old date, and none of them of a very presentable nature. There are, however, some other literary curiosities in it which are worthy of attention, such as the " Pugna Porcorum," Hugbald's " Ecloga," &c.

class is one published by M. Octave Delepierre
(Paris, 1852).

Dunbar's "Testament of Andro Kennedy," reputed to be one of the oldest and best, is written
in Latin and Old Scottish, and of this the following
are the concluding lines :

> " I will na priestis for me sing,
>   Dies illa, Dies irae ;
>   Na yet na bellis for me ring,
>   Sicut semper solet fieri ;
>
> But a bagpipe to play a spring,
>   Et unum ailwisp ante me ;
>   Instead of banners for to bring
>   Quatuor lagenas servisiae :
>
> Within the grave to set sic thing,
>   In modum crucis juxta me.
>   To flee the fiends, then hardily * sing
>   De terra plasmati me."

Lord Hailes remarks of the "Testament:"
"This is a singular performance ; it represents
the character of a graceless, drunken scholar.
The alternate lines are composed of shreds of
the Breviary, mixed with what we call *Dog Latin*,
and the French *Latin de Cuisine*."

Another of the early specimens of macaronic
poetry was written by Drummond of Hawthorn-

---

* With confidence.

den (1585–1649), and is entitled " Polema Mid-
dina," which, though it might then be considered a
piece of exquisite drollery by the author's countrymen, is almost wholly unintelligible to modern
Latinists. Drummond, though his scene and
subject be somewhat disagreeable, and hardly
reproducible nowadays, yet shows in his poem
a certain degree of dignity. Of Drummond's
poem, another macaronic, " The Buggiados," published in 1788, is a manifest imitation, and in this
latter, authors of the day are represented under
the ludicrous imagery of bugs, fleas, and other
pestilent "walkers in darkness." They are engaged in a general battle—the commanders-in-
chief being, for the one side, the Rev. Dr.
Priestley; and, on the other, Mr. Coleman of
the Haymarket Theatre. Various heroes traverse
the field, whom the poet characterises with bold
if not discriminating touches—

> " Geometrical Hutton,
> Atque heavy-brain'd Gillies, and the reverend Arthur
>   O'Leary,
> Tragicomic Jephson, et weak Dicky Cumberlandus;
> Atque alter sapiens blockhead, the deep Jemie Beattie,
> Et Johnny Duncanus, than whom a stupider unquam
> Nullibi crawlavit Loussus, with thick Willy Thompson,
> Et silly Joe Watson, regis qui ticklitat aures."

Heroines, too, are engaged in this war—Mesdames Inchbald, Cowley, Seward, and More appear, with a ferocity disgraceful to their sex, using poisoned weapons and the language of Billingsgate; and the extraordinary contest concludes in a curious manner, for Sir John Hawkins, with the five ponderous volumes of his "History of Music," overwhelmes and smashes the whole of the combatants into nothingness.

One of the best of these older macaronics is the following diploma, written by William Meston, M.A., Professor of Philosophy in Marischal College, Aberdeen, about the beginning of last century, whose works are now rarely to be seen:

VIRI HUMANI, SALSI ET FACETI,

GULIELMI SUTHERLANDI,

MULTARUM ARTIUM ET SCIENTIARUM DOCTORIS DOCTISSIMI.

DIPLOMA.

Ubique gentium et terrarum,
From Sutherland to Padanarum,
From those who have six months of day,
Ad Caput usque Bonæ Spei,
And farther yet, si forte tendat
Ne ignorantiam quis praetendat,—
We doctors of the Merry Meeting,
To all and sundry do send greeting,
Ut omnes habeant compertum,
Per hanc præsentem nostram chartam,

Gulielmum Sutherlandum Scotum
At home per nomen Bogsie notum,
Who studied stoutly at our College,
And gave good specimens of knowledge
In multis artibus versatum,
Nunc factum esse doctoratum.
Quoth Preses, Strictum post examen,
Nunc esto Doctor ; we said, Amen.
So to you all hunc commendamus,
Ut juvenem quem nos amamus,
Qui multas habet qualitates,
To please all humours and ætates.
He vies, if sober, with Duns Scotus,
Sed multo magis si sit potus.
In disputando just as keen as
Calvin, John Knox, or Tom Aquinas.
In every question of theology,
Versatus multum in trickology ;
Et in catalogis librorum
Fraser could never stand before him ;
For he, by page and leaf, can quote
More books than Solomon ere wrote.
A lover of the mathematics
He is, but hates the hydrostatics,
Because he thinks it a cold study
To deal in water, clear or muddy.
Doctissimus est medicinæ,
Almost as Boerhaave or Bellini.
He thinks the diet of Cornaro
In meat and drink too scrimp and narrow,
And that the rules of Leonard Lessius
Are good for nothing but to stress us.

By solid arguments and keen
He has confuted Doctor Cheyne,
And clearly proved by demonstration
That claret is a good collation,
Sanis et ægris, always better
Than coffee, tea, or milk and water ;
That cheerful company, cum risu,
Cum vino forti, suavi visu,
Gustatu dulci, still has been
A cure for hyppo and the spleen ;
That hen and capon, vervecina,
Beef, duck and pasties, cum ferinâ.
Are good stomachics, and the best
Of cordials, probatum est.

 . . . . .

A good French nightcap still has been,
He says, a proper anodyne,
 Better than laudanum or poppy,
Ut dormiamus like a toppy.
Affirmat lusum alearum,
Medicamentum esse clarum,
Or else a touch at three-hand ombre
When toil or care our spirits cumber,
Which graft wings on our hours of leisure,
And make them fly with ease and pleasure.
Aucupium et venationem,
Post longam nimis potationem,
He has discovered to be good
Both for the stomach and the blood.

 . . . . .

He clearly proves the cause of death
Is nothing but the want of breath ;

And that indeed is a disaster
When 'tis occasioned by a plaster
Of hemp and pitch, laid closely on
Somewhat above the collar-bone.

.   .   .   .   .

To this, and ten times more his skill
Extends, when he could cure or kill.
Immensam cognitionem legum
Ne prorsus hic silentio tegam,
Cum soeñs artis, grease his fist
Torquebat illas as you list.
If laws for bribes are made, 'tis plain,
They may be bought and sold again ;
Spectando aurum, now we find
That Madam Justice is stone-blind,
So deaf and dull in both her ears,
The clink of gold she only hears ;
Nought else but a loud party shout
Will make her start or look about.
His other talents to rehearse,
Brevissimè in prose or verse,
To tell how gracefully he dances,
And artfully contrives romances ;
How well he arches, and shoots flying
(Let no man think that we mean lying),
How well he fences, rides, and sings,
And does ten thousand other things ;
Allow a line, nay, but a comma,
To each, turgeret hoc diploma ;
Quare ; ut tandem concludamus,
Qui brevitatem approbamus

(For brevity is always good,
Providing we be understood).
In rerum omnium naturis,
Non minus quam scientia juris
Et medicinæ, Doctoratum
Bogsæum novimus versatum ;
Nor shall we here say more about him,
But you may dacker if you doubt him.
Addamus tamen hoc tantillum,
Duntaxat nostrum hoc sigillum,
Huic testimonio appensum,
Ad confirmandum ejus sensum,
Junctis chirographis cunctorum,
Blyth, honest, hearty sociorum.
Dabamus at a large punch-bowl
Within our proper common school,
The twenty-sixth day of November,
Ten years, the date we may remember,
After the race of Sheriffmuir
(Scotsmen will count from a black hour),
Ab omni probo nunc signetur,
Qui denegabit extrudetur.

FORMULA GRADUS DANDI.

Eadem nos auctoritate,
Reges memoriæ beatæ,
Pontifices et papæ læti,
Nam alii sunt à nobis spreti,
Quam quondam nobis indulserunt,
Quæ privilegia semper erunt,
Collegio nostro safe and sound,
As long's the earth and cups go round.

Te Bogsæum hic creamus,
Statuimus et proclamamus,
Artium Magistrum et Doctorem,
Si libet etiam Professorem ;
Tibique damus potestatem
Potandi ad hilaritatem,
Ludendi porro et jocandi,
Et mœstos vino medicandi,
Ad risum etiam fabulandi ;
In promissionis tuæ signum
Caput, honore tanto dignum
Hoc cyatho condecoramus,*
Ut tibi felix sit oramus ;
Præterea in manum damus
Hunc calicem, ex quo potamus,
Spumantem generoso vino,
Ut bibas more Palatino.
Sir, pull it off and on your thumb
Cernamus supernaculum,
Ut specimen ingenii
Post studia decennii.
(*While he is drinking, the chorus sings*)
En calicem spumantem.
Falerni epotantem ;
En calicem spumantem,
Io, io, io.
(*After he has drunk, and turned the glass on his thumb,
they embrace him, and sing again.*)
Laudamus hunc Doctorem,
Et fidum compotorem ;
Laudamus hunc Doctorem,
Io, io, io.

* Here he was crowned with the punch-bowl.

One of the best modern specimens of macaronic poetry is attributed to Professor Porson, and is said to have owed its origin to the alarm of the French invasion:

LINGO DRAWN FOR THE MILITIA.

Ego nunquam audivi such terrible news,
At this present tempus my sensus confuse;
I am drawn for a miles—I must go cum marte,
And, concinnus esse, engage Bonaparte.

Such tempora nunquam videbant majores,
For then their opponents had different mores;
But we will soon prove to the Corsican vaunter,
Though times may be changed—Britons never mu-
 tantur!

Mehercle! this Consul non potest be quiet,
His word must be lex, and when he says fiat,
Quasi Deus, he thinks we must run at his nod,
But Britons were ne'er good at running, by God!

Per mare, I rather am led to opine,
To meet British naves he would not incline;
Lest he should in mare profundum be drowned,
Et cum algâ, non lauro, his caput be crowned.

But allow that this boaster in Britain should land,
Multis cum allis at his command:
Here are lads who will meet, ay, and properly work
 'em,
And speedily send 'em, ni fallor, in Orcum.

Nunc let us, amici, join corda et manus,
And use well the vires Di Boni afford us :
Then let nations combine, Britain never can fall,
She's—multum in parvo—a match for them all!

The following belongs to the reign of Queen
Elizabeth, and was written on the defeat of the
Spanish Armada :

"A Skeltonical salutation,
  Or condign gratulation,
  At the just vexation
  Of the Spanish nation,
  That in a bravado
  Spent many a crusado
  In setting forth an Armado
  England to invado.
  Pro cujus memoria
  Ye may well be soria,
  Full small may be your gloria,
  When ye shall hear this storia,
  Then will ye cry and roria,
  We shall see her no moria."

A MACARONIC

BY TOM DISHINGTON, SOMETIME CLERK OF CRAIL.

"Horrifero nivium nimbos Aquilone ruente,
  Sic tonuit Thoma Dishingtonus ore rotundo."

Saccum cum sugaro, cum drammibus in a glasseo,
In hoc vervece, est melius quam pipe o' tobacco.
Ælli cum bikero, cum pyibus out o' the oono,
Cum pisce, Crelli nominato vulgo caponem,

Quid mellus, si sit ter unctus butyro?
Virides et beefum, cum nose-nippante sinapi ;
O quam gustabunt ad Maria More's fyr-sydum !
Sin erimus drunki, Deil care ! aras dat medicinum
Qui bibit ex lastis ex firstibus incipit ille.

A work entitled "Wild Sports of the East," published many years ago, contained the following admirable specimen :

"Arma virumque cano qui primo solebo peeping,
Jam nunc cum tabbynox languet to button her eyelids,
Cum pointers et spaniels campos sylvasque pererrant.
Vos mihi—Brontothesi over arms small and great domi-
 nantes,
Date spurs to dull poet qui dog Latin carmina condit,
Artibus atque novis audax dum sportsman I follow
Per stubbles et turnips et tot discrimina rerum,
Dum partridge with popping terrificare minantur
Pauci, namque valent a feather tangere plumbo!
Carmina si hang fire discharge them bag-piping Apollo.
Te quoque, magne cleator, te memorande precamur.
Jam nunc thy fame gallops super Garamantos et Indos,
Nam nabobs nil nisi de brimstone et charcoal loquentur,
Horriferifizque ' Tippoo' sulphurea, sustinet arma.
Induit ecce shooter tunicam made of neat marble drugget,
Quæ bene convenient defluxit to the waistband of breeches,
Nunc paper et powder et silices popped in the side-pocket,
Immemor haud shot-bag graditur comitatus two pointers,
Mellorian retinens tormentum dextra bibarelled :
En stat staunch dog Dingo haud aliter quam steady guide
 post,
Proximus atque Pero per stat si ponere juxta,
With gun cocked and levelled et æva lumine clauso,
Nunc avicida resolves haud double strong parcere powder.

Vos teneri yelpers vos grandivique parentes
Nunc palsy pate Jove orate to dress to the left hand,
Et Veneri tip the wink like a shot to skim down ab alto
Mingere per touch-hole totamque madescere priming.
Nunc lugete dire nunc sportsman plangite palmas,
Ex silis ecce lepus from box cum thistle aperto !
Bang bellowed both barrels, heu ! pronus sternitur each dog,
Et puss in the interim creeps away sub tegmine thornbush."

One of the most celebrated English macaronics is a comedy entitled "Ignoramus," written by a clergyman named Ruggle, and performed before James I. at Cambridge in 1616. James expressed himself as highly delighted with it, and ordered it to be twice afterwards performed for his amusement. The pedantic monarch, educated by Buchanan, one of the purest of Latinists, well under-stood the witty production, which had an additional zest for the King in that it was a satire on the barbarous Law-Latin used by the English jurists of the time—James being attached to the simpler forms and terms of Scotch law. The quotation given is part of one of the speeches of Ignoramus, a lawyer, showing how he will endow his mistress, Rosabella :

"Si posem vellem pro te, Rosa, ponere pellum
Quicquid tu qus crava, et habebis singula brava,
Et dabo, fee simple, si monstras Love's pretty dimple,
Gownos, silkcoatos, kirtellos, et petticoatos,

Farthingales biggos, stomacheros, et perriwiggos,
Buskos et soccos, tiffanas en cambricka smockos,
Pantofflos, cuffos, garteros, Spanica ruffos,   '
Wimpolos, pursos ; ad ludos ibis et ursos."

Dean Swift was somewhat addicted to this style of composition, and the following three are his :

A LOVE SONG.

Apud in is almi de si re,
Mimi tres I ne ver re qui re,
Alo veri findit a gestis,
His miseri ne ver at restis.

TO MY MISTRESS.	MOLL.
O mi de armis tres,	Mollis abuti,
Imi na dis tres.	Has an acuti, '
Cantu disco ver	No lasso finis,
Meas alo ver ?	Molli divinis.

Geddes, a clergyman and translator of the Bible, was a prolific macaronic writer. One of his pieces is a poem of considerable length, describing a dinner of Protestant dissenters at the London Tavern. He thus writes of the tables :

" Sedimus ad ternas tabulas longo ordine postas
Et mappas mundi coveratas, et china-plattis,
Spoonibus, et knivis sharpis, furcisque trisulcis
Stratas ; cum largis glassis, vinoque repletis,
Botellis, saltis, vinegarique cruetis."

The following was written by S. W. Partridge, and appeared originally in *Bentley's Miscellany* about thirty years ago:

TONIS AD RESTO MARE.	TONY'S ADDRESS TO MARY.
O Mare, ævi si forme,	O Mary, heave a sigh for me,
Forme ure tonitru,	For me, your Tony true ;
Iambecum as amandum,	I am become as a man dumb—
Olet Hymen promptu !	Oh, let Hymen prompt you !
Mihi his vetas an ne se,	My eye is vet as any sea,
As humano eribi.	As you may know hereby ;
Olet mecum marito te,	Oh, let me come, Mary, to tea,
Or Eta, Beta, Pi !	Or eat a bit o' pie !
Alas ! plano more meretrix,	Alas ! play no more merry tricks,
Mi ardor vel uno ;	My ardour vel you know ;
Inferiam ure art is base ;	In fear I am your heart is base ;
Tolerat me urebo.	Tolerate me, your beau !
Ahm ! ve ara scillicet	Ah me ! ve are a silly set
To laudu vimen thus ;	To laud you vimen thus ;
Hiatu as arandum sex ;	I hate you as a random sex,
Illuc Ionicus.	Ill-luck I only curse.
Heu ! sed heu ! vixen imago,	You said, you vixen, I may go ;
Mi mises mara sta ;	My missus, Mary, stay ;
O cantu redit in mihi !	Oh, can't you read it in my eye ?
Hibernus arida.	I burn as arid hay.
A veri vafer heri si,	A very vafer here I sigh,
Mihi resolves indu,	My eye resolves in dew ;
Totius olet Hymen cum,	To tie us, oh ! let Hymen come—
Accepta tonitru.	Accept a Tony true.

The next example comes from the columns of a newspaper:

EPITAPH ON A DOG.

Eheu ! hic jacet Crony,	In war he was acerrimus,
A dog of much renown ;	In dog-like arts perite ;
Nec fur, nec macaroni,	In love, alas ! miserrimus,
Though born and bred in town.	For he died of a rival's bite.

His mistress struxit cenotaph,
  And as the verse comes pat in,
Ego qui scribo epitaph,
  Indite it in dog-Latin.

In a comedy by O'Keefe, an inebrious school-master gives a song commencing—

" Amo, amas,
  I love a lass
As cedar tall and slender ;
  Sweet cowslip's grace
  Is her nominative case,
And she's of the feminine gender.
(*Chorus.*) Horum corum
    Sunt divorum
  Harum scarum divo ;
Tagrag, merry-derry, periwig and hatband,
  Hic hoc horum genitivo."

An extraordinary specimen of macaronic " puffing " appeared in a Liverpool newspaper some years ago :

AD KELLIAM.

Parvum Buttyranum cano,
Qui vivit in via Dawsoni,
Sedit pulpito suo
Avec ses Barnacles super nasum
Et turndownibus collaris so natty,
Ibi recipit argentum et aurum,
Atque nova coppercoina distribuit
Ad costomeri qui emunt Buttyram
Suis. Tout le monde purchase

Son beurre sel et son beurre frais ;
Ambo sunt capital.   Melle dulcis
Et Buttyrii Kellii.
Formosæ sunt puellæ quæ milkent
Les belles vaches qui donnent du lait
Du quel Buttyrii Kellii formatur.
Butterus yellowus quam vendit
Octavorum pencium est très bon marché,
Sed Buttyrus optimus uni shillingi
Excellentissimum est.
   O Kellius, mi puer, tu es trumpus !
Brickus concentratus sublimatus,
Et no mistake !   In "Loco" Butteryii
Super longum counterums sunt all sorts dis-
   played—
Tempting veritabile appetitum.
Canamus et Laudamus Kellii
Benefactorum toto Liverpudlio,
Qui sells Butteryun cheap et bonum,
Et omnibus dat capital weight !

The winter of 1837–38 is memorable in the
annals of Edinburgh for a series of snowball riots
which were only finally quelled by a detachment
of the 79th Regiment.   The defiance of all con-
stituted authorities, more especially of town coun-
cillors, was no new thing to the Edinburgh youth,
and when, in the beginning of 1838, a simple
snowball "bicker" merged into a bold and deter-
mined opposition to all authority, it only followed
the usual course of such displays, where the

customary interference of the civic power tends
to magnify a mere academical exercise into a
serious public riot. Snow had fallen thickly on
the evening of the 10th of January. Next morning
the street in front of the University was thronged
with boys and idlers, who began a short and comparatively trifling disturbance by throwing snowballs at the students going to and from their classes.
The snowballing recommenced with greater fury
in the afternoon, business was soon at a standstill
and the streets impassable ; the disturbance not
being quelled until the students had learned to
expect little protection from the police, and possibly further annoyance from the public. The
following day it began anew ; a body of police
sent for the protection of the students sided with
the mob, and there ensued a succession of sallies
from either side and hand-to-hand conflicts on the
street and in the porches of the College, which
lasted for several hours. Staffs, sticks, stones,
and snowballs were plied in all directions—many
severe wounds were inflicted, more especially on
the hats and heads of the police ; until at last
matters seemed getting so serious that the Lord
Provost and Bailies of the city thought themselves
called upon to send to the Castle for a detachment

of soldiers.   The appearance of the Redcoats and
the bayonets soon brought the riot to an end.   In
the course of the second day thirty-five students
had been arrested and marched to the police-office.
Many, indeed, were seized who had not been engaged in the tumult, and though all were remanded
to a future day, the prosecution was finally directed
against five only.   Six weeks passed away before a
trial could be arranged ; the case was at last heard
before the Sheriff Court, occupied three days, and
terminated in a full acquittal.   During these six
weeks squibs in all sorts of rhyme and measure were
printed in broadsheets and handed about the
streets.   Of these, the best were written by Edward
Forbes, then a student, but afterwards Professor
of Natural History in Edinburgh, and amongst
them was the following :

FROSTEÏDOS.—LIBER SOLUS.

Frosty policeque cano, Reekie qui primus ab office
In High Street, ad College venibant quellere riot,
Regiment assistente novem et septuaginta,
Bayonetibus fixis, shottisque et powdere multo ;
Musa, mihi causas memora, what Student offended,
Quidve dolens parentis Provosti, tot askere queries
Insignem foolery Lord Rector, tot adire so much slang
Impulerit.   Tantaene animis Studentibus Irae !

Urbs antiqua fuit (Bailies tenuere coloni),
Edina, Burntisland contra, Fortharenaque longa
Ostia, very poor, Studisque asperrima physic,
Hinc erat collegium, edificum very superbum ;
Hinc erant Studentes, collected from every terra,
De first-rate Magistros qui sapientia tucked in,
Distincti juvenes amantes scienceque mischief,
Spes Scotiae erant, spes atque Brittaniæ magnæ.
Hinc etiam erant animalia batonibus ar-med,
Studentes arrestere toujours et frangere pacem,
" Policemen " Dii, " Charlies " qui homines vocant.
Hinc erant Bailies, Frosty et alia mobbi.

Anno incipiente happenabit, snowere multum
Et gelu intensum streetas coverabit wi' slidas,
Constanterque little boys, slided et pitched about snow-
    balls,
Quorum not-a-few bunged up the eyes of Studentes,
Irritate, Studentes chargebant policemen to take up
Little boyos, sed Charlies refusabant so for to do then,
Contemptim Studentes appellabant " Pedica*tores*."
Studentes indignant, reverberant complimenta.
Cum multi homines "blackguards" qui gentlemen
    vocant.
Bakers, et Butchers, et Bullies, et Colliers, atres,
Et alios, cessatores qui locus ecclessiæ frequent
" Tron Church " et Cowgate cum its odoriferous abyss,
Assaultant Studentes stickis et umberelibus.
" Hit 'em hard ! hit 'em hard ! " shoutant, "damnatos
    puppies,"
" Catamitos que torios " appellant et various vile terms,
Studentes audiebant, sed devil an answer retur-ned.
Mobbus Policeque runt downpullere portas ;

Studentes cudgellis thickheados populi crackunt,
Et smashunt fenestras interim snowballs volitantes,
Spemque metumque interdubii, on which side the
    triumph,
Undique Policemen sinkunt sub whackibus stickum
Undique Butchers, et Bakers, et Colliers floorabunt.
Thomsonus, bullyus in domus ill-famæ Cowgatus,
Armatus umbrello poket Studentes frustra,
Umbrella shiverabunt, et Thomson cuts like the devil;
Veluti doggum cum little boys animal plagant
Et tieunt ad talum tinkettlelum loudly clinkatum,
Currit, et barkat, et *bow-wow, bow-wow* shoutat.
Provost riot-acto cum Dymock quadrangulo rushet,
Sed frustra endeavorat to put a stop to the rowam;
Studentes inquirant, "Si mater sua cognoscit
Filum out-esse?"   Sed Frosty respondit nihil!
Concurrit ad shoppum Bailie cognominat Grievum
(Asinus sed hominus) et cum boulanger Sawers,
Ad Castrum militibus Major Young atque they sendunt,
Militibus mille, annihilitare Studentes.
Horribile dictu! regimentum vite arrivat,
Et in Quadrangulam ruit at double-quick time,
Bayonetibus fixis, et musketis loaded cum shottis,
Subito Policemen, qui nuper were sadly frightened
Magnanimi fiunt, et right and left seize on Studentes.
Arrestant Dalrymple et Kellat, fortissimos vires;
Arrestant Aikenhead, Skirving que, Westmacott aussi,
Et luggant Studentes plures ad office in High Street,
Oh pudor! videre gentlemen very ill-treated!

The next example given is from *Notes and
Queries :*

Mi Molle Anni.

O pateo tulis aras cale fel O,
Hebetis vivis id, an sed "Aio puer vello!"
Vittis nox certias in erebo de nota olim,—
A mite grate sinimus tonitis ovem:
"Præ sacer, do tellus, hausit," sese,
"Mi Molle anni cano te ver ægre?"
Ure Molle anu cano te ver ægre.
Vere truso aio puellis tento me;
Thrasonis plano "cum Hymen" (heu sedit),
"Diutius toga thyrso" Hymen edidit;—
Stentior mari aget O mare nautis alter id alas!
Alludo isto terete ure daris pausas anas.
"O pater hic, heu vix en," ses Molle, and vi?
Heu itera vere grates troche in heri.
Ah Moliere arti fere procaciter intuitis!
Vos me! for de parte da vas ure arbuteis.
Thus thrasonis planas vel huma se,
Vi ure Molle anu cano te ver ægre.
Betœ Molle indulgent an suetas agile,—
Pares pector sex, uno vimen ars ille;
"Quietat ure servis Iam," sato heras heu pater,
"Audio do missus Molle, an vatis thema ter?
Ara mi honestatis, vetabit, diu se,—
O mare, mi dare, cum specto me:
Ago in a vae aestuare, vel uno more illic,
O mare, mi dare, cum pacto ure pater hic."
Beavi ad visu civile, an socia luse,
Ure Molle an huma fore ver ægre.

Which, being interpreted, is:

My Molly · and I.

O Patty O'Toole is a rascally fellow,
He beat his wife's head, and said, "I hope you are well, O!"
With his knocks, sir, she has in her body not a whole limb,—
A mighty great sin I must own it is of him.
" Pray, say, sir, do tell us, how is it," says he,
" My Molly and I cannot ever agree ? "
Your Molly and you cannot ever agree :
Very true, so I hope you will listen to me ;
The *rason* is plain, " O come Hymen " (you said it),
"Do ye tie us together."   So Hymen he did it.
Since your marriage to Mary now 'tis altered, alas !
All you do is to *trate* your dear spouse as an ass.
"O Patrick ! you vixen," says Molly, and why ?
You hit her a very great stroke in her eye.
Ah Molly ! her heart I fear *proke* as 'twere in two it is !
Woes me ! for departed away sure her beauty is.
Thus the *rason* is plain, as well you may see,
Why your Molly and you cannot ever agree.
Be to Molly indulgent and *swate* as a jelly,—
Pay respect to her sex, you know women are silly :
" Quite at your service I am," say to her as you pat her,
" How d'ye do, Missus Molly, and what is the matter?
Arah, my honey ! stay, 'tis wait a bit, d'ye see,
O Mary, my *dary*, come *spake* to me :
A-going away is't you are, well you no more I'll lick,
O Mary, my *dary*, come *pack* to your Patrick.'
Behave, I advise you, and so you shall see,
Your Molly and you may for ever agree.

The following appeared in *Punch* some years
ago, and, though not exactly macaronic, deserves
a place as a literary curiosity :

ΤΟ ΘΕ ΛΕΑΔΙΝΓ ΠΕΡΙΟΔΙΚΑΛ.

Θις κομπλιμεντ, γρεατ σιρ, ο τακε,
Τρε α βρικ, ανδ νο μιστακε·
Ενεμι το καντ ανδ φυδγε,
Τιμε το θεε Ι νε'ερ βεγρυδγε·
Ανδ Ι ωπε το σεε υρε ναμε
Φωρεμοστ ιν θε λιστς οφ φαμε
            Τομ Σμιθ, Γρυβ Στρεετ.

A juvenile specimen may find room here:

LITTLE JACK HORNER.

Parvus Jacobus Horner
Sedebat in corner,
Edens a Christmas pie:
Inferuit thumb,
Extraherit plum—
Clamans, "Quid sharp puer am I!"

The "Breitmann Ballads" * of Mr. Charles G. Leland are of a very humorous nature, and many are also in a certain degree macaronic—in so far, at least, that they combine two languages. They are written in the curious broken English spoken by many thousands of Germans in America, and are all of them full of happy phrases and curious combinations of English words with German forms and idioms, as:

"Got well ge-cooked his goose."

We give one short poem—not perhaps the best

* Trübner & Co., London.

macaronic specimen, but one showing well the author's humour and style:

LOVE SONG.

O vere mine lofe a sugar-powl,
　　De fery shmallest loomp
Vouldt shveet de seas, from pole to pole,
　　Und make de shildren shoomp.
Und if she vere a clofer-field,
　　I'd bet my only pence,
It vouldn't pe no dime at all
　　Pefore I'd shoomp the fence.

Her heafenly foice, it drill me so,
　　It oft-dimes seems to hoort,
She is de holiest animale
　　Dat roons oopon de dirt.
De renpow rises vhen she sings,
　　De sonnshine vhen she dalk;
De angels crow und flop deir wings
　　Vhen she goes out to valk.

So livin white, so carnadine,
　　Mine lofe's gomblexion show;
It's shoost like Abendcarmosine,
　　Rich gleamin on de shnow.
Her soul makes plushes in her sheek
　　Ash sommer reds de wein,
Or sonnlight sends a fire life troo
　　An blank Karfunkelstein.

De überschwengliche idées
　　Dis lofe poot in my mind,

Vouldt make a foost-rate philosoph
   Of any human kind.
'Tis schudderin schveet on eart to meet
   An himmlisch-hoellisch Qual ;
Und treat mitwhiles to Kümmel Schnapps
   De Schoenheitsidéal.
Dein Füss seind weiss wie Kreiden,
   Dein Ermlein Helfenbein,
Dein ganzer Leib ist Seiden,
   Dein Brust wie Marmelstein—
Ja—vot de older boet sang,
   I sing of dee—dou Fine !
Dou'rt soul und pody, heart und life :
   Glatt, zart, gelind, und rein.*

Wendell Holmes, in the "Autocrat of the Breakfast Table," † gives a macaronic poem, which is thus introduced : "Your talking Latin reminds me of an odd trick of one of my old tutors. He read so much of that language, that his English half turned into it. He got caught in town, one hot summer, in pretty close quarters, and wrote, or began to write, a series of city pastorals. Eclogues, he called them, and meant

* " Thy feet are white as chalk, my love,
   Thy arms are ivory bone,
Thy body is all satin soft,
   Thy breast of marble stone.

   .   .   .   .   .

Smooth, tender, pure, and fair."

† London: Routledge & Sons.

to have published them by subscription. I remember some of his verses, if you want to hear them. . . . The old man had a great deal to say about 'æstivation,' as he called it, in opposition, as one might say, to *hibernation.* Intra-mural æstivation, or town-life in summer, he would say, is a peculiar form of suspended existence or semi-asphyxia. One wakes up from it about the beginning of the last week in September. This is what I remember of his poem :

ÆSTIVATION.

In candent ire the solar splendor flames ;
The foles, languescent, pend from arid rames ;
His humid front the cive, anheling, wipes,
And dreams of erring on ventiferous ripes.

How dulce to vive occult to mortal eyes,
Dorm on the herb with none to supervise,
Carp the suave berries from the crescent vine,
And bibe the flow from longicaudate kine !

To me, alas ! no verdurous visions come,
Save yon exiguous pool's conferva-scum—
No concave vast repeats the tender hue
That laves my milk-jug with celestial blue.

Me wretched ! let me curr to quercine shades !
Effund your albid hausts, lactiferous maids !
Oh, might I vole to some umbrageous clump,—
Depart—be off,—excede,—evade,—erump !

We conclude the notice of Macaronic Verse with a ridiculous specimen of a hybrid language, written by Pinkerton the antiquary. It is a version of a portion of the beautiful "Vision of Mirza," having Italian terminations to English words:

"When I was ato Grand Cairo, I picked up several orientala manuscripta, whica I have still by me. Among othera, I met with one entitulen, Thea Visiona of Mirza, whica I have redd ove with great pleasure. I intend to give ito to the publico, when I have no other entertain, mento fo them: ando shall begin with the first vision, whico I have translaten wordo fo wordo az followeth:

"On the fifth day of the moon, whico according to the customo of mya forefathera I always keep holi, aftero having washen myself, ando offeren up mya morninga devotiona, I ascended thea hia hilla of Bagdad, in ordero to pas the resto of the dayo in meditation. Az I waz here airing myself on thea topa of thea mountaina, I fell into a profound contemplation of the vanité of human life; ando passing fro one thote to anothero; surely, said I, man iz buto a shado ando life a dreamo. While I waz thuso muzing, I cast mea eyea towardo the summito of a roco, tha waz noto faro fro me, where I discovered one, in the habito of a shepherdo, with a litel musical instrument in hiz hando. Az I looked upo him, he applied ito to hiza lipa, ando began to play upo it. Thea soundo of ito waz exceeding sweet, ando wrote into a varieté of tuna tha were inexpressibly melodiouza, ando alto differenta fro any thinga I had eve heard," &c.

CHRONOGRAMS.

ANOTHER kind of puzzling ingenuity to which our ancestors were occasionally addicted was the indicating of dates in the manner known as Chronograms or Chronographs. This was done by the device of *capitalising* certain letters in the words of a sentence; take, as a primary example, and as giving at once a key to the meaning of this kind of literary frivolity, the line from Horace:

. . . . feriaM siDera VertIce;

the capital letters here, MDVI, give the year 1506. As a source of amusement this fashion prevailed in some degree among the Romans, and more recently among the French literati—the epigrammatic qualities of the language of the latter being perhaps somewhat of an inducement to this literary frivolity. We all know such puzzles as XL, which will serve for either 40 or for "excel;" and MIX, which answers alike for 1009 and for "mix."

Shakespeare evidently knew something of Chronograms, for in "Love's Labour's Lost" (iv. sc. 2),
Holofernes makes one of his quips in this way in
conversation with Sir Nathaniel and Dull. He
boasts: "This is a gift that I have, simple, simple;
a foolish extravagant spirit, full of forms, figures,
shapes, objects, ideas, apprehensions, motions,
revolutions;" and in making letters serve as
numerals, Holofernes says:

"If sore be sore, then L to sore makes fifty sores; O sore L!
Of one sore I an hundred make, by adding but one more L."

Chronograms have been more used in ecclesiastical inscriptions than otherwise, and are to be
found engraven plentifully in churches and cathe-
drals in cities on the banks of the Rhine. The
regular order of the letters composing the date
frequently seems never to have been taken into
account, the selection in many cases being somewhat arbitrary. The following is one done in this
way, and is made up from the Latinised name of
George Villiers, Duke of Buckingham· .

"GeorgIVs DVX ʙVCkIngaMIe,"

which gives MDCXVVVIII (1628), the year of
the Duke's assassination by Lieutenant Felton. It
must be evident from this example that no great

difficulty exists in indicating any date by capitalising letters at intervals.

There is an inscription on a church at Cologne, giving the date of 1722—

> " pIa VIrgInIs MarIæ soDaLItas annos
> sæCVLarI renoVat."

On the minster at Bonn is the following, chronographically indicating the date of 1611:

> "glorifiCate
> et
> portate DeVM
> In Corpore Vestro
> 1 Cor. 6."

The close of the Seven Years' War is thus expressed:

> "Aspera beLLa sILent; reDIIt bona gratIa paCIs;
> O sI parta foret seMper In orbe qVIes."

On a fountain near the Church of St. Francesco di Paola is this:

> "D. O. M.
> Imperante Carlo VI., Vicregente Comite de Palma,
> Gubernante Civitate Comite de Wallis.
> P. P. P.
> Vt aCtIonIbVs nostrIs IVste proCeDaMVs."

The last line gives VCIIVIIVCDMV, which, added together, is 1724.

The following Chronogram is said to be in Albury Church, and gives the date of death in 1646 of George Duncome of Weston, founder of that branch of the family in Surrey:

"ResVrgent eX Isto pVLVere qVI IbI sepVLtI DorMIVnt.
My body, pawned to death, doth here remaine,
As surety for the soul's return againe."

The capitals taken in the order in which they stand, are VXIVLVVIIIVLIDMIV, but rearranged in the order of their relative importance are MDLLXVVVVVVIIIIII, or 1646.

Coins and medals were not unfrequently made the subject of chronographic inscriptions; as, for example, after the opening of the gold mines at Fiume-di-Nisi in Sicily, the Messinese coins bore this:

"EX VIsCerIbVs MeIs haeC fVnDItVr" (1734?)

Addison, in one of his pleasant papers (No. 60 of the "Spectator"), has the following passage on this subject: "This kind of wit appears very often on modern medals, especially those of Germany, when they represent in the inscription the year in which they were coined. Thus we see on a medal of Gustavus Adolphus the following words— 'ChrIstVs DuX ergo triVMphVs.' If you take the pains to pick the figures out of the several words and range them in their proper order, you will find they amount to MDCXVVVII, or 1627, the year in which the medal was stamped; for, as some of the letters distinguish themselves from the rest and overtop their fellows, they are to be considered in a double capacity, both as letters and as figures. Your laborious German wits will turn over a whole dictionary for one of these ingenious devices. A man would think they are searching after an apt classical term; but instead of that, they are looking out a word that has an L, an M, or a D in it. When, therefore, we meet with any of these inscriptions, we are not so much to look in them for the thought as for the year of our Lord."

In Thomas Fuller's "Worthies" there is to be found a notice of the death of Bishop Prideaux, which indicates 1650 as the year of his death: " Iohannes PrIDeaVXVs EpIsCopVs VVIgornIæ MortVVs est." There are very few English Chronograms, and but one of any note, which gives the date of the death of Queen Elizabeth:

"My Day Closed Is In Immortality."

The capital letters in the above giving MDCIII or 1603, the year the great Queen died.

This brief notice of Chronograms—of which we have limited the examples—cannot be better concluded than by the following anecdote, related by Wheatley in his little book upon Anagrams. "A passage of Scripture, arranged chronogrammatically, was made the vehicle for a prophecy by Michael Stifelius, a Lutheran minister at Wirtemberg, who foretold that on the 3d of October 1533, at ten o'clock, the world would come to an end. The passage from which he elicited this wonderful, and, as it proved, inaccurate prediction, is in John xix. 37—'They shall look on Him whom they pierced' —VIDebVnt In qVeM transfIXerVnt, making MDXVVVVIII or 1533; but the month, the day, and the hour seem only to have existed in the excited imagination of the worthy Stifelius himself. There is a rider to this anecdote which may be thus related: On the day that Stifelius predicted the end of the world, a very violent storm arose while he was preaching to his congregation, who believed his prophecy was coming to pass, when lo! suddenly the clouds disappeared, the sky became clear, and all was calm except the people, whose indignation was aroused, and they dragged the prophet from his pulpit, and beat him sorely for thus disappointing them."

ECHO VERSES.

HE writing of Echo Verses was another of the methods in which our bygone poets often displayed an occasional poetical beauty, as well as a quaint ingenuity—the aim of such compositions being that the last syllable, when repeated as by an echo, should convey a different yet appropriate meaning. Butler seems to have been rather opposed to this literary frivolity, for in the following extract from "Hudibras," in which Orsin is lamenting for his bear, he terms them "splay-foot" rhymes:

> " He beat his breast and tore his hair,
> For loss of his dear crony bear
> That Echo, from the hollow ground,
> His doleful wailings did resound
> More wistfully, by many times,
> Than in small poets' splay-foot rhymes.
> Quoth he, ' O whither, wicked bruin,
> Art thou fled ? to my '—Echo, ' *Ruin*,'
> ' I thought thou 'ads't scorned to budge a step
> For fear.' Quoth Echo, ' *Marry quep*.'

'Am I not here to take thy part,
Then what has quailed thy stubborn heart ?
Have these bones rattled, and this head
So often in thy quarrel bled ?
Nor did I ever wince or trudge it
For thy dear sake.'   Quoth she, ' *Mum budget.*'
' To run from those thou hadst o'ercome
Thus cowardly.'   Quoth Echo, '*Mum !*
' Yet shame and honour might prevail
To keep thee thus from turning tail,
For who would grudge to spend his blood in
His honour's cause ? '   Quoth she, ' *A puddin' !* ' "

This kind of verse was at one time frequently
used in political affairs, and the following was
written by a Royalist during the struggle between
Charles I. and the Parliamentarians :

" What wantest thou, that thou art in this sad taking ?
              Echo—A king.
What made him first remove hence his residing ?
                       Siding.
Did any here deny him satisfaction ?
                       Faction,
Tell me wherein the strength of faction lies ?
                       On lies.
What didst thou when the king left his Parliament ?
                       Lament.
What terms wouldst give to gain his company ?
                       Any.
What wouldst thou do if here thou mightst behold him ?
                       Hold him.

But wouldst thou save him with thy best endeavour?
　　　　　　　Ever.
But if he comes not, what becomes of London?
　　　　　　　Undone."

Another Royalist production of this nature is given by Disraeli in his "Curiosities," as having been recited at the end of a comedy played by the scholars of Trinity College, Cambridge, in March 1641:

THE ECHO.

Now, Echo, on what's religion grounded?
　　　　　　　Roundhead!
Whose its professors most considerable?
　　　　　　　Rabble!
How do these prove themselves to be the godly?
　　　　　　　Oddly.
But they in life are known to be the holy.
　　　　　　　O lie!
Who are these preachers, men or women common?
　　　　　　　Common!
Come they from any universitie?
　　　　　　　Citie.
Do they not learning from their doctrine sever?
　　　　　　　Ever.
Yet they pretend that they do edifie;
　　　　　　　O fie!
What do you call it then, to fructify?
　　　　　　　Ay.
What church have they, and what pulpits?
　　　　　　　Pitts!

But now in chambers the Conventicle ;
> Tickle !

The godly sisters shrewdly are belied.
> Bellied !

The godly number then will soon transcend.
> End !

As for the temples they with zeal embrace them.
> Rase them !

What do they make of bishop's hierarchy ?
> Archie ! *

Are crosses, images, ornaments their scandall ?
> All.

Nor will they leave us many ceremonies,
> Monies.

Must even religion down for satisfaction,
> Faction.

How stand they affected to the government civil ?
> Evil.

But to the king they say they are most loyal.
> Lye all !

Then God keep king and State from these same men.
> Amen !

The following belongs to the same period. All our readers, however, may not agree with the sentiments of the author, and, though not properly

---

* "An allusion, probably, to Archibald Armstrong, the fool or privileged jester of Charles I., usually called *Archy*, who had a quarrel with Archbishop Laud, and of whom many *arch* things are on record : there is a little jest-book very high-priced and of little worth which bears the title of *Archie's Jests*."—*Disraeli.*

belonging to the class of Echo Verses, the poem
has generally been referred to as deserving a place
amongst them :

> "O faithless world, and thy most faithless part,
>   A woman's heart ;
> The true shop of variety, where sits
>   Nothing but fits
> And fevers of desire, and pangs of love,
>   Which toys remove.
> Why was she born to please, or I to trust
>   Words writ in dust ?
> Suffering her looks to govern my despair,
>   My painful air ;
> And fruit of time rewarded with untruth,
>   The food of youth.
> Untrue she was, yet I believed her eyes,
>   Instructed spies ;
> Till I was taught that love is but a school
>   To train a fool.
> Could it be absence that did make her strange,
>   Base flower of change ?
> Or sought she more than triumph of denial ?
>   To see a trial,
> How far her smile commanded on my weakness
>   To yield and confess.
> Excuse not now the folly, nor her nature,
>   Blush and endure
> As well thy shame, as passions that were vain,
>   And think thy gain,
> To know that love, lodged in a woman's breast,
>   Is but a guest."

The next is a Dialogue between Glutton and Echo, taken from "Hygiasticon: or the Right Course of Preserving Life and Health unto extream old Age: together with soundnesse and integritie of the Senses, Judgement, and Memorie. Written in Latine by Leonard Lessius, and now done into Englishe. 24ᵐᵒ, Cambridge. 1634."

DIALOGUE BETWEEN A GLUTTON AND ECHO.

Glutton. My bellie I do deifie.
Echo.   Fie!
Gl. Who curbs his appetite's a fool.
Echo.   Ah fool!
Gl. I do not like this abstinence.
Echo.   Hence!
Gl. My joy's a feast, my wish is wine.
Echo.   Swine.
Gl. We epicures are happie truly.
Echo.   You lie.
Gl. Who's that which giveth me the lie?
Echo.   I.
Gl. What! Echo, thou that mock'st a voice?
Echo.   A voice.
Gl. May I not, Echo, eat my fill?
Echo.   Ill.
Gl. Wilt hurt me if I drink too much?
Echo.   Much.
Gl. Thou mock'st me, nymph; I'll not believe it.
Echo.   Believe't.

Gl.   Dost thou condemn then what I do?
Echo.   I do.
Gl.   I grant it doth exhaust the purse.
Echo.   Worse.
Gl.   Is't this which dulls the sharpest wit?
Echo.   Best wit.
Gl.   Is't this which brings infirmities?
Echo.   It is.
Gl.   Whither will't bring my soul? canst tell?
Echo.   T'hell.
Gl.   Dost thou no gluttons virtuous know?
Echo.   No.
Gl.   Would'st have me temperate till I die?
Echo.   Ay.
Gl.   Shall I therein finde ease and pleasure?
Echo.   Yea, sure.
Gl.   But is't a thing which profit brings?
Echo.   It brings.
Gl.   To mind or body? or to both?
Echo.   To both.
Gl.   Will it my life on earth prolong?
Echo.   Oh long!
Gl.   Will it make me vigorous until death?
Echo.   Till death.
Gl.   Will't bring me to eternal blisse?
Echo.   Yes.
Gl.   Then, sweetest Temperance, I'll love thee.
Echo.   .   I love thee.
Gl.   Then, swinish Gluttonie, I' leave thee.
Echo.   I'll leave thee.
Gl.   I'll be a belly-god no more.
Echo.   No more.

Gl. If all be true which thou dost tell,
They who fare sparingly, fare well.
Echo.   Farewell.

At the time when Napoleon was supreme over Germany, in the spring of 1806, one Palm, a book-seller in Nuremberg, published a pamphlet entitled "Germany in its Deepest Humiliation," which contained some bitter truths concerning Napoleon, criticising his policy with considerable severity. Palm was seized by French gendarmes, and transferred to Brunau, where he was tried before an extraordinary court-martial for a libel on the Emperor of France, and condemned to death, without any advocate being heard in his defence. All intercession on his behalf failing, he was shot on August 26, in terms of his sentence—the very day of his trial! The murder of this poor man, for such it literally was, whether immediately follow-ing from Napoleon's mandate, or the effect of the furious zeal of some of his officers, excited deep and universal indignation. Napoleon himself afterwards said regarding Palm's execution—"All that I recol-lect is, that Palm was arrested by order of Davoust, I believe, tried, condemned, and shot, for having, while the country was in possession of the French and under military occupation, not only excited rebellion amongst the inhabitants, and urged them to rise and massacre the soldiers, but also attempted to instigate the soldiers themselves to refuse obedience to their orders, and to mutiny against their generals. *I believe* that he met with a fair trial." * An Echo Poem appeared with the pamphlet, of which the following is a translation :

BONAPARTE AND THE ECHO.

Bon. Alone, I am in this sequestered spot not overheard.
Echo. Heard !
Bon. 'Sdeath ! Who answers me ? What being is there nigh ?
Echo. I.
Bon. Now I guess ! To report my accents Echo has made her task.
Echo. Ask.
Bon. Knowest thou whether London will henceforth continue to resist ?
Echo. Resist.
Bon. Whether Vienna and other Courts will oppose me always ?
Echo. Always.
Bon. O Heaven ! what must I expect after so many reverses ?
Echo. Reverses.
Bon. What ! should I, like a coward vile, to compound be reduced ?
Echo. Reduced.
Bon. After so many bright exploits be forced to restitution ?
Echo. Restitution.
Bon. Restitution of what I've got by true heroic feats and martial address ?
Echo. Yes.
Bon. What will be the fate of so much toil and trouble ?
Echo. Trouble.
Bon. What will become of my people, already too unhappy ?
Echo. Happy.

---

* "Voice from St. Helena," vol. i. p. 432.

Bon. What should I then be, that I think myself immortal?
Echo.   Mortal.
Bon. The whole world is filled with the glory of my name, you
       know.
Echo.   No.
Bon. Formerly its fame struck this vast globe with terror.
Echo.   Error.
Bon. Sad Echo, begone! I grow infuriate! I die!
Echo.   Die!

The next example is a Song by Addison:

> " Echo, tell me, while I wander
>   O'er this fairy plain to prove him,
> If my shepherd still grows fonder,
>   Ought I in return to love him?
>   Echo—Love him, love him!
>
> If he loves, as is the fashion,
>   Should I churlishly forsake him?
> Or in pity to his passion,
>   Fondly to my bosom take him?
>   Echo—Take him, take him!
>
> Thy advice then, I'll adhere to,
>   Since in Cupid's chains I've led him;
> And with Henry shall not fear to
>   Marry, If you answer, 'Wed him!'
>   Echo—Wed him, wed him!"

William Browne (1590–1645), a poet of whom comparatively little is known, in one of his poems, " Britannia's Pastorals," introduces in his " Fifth Song" some Echo verses; apostrophising Heaven, Browne writes—

" O sacred Essence, light'ning me this houre !
How may I rightly stile thy great power ?
          Echo—Power.

Power ! but of whence ? under the greene-wood spray,
Or liv'st in Heaven ? say :
          Echo—In Heavens aye.

In Heavens aye ! tell, may I it obtaine
By almes, by fasting, prayer, by paine ?
          Echo—By paine.

Show me the paine, it shall be undergone :
I to mine end will still go on.
          Echo—Go on.

But whither ? On ! Show me the place, the time :
What if the mountaine I do climbe ?
          Echo—Climbe.

Is that the way to joyes which still endure ?
Oh bid my soul of it be sure !
          Echo—Be sure.

Then, thus assured, doe I climbe the hill,
Heaven be my guide in this Thy will.
          Echo—I will."

The next is taken from an old newspaper (_circa_ 1760):

    " If I address the Echo yonder,
      What will its answer be, I wonder?
          Echo—I wonder.

O wondrous Echo, tell me, *blessé,*
Am I for marriage or celibacy?
> Echo—Silly Bessy.

If then to win the maid I try,
Shall I find her a property?
> Echo—A proper tie.

If neither being grave nor funny
Will win the maid to matrimony?
> Echo—Try money.

If I should try to gain her heart,
Shall I go plain, or rather smart?
> Echo—Smart.

She mayn't love dress, and I, again, then
May come too plain, and she'll complain then?
> Echo—Come plain, then.

To please her most, perhaps 'tis best
To come as I'm in common dressed?
> Echo—Come undressed.

Then, if to marry me I tease her,
What will she say if that should please her?
> Echo—Please, sir.

When cross nor good words can appease her—
What if such naughty whims should seize her?
> Echo—You'd see, sir.

When wed she'll change, for Love's no stickler,
And love her husband less than liquor?
> Echo—Then lick her.

To leave me then I can't compel her,
Though every woman else excel her.
                    Echo—Sell her.

The doubting youth to Echo turned again, sir,
To ask advice, but found it did not answer."

The following appeared in an Edinburgh newspaper some years ago, and is of a similar nature to
the preceding:

EGO AND ECHO.

I asked of Echo, t'other day,
    Whose words are few and often funny,
What to a question she should say
    Of courtship, love, and matrimony.
            Quoth Echo, plainly, " Matter o' money."

Whom should I marry? Should it be
    A dashing damsel, gay and pert,
A pattern of consistency,
    Or selfish, mercenary flirt?
            Quoth Echo, sharply, "Nary flirt."

What if, a-weary of the strife
    That long has lured the gay deceiver,
She promised to amend her life
    And sin no more—can I believe her?
            Quoth Echo, with decision, "Leave her."

But if some maiden with a heart
    On me should venture to bestow it,

Pray, should I act the wiser part,
    To take the treasure or forego it?
        Quoth Echo, very promptly, "Go it."

But what, if seemingly afraid
    To bind her fate in Hymen's fetter,
She vows she means to die a maid,
    In answer to my loving letter?
        Quoth Echo, very coolly, "Let her."

What if, in spite of her disdain,
    I find my heart entwined about
With Cupid's dear, delicious chain,
    So closely that I can't get out?
        Quoth Echo, laughingly, "Get out."

But if some maid with beauty blest,
    As pure and fair as Heaven can make her,
Will share my labour and my rest
    Till envious Death shall overtake her?
        Quoth Echo (*sotto voce*), "Take her."

This appeared in a periodical but a short time ago, and is by R. E. Francillon:

" *Lady.* Echo, what giveth maiden's best address?
Echo.   A dress.
Lady. And, of their songs, which is the best for tune?
Echo.   Fortune.
Lady. Whereto must trust poor maids to it?
Echo.   To wit.
Lady. But if they be nor rich nor yet too wise?
Echo.   To eyes."

An Echo Poem by good George Herbert runs as follows:

⸱ HEAVEN.

O who will show me those delights on high?
> Echo—I.

Thou, Echo? Thou art mortal, all men know.
> Echo—No.

Wert thou not born among the trees and leaves?
> Echo—Leaves.

And are there any leaves that still abide?
> Echo—Bide.

What leaves are they? Impart the matter wholly.
> Echo—Holy.

Are holy leaves the Echo then ot bliss?
> Echo—Yes.

Then tell me, what is that supreme delight?
> Echo—Light.

Light to the mind: what shall the will enjoy?
> Echo—Joy.

But are there cares and business with the pleasure?
> Echo—Leisure.

Light, joy, and leisure! but shall they persever?
> Echo—Ever!

The beautiful verses next given are taken from a volume entitled "The Changed Cross,"* a collec-

* London: Sampson Low & Co.

tion of religious poems gathered chiefly from American sources, and bear the name of

The Christian and his Echo.

True faith, producing love to God and man,
Say, Echo, is not this the Gospel plan?
> The Gospel plan.

Must I my faith and love to Jesus show,
By doing good to all, both friend and foe?
> Both friend and foe.

But if a brother hates and treats me ill,
Must I return him good, and love him still?
> Love him still.

If he my failings watches to reveal,
Must I his faults as carefully conceal?
> As carefully conceal.

But if my name and character he blast,
And cruel malice, too, a long time last;
And if I sorrow and affliction know,
He loves to add unto my cup of woe;
In this uncommon, this peculiar case,
Sweet Echo, say, must I still love and bless?
> Still love and bless.

Whatever usage ill I may receive,
Must I be patient still, and still forgive?
> Be patient still, and still forgive.

Why, Echo, how is this? thou'rt sure a dove!
Thy voice shall teach me nothing else but love?
> Nothing else but love.

Amen ! with all my heart, then be it so ;
'Tis all delightful, just, and good, I know ;
And now to practise I'll directly go.
    Directly go.

Things being so, whoever me reject,
My gracious God me surely will protect.
    Surely will protect.

Henceforth I'll roll on Him my every care,
And then both friend and foe embrace in prayer.
    Embrace in prayer.

But after all those duties I have done,
Must I, in point of merit, them disown,
And trust for heaven through Jesus' blood alone ?
    Through Jesus' blood alone.

Echo, enough ! thy counsels to mine ear
Are sweeter than, to flowers, the dew-drop tear ;
Thy wise instructive lessons please me well :
I'll go and practise them. Farewell, farewell !
    Practise them. Farewell, farewell !

The following beautiful poem has been ascribed to various authors—amongst others, to James I. and Bishop Andrewes. It is not an Echo Poem, but its composition being somewhat similar, it merits a place here.

THE LORD'S PRAYER.

If any be distressed, and fain would gather
Some comfort, let him haste unto

Our Father,
For we of hope and help are quite bereaven
Except Thou succour us
Who art in heaven.
Thou showest mercy, therefore for the same
We praise Thee, singing
Hallowed be Thy name.
Of all our miseries cast up the sum ;
Show us Thy joys, and let
Thy kingdom come.
We mortal are, and alter from our birth ;
Thou constant art.
Thy will be done on earth.
Thou mad'st the earth, as well as planets seven,
Thy name be blessed here
As 'tis in Heaven.
Nothing we have to use or debts to pay,
Except Thou give it us.
Give us this day
Wherewith to clothe us, wherewith to be fed,
For without Thee we want—
Our daily bread.
We want, but want no faults, for no day passes
But we do sin—
Forgive us our trespasses.
No man from sinning ever free did live,
Forgive us, Lord, our sins
As we forgive.
If we repent our faults, Thou ne'er disdainest us ;
We pardon them
That trespass against us.
Forgive us that is past, a new path tread us ;

Direct us always in Thy faith,
  And lead us—
We, Thine own people, and Thy chosen nation,
Into all truth, but
  Not into temptation.
Thou that of all good graces art the giver,
Suffer us not to wander,
  But deliver
Us from the fierce assaults of world and devil
And flesh, so shalt Thou free us
  From all evil.
To these petitions let both Church and laymen,
With one consent of heart and voice, say
  Amen.

One of the most peculiar poems we have met with follows, and being the same in subject as the preceding, it is placed here, though properly belonging neither to this section nor any other. The initial letters of the lines form an acrostic of "My boast is in the glorious Cross of Christ." The words in Italics, when read on the left-hand side from top to bottom, and on the right hand from bottom to top, form the whole of the Lord's Prayer.

MY BOAST IS IN THE GLORIOUS CROSS OF CHRIST.
Make known the gospel truth, *our* Father King;
  Yield up Thy grace, dear *Father*, from above;
Bless us with hearts *which* feelingly can sing,
  " Our life Thou *art* for *ever*, God of love."

Assuage our grief *in* love *for* Christ, we pray,
  Since the Prince of *Heaven* and *glory* died,
Took away all sins, and *hallowed the* display,
  Infinite *be*ing, first man, *and* then was crucified.
Stupendous God ! *Thy* grace and *power* make known ;
  In Jesus' *name* let all *the* world rejoice,
Now labour in *Thy* heavenly *kingdom* own—
  That blessed *kingdom*, of Thy saints *the* choice.
How vile to *come* to Thee, *is* all our cry ;
  Enemies to *Thy* self, and all that's *Thine* ;
Graceless our *will*, we live *for* vanity ;
  Loathing the very *be*ing, *evil* in design—
O God, Thy will be *done from* earth to heaven ;
  Reclining *on* the gospel let *us* live,
In *earth*, from sin *deliver*ed and forgiven,
  Oh, *as* Thyself, *but* teach us to forgive ;
Unless *it*s power *temptation* doth destroy,
  Sure *is* our fall *into* the depths of woe.
Carnal *in* mind, we have *not* a glimpse of joy
  Raised against *Heaven ;* in *us* no hopes we know.
Oh, *give* us grace, and *lead* us on the way ;
  Shine on *us* with Thy love, and give *us* peace.
Self, and *this* sin that rise *against* us, slay.
    Oh, grant each *day* our *trespass*es may cease ;
Forgive *our* evil deeds *that* oft we do ;
  Convince us *daily of them* to our shame ;
Help us with heavenly *bread, forgive* us, too,
  Recurrent lusts ; *and we'*ll adore Thy name.
In Thy *forgive*ness we *as* saints can die,
  Since for *us*, and our *trespasses* so high,
Thy Son, *our* Saviour, died on Calvary.

Similar to the above is this verse by George Herbert :

"OUR LIFE IS HID WITH CHRIST IN GOD."

(Colos. iii. 3.)

My words and thoughts do both express this notion,
That *Life* hath with the sun a double motion.
The first *Is* straight, and our diurnal friend ;
The other *Hid*, and doth obliquely bend.
One life is wrapt *In* flesh, and tends to earth :
The other winds toward *Him*, whose happy birth
Taught me to live here so, *That* still one eye
Should aim and shoot at that which *Is* on high ;
Quitting with daily labour all *My* pleasure,
To gain at harvest an eternal *Treasure.*

JESUITICAL VERSES.

JESUITICAL, or, as they are sometimes called, Equivocal Verses, had their origin very much in the political and religious feuds of our ancestors. They are designed to give two very different meanings, according as they are read downwards or across. Thus, the following lines, if read as they stand, must be admired for their loyalty, but if perused in the order of the figures prefixed, a very different result is obtained :

1. I love my country—but the King
3. Above all men his praise I sing,
2. Destruction to his odious reign
4. That plague of princes, Thomas Paine ;
5. The royal banners are displayed
7. And may success the standard aid
6. Defeat and ruin seize the cause
8. Of France, her liberty, and laws.

The foregoing relic of a revolutionary period may be well followed by one pertaining to Reformation times, which may be read either across or down the columns:

THE DOUBLE-FACED CREED.

I hold for sound faith	What England's church allows,
What Rome's faith saith	My conscience disavows,
Where the king's head	The flock can take no shame
The flock's misled	Who hold the Pope supreme.
Where the altar's dressed	The worship's scarce divine
The people's blessed,	Whose table's bread and wine,
He's but an ass	Who their communion flies
Who shuns the mass	Is catholic and wise.

We find in another work the foregoing lines rendered into a kind of monkish Latin; thus lending an artful aid to the cause of anarchy:

1. Pro fide teneo sana
3. Quæ docet Anglicana
2. Affirmat quæ Romana
4. Videntur mihi vana
5. Supremus quando rex est
7. Tum plebs est fortunata
6. Seductus ille grex est
8. Cui Papa imperator.
9. Altare cum ornatur
11. Communio fit inanis
10. Populus tum beatur
12. Cum mensa, vinum, panis,
13. Asini nomen meruit
15. Hunc morem qui non capit
14. Missam qui deseruit
16. Catholicus est et sapit.

These Equivocal Verses are mostly all of the same nature, and the next seems to have been composed during the Revolution period :

" I love with all my heart
The Hanoverian part
And for the Settlement
My conscience gives consent
Most righteous in the cause
To fight for George's laws
It is my mind and heart
Though none will take my part

The Tory party here
Most hateful do appear
I ever have denied
To be on James's side
To fight for such a king
Will England's ruin bring
In this opinion I
Resolve to live and die."

The promulgation of the new constitution at the first French Revolution gave birth to the next Equivocal lines :

" The newly-made law
From my soul I abhor
My faith to prove good
I maintain the old code
May God give you peace
Forsaken Noblesse
May He ever confound
The Assembly all round

'Tis my wish to esteem
The ancient regime
I maintain the new code
Is opposed to all good
Messieurs Democrats
To the Devil go hence
All the Aristocrats
Are the sole men of sense."

At the beginning of the Civil War in the United States, the following curious production appeared in one of the newspapers, professedly arranged to suit all parties. The first column is the Secession, the second the Abolition Platform, read across it is the Democratic Platform, thus also representing the whole Union :

K

The Platform.

Hurrah for	The old Union
Secession	Is a curse
We fight for	The Constitution
The Confederacy	Is a league with hell
We love	Free speech
The rebellion	Is treason
We glory in	A free press
Separation	Will not be tolerated
We fight not for	The negro's freedom
Reconstruction	Must be obtained
We must succeed	At every hazard
The Union	We love
We love not	The negro
We never said	Let the Union slide
We want	The Union as it was
Foreign intervention	Is played out
We cherish	The old flag
The stars and bars	Is a flaunting lie
We venerate	The *habeas corpus*
Southern chivalry	Is hateful
Death to	Jeff Davis
Abe Lincoln	Is'nt the Government
Down with	Mob law
Law and order	Shall triumph.

The next is not political, but is a curious specimen of Equivocal Versification which may be
read in several ways:

ADDRESS TO MY SWEETHEART.

Your face,	your tongue,	your wit,
So fair,	so sweet,	so sharp,
First bent,	then drew,	then hit
Mine eye,	mine ear,	my heart.
Mine eye,	mine ear,	mine heart,
To like,	to learn,	to love,
Your face,	your tongue,	your wit,
Doth lead,	doth teach,	doth move.
Your face,	your tongue,	your wit,
With beams,	with sound,	with art,
Doth blind,	doth charm,	doth rule
Mine eye,	mine ear,	mine heart.
Mine eye,	mine ear,	mine heart,
With life,	with hope,	with skill,
Your face,	your tongue,	your wit,
Doth feed,	doth feast,	doth fill.
O face !	O tongue !	O wit !
With frowns,	with check,	with smart,
Wrong not,	vex not,	wound not
Mine eye,	mine ear,	mine heart.
This eye,	this ear,	this heart,
Shall joy, ·	shall bend,	shall swear,
Your face,	your tongue	your wit
To serve,	to trust,	to fear."

Amongst various other ingenious contrivances
adopted by the proprietors of the *rosoglio* houses

(Anglice, dram-shops) in Valetta, to attract the custom and patronage of the gallant red-jackets that occasionally swarm the streets, one individual distributed among the soldiers the following puzzle. A little study will suffice to master the mysterious document.

THE INVITATION.

Here's to Pand's Pen.   DASOCI.
Alhou Rinha? R. M. (Les Smirt)
Ha ! N. D. F.   Unlet fri.   Ends.
HIPRE ! ign.   Beju !   Standk.
Indan !   DEVIL'S PEAKO !   F. N.
(One.)

We conclude with a "Panegyric on the Ladies," which may be read in two ways, giving totally different meanings, and we leave the reader to find out these for himself, premising that it is not at all difficult, after the examples already given.

> " That man must lead a happy life
>   Who's free from matrimonial chains,
> Who is directed by a wife
>   Is sure to suffer for his pains.
>
> Adam could find no solid peace
>   When Eve was given for a mate ;

Until he saw a woman's face
Adam was in a happy state.

In all the female race appear
Hypocrisy, deceit, and pride;
Truth, darling of a heart sincere,
In woman never did reside.

What tongue is able to unfold
The failings that in woman dwell;
The worth in woman we behold
Is almost imperceptible.

Confusion take the man, I say,
Who changes from his singleness,
Who will not yield to woman's sway,
Is sure of earthly blessedness."

MONOSYLLABIC VERSE.

ONE of the most curious foibles of eighteenth century poets was their dislike to monosyllables in their verses—a dislike strikingly antagonistic to the opinion entertained by poets of an earlier age. In the estimation of those of more modern days, however, monosyllables occasionally add to the force and rhythm of a passage. Pope, in speaking of their use, rather contemptuously exclaims in the " Dunciad :"

" And ten low words creep on in one dull line."

Churchill afterwards, in the " Rosciad," where he censures Mossop, the actor, hints also at something of this nature :

" With studied impropriety of speech,
    He soars beyond the hackney'd critic's reach ;
    To epithets allots emphatic state,
    Whilst principals, ungraced, like lackeys wait ;
    In ways first trodden by himself excels,
    And stands alone in indeclinables ;

Conjunction, preposition, adverb, join
To stamp new vigour on the nervous line ;
In monosyllables his thunders roll,
He, she, it, and we, ye, they, affright the soul."

Rogers and Moore thought somewhat more highly than either Pope or Churchill regarding this feature in poetry, and Lord Russell's "Life of Moore" records a conversation between Crowe (author of a book on the "Structure of English Verse"), Rogers, and Moore on the use of mono-syllables, and phrases like "He jests at scars," "Sigh on my lip," "Give all thou canst," and many others, were referred to as most musical and vigo-rous. In the works of Moore himself there is a very fine specimen of the effective use of monosyllables, in a passage which occurs in the Fire-Worshippers in "Lalla Rookh"—

" I knew, I knew it could not last—
'Twas bright, 'twas heavenly, but 'tis past !
Oh ! ever thus, from childhood's hour,
    I've seen my fondest hopes decay ;
I never loved a tree or flower.
    But 'twas the first to fade away.
I never nursed a dear gazelle
    To glad me with its soft black eye,
But when it came to know me well,
    And love me, it was sure to die !

Now, too—the joy most like divine
   Of all I ever dreamt or knew,
To see thee, hear thee, call thee mine,—
   Oh misery ! must I lose *that* too ?
Yet go ! On peril's brink we meet ;
   Those frightful rocks—that treach'rous sea—
No, never come again—though sweet,
   Though Heaven, it may be death to thee!"

This passage contains 126 words, 110 of which are monosyllables.

The readers of "John Halifax, Gentleman," will easily recollect how highly Miss Muloch speaks in that work regarding the brothers Fletcher and their poetry. In the little-known poem of Phineas Fletcher (died about 1650) entitled "The Purple Island"—a work which, though grotesque and prolix, is smoothly versified, and has rich descriptive and moral passages—there is this fine specimen of monosyllabic and alliterative power in Canto I. stanza 7 :

" New light new love, new love new life hath bred ;
   A life that lives by love, and loves by light ;
  A love to Him to whom all loves are wed ;
  A light to whom the sun is darkest night :
Eye's light, heart's love, soul's only life He is ;
Life, soul, love, heart, light, eye, and all are His ;
He eye, light, heart, love, soul ; He all my joy and
   bliss."

Of the seventy words contained in this verse only two are of more than one syllable. Giles Fletcher, as well as his brother Phineas, furnishes numerous examples of monosyllabic versification, and one specimen is selected from him also, quoted from " Christ's Victory and Triumph in Heaven and Earth over and after Death," a work which, though somewhat affected, rises occasionally into lofty imaginative poetry :

> " Love is the blossom where there blows
> Everything that lives or grows ;
> Love doth make the Heav'ns to move,
> And the Sun doth burn in love :
> Love the strong and weak doth yoke,
> And makes the ivy climb the oak ;
> Under whose shadows lions wild,
> Soften'd by love, grow tame and mild.
>
> Love no med'cine can appease,
> He burns the fishes in the seas ;
> Not all the skill his wounds can stench,
> Not all the sea his fire can quench :
> Love did make the bloody spear,
> Once a leafy coat to wear."

From these two brothers many similar instances might be given, but to proceed to poets better known, we give two quotations from the " saintly " George Herbert :

Virtue.

Sweet Day, so cool, so calm, so bright,
The bridal of the earth and sky,
The dew shall weep thy fall to-night;
        For thou must die.

Sweet Rose, whose hue angry and brave,
Bids the rash gazer wipe his eye,
Thy root is ever in the grave,
        And thou must die.

Sweet Spring, full of sweet days and roses,
A box where sweets compacted lie,
My music shows ye have your closes,
        And all must die.

Only a sweet and virtuous soul,
Like season'd timber, never gives;
But though the whole world turn to coal,
        Then chiefly lives.

The Call.

Come, my Way, my Truth, my Life;
Such a Way, as gives us breath:
Such a Truth, as ends all strife:
Such a Life, as killeth death.

Come, my Light, my Feast, my Strength;
Such a Light, as shows a feast:
Such a Feast, as mends in length:
Such a Strength, as makes his guest.

Come, my Joy, my Love, my Heart;
Such a Joy, as none can move:

Such a Love, as none can part :
Such a Heart, as joys in love.

Herbert's poems are full of similar passages. Shakespeare gives an instance which shows that the abrupt and broken language of passion is generally monosyllabic, as in "King John," when the widowed Constance says :

" Thou may'st, thou shalt ; I will not go with thee :
  I will instruct my sorrows to be proud ;
  For grief is proud, and makes his owner stout.
  To me, and to the state of my great grief,
  Let kings assemble ; for my grief's so great,
  That no supporter but the huge firm earth
  Can hold it up : here I and sorrow sit ;
  Here is my throne, bid kings come bow to it."

In this there are only six words of more than one syllable.

In the Library of the British Museum there is a tract of great rarity, from which Shakespeare is said to have borrowed the plot of " As You Like It." The tract is entitled " Euphue's Golden Legacy," by Thomas Lodge, a poet of the Elizabethan age, who was also the author of a variety of valuable productions both in prose and verse. Ellis, in his " Specimens of Early English Poets," gives three of Lodge's poems from the " Pleasant

Historie of Glaucus and Scilla," but has omitted to mention the following madrigal, the most beautiful, perhaps, of all Lodge's compositions, and it is given here as an excellent illustration of monosyllabic verse, few words of more than one syllable appearing in it.

MADRIGAL.

Love in my bosom, like a bee,
   Doth sucke his sweete ;
Now with his wings he plays with me,
   Now with his feete.

Within mine eyes he makes his nest,
His bed amid my tender breast ;
My kisses are his daily feast,
And yet he robs me of my rest.

Strike I my lute—he tunes the string,
He music plays, if I do sing ;
He lends me every living thing,
Yet cruel he my heart doth sting.

What, if I beat the wanton boy
   With many a rod,
He will repay me with annoy,
   Because a god.

Then sit thou safely on my knee,
And let thy bower my bosom be ;
O Cupid ! so thou pity me,
I will not wish to part from thee.

Coleridge considered that the most beautiful verse, and also the most sublime, in the Bible was that in the book of Ezekiel which says—"And He said unto me, Son of man, can these bones live? And I answered, O Lord God, thou knowest." Here are seventeen monosyllables, and only three words of two syllables.

The author of the "Night Thoughts," also, in a very impressive passage, says—

> "The bell strikes one. We take no note of time
> Save by its loss; to give it then a tongue
> Was wise in man."

The following lines of Hall, satirising the vanity of those who take pleasure in adding house to house and field to field,—

> "Fond fool, six feet shall serve for all thy store,
> And he that cares for most shall find no more"—

gave occasion for the historian Gibbon's appreciative remark, "What harmonious monosyllables!"

NONSENSE VERSE, &c.

THE French had at one time a favourite and ingenious kind of versification called Amphigourie, or Nonsense Verse. The word is derived from two Greek words signifying *about* and *circle*, and the object was to give verses the appearance of good sense and fine poetry, while in reality meaning nothing whatever! The primary example given is richly-rhymed, elegantly expressed, but actual nonsense! It is taken from Disraeli's "Curiosities of Literature."

AMPHIGOURIE.

Qu'il est heureux de se défendre
Quand le cœur ne s'est pas rendu !
Mais qu'il est fâcheux de se rendre
Quand le bonheur est suspendu !
Par un discours sans suite et tendre,
Égarez un cœur eperdu ;
Souvent par un mal-entendu
L'amant adroit se fait entendre.

IMITATED.

How happy to defend our heart,
When Love has never thrown a dart!
But ah! unhappy when it bends,
If pleasure her soft bliss suspends!
Sweet in a wild disordered strain,
A lost and wandering heart to gain,
Oft in mistaken language wooed
The skilful lover's understood.

The preceding was sung by the celebrated Madame Tencin one evening to Fontenelle, and they bore such a resemblance to meaning that Fontenelle requested they should be repeated. "Do you not perceive," said the witty authoress, "that they are nonsense?" "Ah," replied the poet, sarcastically, "they are so much like the fine verses I have heard here, that it is not surprising I should be for once mistaken!"

Pope furnishes the best English specimen of this kind of poetry—the "Song by a Person of Quality," and it is believed to have been written to ridicule certain namby-pamby poets of his day. The lines are as follow:

SONG, BY A PERSON OF QUALITY.

Fluttering spread thy purple pinions,
Gentle Cupid, o'er my heart,

I a slave in thy dominions,
   Nature must give way to art.

Mild Arcadians, ever blooming,
   Nightly nodding o'er your flocks,
See my weary days consuming,
   All beneath yon flowery rocks.

Thus the Cyprian goddess weeping,
   Mourned Adonis, darling youth :
Him the boar, in silence creeping,
   Gored with unrelenting tooth.

Cynthia, tune harmonious numbers ;
   Fair Discretion, tune the lyre ;
Soothe my ever-waking slumbers ;
   Bright Apollo, lend thy choir.

Gloomy Pluto, king of terrors,
   Armed in adamantine chains,
Lead me to the crystal mirrors,
   Watering soft Elysian plains.

Mournful Cypress, verdant willow,
   Gilding my Aurelia's brows,
Morpheus, hovering o'er my pillow,
   Hear me pay my dying vows.

Melancholy, smooth Mæander,
   Swiftly purling in a round,
On thy margin lovers wander
   With thy flowery chaplets crowned.

Thus when Philomela, drooping,
   Softly seeks her silent mate,

So the bird of Juno stooping;
Melody resigns to fate.

Gilbert Wakefield, Pope's talented commentator, actually misapprehended the nature of the above composition, and wrote some pages of his Commentary to support his assertion that the poem was disjointed and obscure!*

Examples of true Nonsense Verse are not numerous, but we find the following two in the pages of "Fun."

A Chronicle.

Once—but no matter when—
　There lived—no matter where—
A man, whose name—but then
　I need not that declare.

He—well, he had been born,
　And so he was alive;
His age—I details scorn—
　Was somethingty and five.

He lived—how many years
　I truly can't decide;
But this one fact appears
　He lived—until he died.

" He died," I have averred,
　But cannot prove 'twas so,

* This song, though generally attributed to Pope, is believed by some to have been the work of Swift, and it appears in some editions of his works. (*Vide* Pickering's, 3 vols. 1833.)

But that he was interred,
   At any rate, I know.

I fancy he'd a son,
   I hear he had a wife :
Perhaps he'd more than one,
   I know not, on my life !

But whether he was rich,
   Or whether he was poor,
Or neither—both—or which,
   I cannot say, I'm sure.

I can't recall his name,
   Or what he used to do :
But then—well, such is fame !
   'Twill so serve me and you.

And that is why I thus,
   About this unknown man
Would fain create a fuss,
   To rescue, if I can,

From dark oblivion's blow,
   Some record of his lot :
But, ah ! I do not know
   Who—where—when—why—or what.

MORAL.

In this brief pedigree
   A moral we should find—
But what it ought to be
   Has quite escaped my mind !

Lines by a Medium

In communication with the late L. Murray.

I might not, if I could ;
 I should not, if I might ;
Yet if I should I would,
 And, shoulding, I should quite !

I must not, yet I may ;
 I can, and still I must ;
But ah ! I cannot—nay,
 To must I may not, just !

I shall, although I will,
 But be it understood,
If I may, can, shall—still
 I might, could, would, or should !

Some authors, however, write Nonsense Verses without intending it—as, for instance, Stonihurst, in his translation of Virgil, rendered a really sublime passage into the following extraordinary lines :

" Then did he make Heaven's vault to rebound
With rounce robble bobble,
Of ruffee raffe roaring,
With thicke thwacke thurly bouncing."

The following curious verse is said to have been on a gravestone at one time in the churchyard of Homersfield, Suffolk, over the body of Robert

Crytoft, who died November 17, 1810, and it is very like nonsense:

MYSELF.

As I walked by myself I talked to myself,
  And thus myself said to me,
Look to thyself and take care of thyself,
  For nobody cares for thee.
So I turned to myself, and I answered myself,
  In the self-same reverie,
Look to myself or look not to myself,
  The self-same thing will it be.

One of Theodore Hook's witty associates, the Rev. Edward Cannon, wrote the following piece of unparalleled nonsense:

IMPROMPTU.

If down his throat a man should choose
  In fun, to jump or slide,
He'd scrape his shoes against his teeth,
  Nor dirt his own inside.

Or if his teeth were lost and gone,
And not a stump to scrape upon,
He'd see at once how very pat,
His tongue lay there, by way of mat,
And he would wipe his feet on *that!*

There are strung together here a variety of curious nonsensical pieces, not in the sense of their being Amphigouries, but because they deserve a place for their excellence in some ludicrous point or feature. The first is credited to Alfred Crowquil:

To My Nose.

Knows he, who never took a pinch,
Nosey! the pleasure thence which flows?
Knows he the titillating joy
      That my nose knows?

O nose! I am as proud of thee,
As any mountain of its snows;
I gaze on thee, and feel that pride
      A Roman knows.

The description here given of Bridget Brady by her lover, Thaddeus Ruddy, a bard who lived about the middle of the seventeenth century, is excellent:

"She's as straight as a pine on the mountain of Kilmannon;
She's as fair as the lilies on the banks of the Shannon;
Her breath is as sweet as the blossoms of Drumcallan,
And her breasts gently swell like the waves of Lough Allan;
Her eyes are as mild as the dews of Dunsany,
Her veins are as pure as the blue bells of Slaney;
Her words are as smooth as the pebbles of Terwinny,
And her hair flows adown like the streamlets of Finney."

Our life-long friend, Mr. Punch, some years ago furnished his readers with this single-rhymed verse:

A Word of Welcome.

A Commissioner from Pondicherry, named Checkabendalcadermarecar, has arrived in Paris, bringing a lac of rupees (125,000 francs) for the emigrants from Alsace-Lorraine.

> Come, Frenchmen, sound his fame afar,
> Checkabendalcadermarecar !
> Due your best words of welcome are
> To Checkabendalcadermarecar !
> Greet him with gittern or guitar,
> Checkabendalcadermarecar !
> Let his long name be ne'er a bar,
> Checkabendalcadermarecar !
> In brightest salons bid him star,
> Checkabendalcadermarecar !
> He comes to heal the wounds of war,
> Checkabendalcadermarecar !
> He helps to raise your funds to par,
> Checkabendalcadermarecar !
> So let no cloud your welcome mar
> Of Checkabendalcadermarecar !

The custom of using compound words was very prevalent in Ben Jonson's time, and he called them "un-in-one-breath-utterable." This practice was also common among the Sophists, and Scaliger has an epigram satirising them as—

> " Lofty-brow-flourishers,
> Nose-in-beard-wallowers,
> Bag-and-beard-nourishers,
> Dish-and-all-swallowers.

  Old-cloak-investitors,
   Barefoot-look-fashioners,
  Night-private-feast-eaters,
   Craft-lucubrationers,
Youth-cheaters, word-catchers, vain-glory-osophers,
Such are your seekers-of-virtue philosophers."

The following Jingling Rhymes deserve a place as a curiosity:

 " A fly got caught, once in a web,
  And soon the spider spied her.
 A donkey pricked her ears and brayed,
  Just to deride her rider.
 Quite oft a lady, when she's vexed,
  Will make a feint in fainting,
 She uses it but to deceive,—
  As she does paint in painting.
 If you will eat too much, 'tis plain,
  You sure will grow, sir, grosser :
 If you persist in drinking rum,
  'Twill paint your nose, sir, know, sir !
 To sober keep, I signed the pledge—
  My sole design in signing ;
 Some men throw all their cash away,
  But I spend mine in mining.
 I must confess I love the weed,
  And when I choose, sir, chew, sir.
 I don't play cards—I find that I,
  When I play loo, sir, lose, sir.
 Although I'm tempted to transgress,
  Each day instead, I stead eye,

Forswear gay pleasure's blandishments—
Turn from the ready 'red eye.'
I can't play billiards—when I miss
I don't accuse a cue, sir.
If you can play a better game
I'll take a view of you, sir.
Some rhymes may more mellifluent sound,
But you can't meet a metre
Will puzzle you much more than this,
Though quite as sweet or sweeter."

There appears to be no end to the vagaries and
nonsensical notions of poets, and the next examples are from the other side of the Atlantic—
the first being a hit at the curious names of American rivers, which, though with features in nature
frequently excelling those of Europe in beauty and
sublimity, yet have been named in the New World
in a most unfortunate manner. Witness Bigmuddy
River and Littlemuddy River, Little Shallow River,
Good Woman River, Little Woman River, Blowing
Fly Creek, and many others to the same tune.
When the western parts of the United States shall
have a full quota of civilised inhabitants, cities,
scholars, and poets, how sweetly shall such names
sound in their verse!

" Ye plains where sweet Bigmuddy rolls along,
And Teapot, one day to be famed in song ;

Where swans on Biscuit and on Grandstone glide,
And willows wave on Good Woman's side;
How shall your happy streams in after time,
Tune the soft lay and fill the sonorous rhyme!
Blest bards, who in your amorous verse will call
On murmuring Pork and gentle Cannon Ball,
Split Rock, and Stick Lodge, and Two Thousand Mile,
White Lime, and Cupboard, and Bad Humoured Isle!
Flow, Little Shallow, flow, and be thy stream
Their great example as 'twill be their theme!
Isis with Rum and Onion must not vie,
Cam shall resign the palm to Blowing Fly,
And Thames and Tagus yield to Big Little Dry!"

LINES TO MISS FLORENCE HUNTINGDON.

(*Passamaquoddy, Maine.*)

Sweet maiden of Passamaquoddy,
    Shall we seek for communion of souls
Where the deep Mississippi meanders,
    Or the distant Saskatchewan rolls?

Ah no,—for in Maine I will find thee
    A sweetly sequestrated nook,
Where the far-winding Skoodoowabskooksis
    Conjoins with the Skoodoowabskook.

There wander two beautiful rivers,
    With many a winding and crook;
The one is the Skoodoowabskooksis,
    The other—the Skoodoowabskook.

Ah, sweetest of haunts! though unmentioned
    In geography, atlas, or book,

How fair is the Skoodoowabskooksis,
  When joining the Skoodoowabskook !

Our cot shall be close by the waters
  Within that sequestrated nook—
Reflected in Skoodoowabskooksis,
  And mirrored in Skoodoowabskook.

You shall sleep to the music of leaflets,
  By zephyrs in wantonness shook,
And dream of the Skoodoowabskooksis,
  And, perhaps, of the Skoodoowabskook.

When awaked by the hens and the roosters,
  Each morn, you shall joyously look
On the junction of Skoodoowabskooksis,
  With the soft gliding Skoodoowabskook.

Your food shall be fish from the waters,
  Drawn forth on the point of a hook,
From murmuring Skoodoowabskooksis,
  Or wandering Skoodoowabskook !

You shall quaff the most sparkling of water,
  Drawn forth from a silvery brook
Which flows to the Skoodoowabskooksis,
  And then to the Skoodoowabskook !

And *you* shall preside at the banquet,
  And *I* will wait on thee as cook ;
And we'll talk of the Skoodoowabskooksis,
  And sing of the Skoodoowabskook !

Let others sing loudly of Saco,
  Of Quoddy, and Tattamagouche,

Of Kennebeccasis, and Quaco,
  Of Merigonishe, and Buctouche,

Of Nashwaak, and Magaguadavique,
  Or Memmerimammericook,—
There's none like the Skoodoowabskooksis,
  Excepting the Skoodoowabskook !

AUTUMN DAYS.

(Manufactured by Peleg Wale's Machine.)

The melancholy days have come,
  The saddest of the year ;
Gone are the partridge and the plum,
  The falling leaves are sere ;
The partridge now forgets to drum,
  The squirrel to uprear
His merry tail, the brooks are glum :
  The angels disappear ;
The crow pursues the vagrant crumb,
  Too grateful for the cheer ;
The top has ceased its summer hum,
  The kites are out of gear ;
O'er mother Earth a fierce autumn
  Inverts its icy spear.
Each morning some imbibe their rum,
  And some absorb their beer ;
Young soldiers mumble " fi-fo-fum,"
  To drive away their fear.
Blithe, happy, joyous school-girls thrum
  Pianos far and near,

Or eat the cake of Sally Lunn,
    Or Clara Vere de Vere;
While others go to chewing gum,
    Or check the truant tear.
A blind young man did once calum-
    Niate his precious dear,
And railed, instead of being mum,
    Because he did not see her.
Another man got deaf and dumb
    Because he could not hear;
But when with cold his feet got numb,
    He turned in his career,
And danced a polka on his thumb,
    And walked off on his ear.

$\left\{\begin{array}{c}\text{Something broken} \\ \text{in the} \\ \text{machine!}\end{array}\right.$ $\left.\begin{array}{c}\quad \\ \quad \\ \quad\end{array}\right\}$ . . . . . . plumb,
    . . . . . . queer,
    . . . . . . tum-ti-tum!

    K-ch-k-r-r-r-r-r-e-er!

A Dr. Fitzgerald at one time wrote a poem upon his native village of Tipperary, in which occur these two lines—

    "And thou! dear village, loveliest of the clime,
    Fain would I name thee, but I scant in rhyme."

Dr. Fitzgerald's failure to find a rhyme for Tipperary drew forth the following curious composition:

    "A poet there was in sad quandary,
    To find a rhyme for Tipperary.

Long laboured he through January,
Yet found no rhyme for Tipperary;
Toiled every day in February,
But toiled in vain for Tipperary;
Searched Hebrew text and commentary,
But searched in vain for Tipperary;
Bored all his friends in Inverary,
To find a rhyme for Tipperary;
Implored the aid of ' Paddy Cary,'
Yet still no rhyme for Tipperary;
He next besought his mother Mary
To tell him rhyme for Tipperary;
But she, good woman, was no fairy,
Nor witch,—though born in Tipperary;
Knew everything about her dairy,
But not the rhyme for Tipperary;
The stubborn muse he could not vary,
For still the lines would run contrary
Whene'er he thought on Tipperary.
And though of time he was not chary,
'Twas thrown away on Tipperary.
Till of his wild-goose chase most weary,
He vowed he'd leave out Tipperary.
But, no—the theme he might not vary,
His longing was not temporary,
To find meet rhyme for Tipperary.
He sought among the gay and airy,
He pestered all the military.
Committed many a strange vagary,
Bewitched, it seemed, by Tipperary.
He wrote, post-haste, to Darby Leary,
Besought with tears his Aunty Sairie;

But sought he far, or sought he near, he
Ne'er found a rhyme for Tipperary.
He travelled sad through Cork and Kerry,
He drove like mad through sweet Dunleary,
Kicked up a precious tantar-ara,
But found no rhyme for Tipperary ;
Lived fourteen weeks at Stan-ar-ara,
Was well-nigh lost in Glenègary,
Then started slick for Demerara,
In search of rhyme for Tipperary.
Through Yankee-land, sick, solitary,
He roamed by forest, lake, and prairie,
He went *per terram et per mare*,
But found no rhyme for Tipperary.
Through orient climes on dromedary,
On camel's back through great Sahara ;
His travels were extraordinary
In search of rhyme for Tipperary.
Fierce as a gorgon or chimæra,
Fierce as Alecto or Megæra,
Fiercer than e'er a love-sick bear, he
Ranged through the 'londe' of Tipperary.
His cheeks grew thin and wondrous hairy,
His visage long, his aspect ' eerie,'
His *tout ensemble*, faith, would scare ye,
Amidst the wilds of Tipperary.
Becoming hypochon-dri-ary,
He sent for his apothecary,
Who ordered 'balm' and 'saponary,'
Herbs rare to find in Tipperary.
In his potations ever wary,
His choicest drink was 'home gooseberry.'

On swipes, skim-milk, and smallest beer, he
Scanted rhyme for his Tipperary.
Had he imbibed good old Madeira,
Drank pottle-deep of golden sherry,
Of Falstaff's sack, or ripe Canary,
No rhyme had lacked for Tipperary.
Or had his tastes been literary,
He might have found extemporary
Without the aid of dictionary,
Some fitting rhyme for Tipperary.
Or had he been an antiquary,
Burnt midnight oil in his library,
Or been of temper less 'camstary,'
Rhymes had not lacked for Tipperary.
He paced about his aviary,
Blew up, sky-high, his secretary,
And then in wrath and anger sware he,
There was *no* rhyme for Tipperary."

CENTONES OR MOSAICS.

CENTO is properly a piece of patchwork, and hence the term has been applied to poems composed of selected verses or passages from an author, or from different authors, strung together in such a way as to present an entirely new reading. This trick of verse-manufacture was a favourite pastime in the Middle Ages, and popular among the Romans during the declining years of the Empire. Of the earliest of these were the " Homero-Centones," a patchwork of lines from Homer (edited by Teucher at Leipsic, 1793), the " Cento Nuptialis " of Ausonius, and the " Cento Virgilianus " of Proba Falconia in the fourth century. Another early Cento was one of spiritual hymns made up from lines in the works of Horace and Virgil by a monk named Metillus in the twelfth century. The Cento of Proba Falconia is also selected from the works of Virgil, and contains the history of Adam and Eve, together with a life of our Saviour. The authoress was the wife of a Roman proconsul, and belonged to the Anician family, one of the first in the senatorial rank to embrace the doctrines of Christianity in the days of Constantine. A brief notice of this lady will be found in the 31st chapter of Gibbon's " Decline and Fall of the Roman Empire." A passage from this Cento by Proba Falconia may be given :

EXPULSIO ADAMI ET EVÆ DE PARADISO.

At juveni primùm sævus circumstetit horror,
Diriguêre oculi, nec se celare tenebris
Amplius, aut notas audire et reddere voces.
Haud morâ festinant jussi, rapidisque feruntur
Passibus, et pariter gressi per opaca viarum,
Corripiunt spatium medium, limenque relinquunt,
Flentes, et paribus curis vestigia figunt.
Tunc victum in sylvis baccas, lapidosaque corna
Dant rami, et vulsis pascunt radicibus herbæ.

The second part of Proba's work concludes with the following verse :

CHRISTUS ASCENDIT AD CŒLOS.

His demùm exactis, spirantes dimovet auras
Aera per tenuem, cœloque invectus aperto,
Mortales visus medio in sermone reliquit,
Infert se septus nebulâ (mirabile dictu)
Atque illum solio stellantis regia cœli
Accipit, æternumque tenet per sæcula nomen.

Those desirous of further information regarding

M

the work of Proba Falconia and of various others who "wrote" poems of this class in Latin, may consult a French work entitled "Tableau de la Litterature du Centon," by Octave Delepierre (2 vols., Trübner & Co., 1875). In that work there is also mention of a Latin Cento by the Scottish poet, Alexander Ross (1590–1654), who wrote a number of works, most of which are entirely forgotten. His Cento was called "Virgilius Evangelizans," being a life of Christ, taken wholly from the works of Virgil; but Ross is perhaps best remembered by the lines in Butler's "Hudibras":

> "There was an ancient sage philosopher,
> And he had read Alexander Ross over."

What appears to be the earliest English Cento was communicated by Dodsley to his friend Berenger, as the composition of one of the members of a society which met annually to celebrate the birth of Shakespeare.

On the Birthday of Shakespeare.

(A Cento taken from his Works.)

Peace to this meeting,
Joy and fair time, health and good wishes.
Now, worthy friends, the cause why we are met,
Is in celebration of the day that gave

Immortal Shakespeare to this favoured isle,
The most replenished sweet work of Nature
Which from the prime creation e'er she framed.
O thou, divinest Nature! how thyself thou blazon'st
In this thy son! formed in thy prodigality
To hold thy mirror up, and give the time
Its very form and pressure! When he speaks,
Each aged ear plays truant at his tales,
And younger hearings are quite ravished;
So voluble is his discourse. Gentle
As zephyr blowing underneath the violet,
Not wagging its sweet head—yet as rough
His noble blood enchafed, as the rude wind,
That by the top doth take the mountain pine,
And make him stoop to the vale. 'Tis wonderful
That an invisible instinct should frame him
To loyalty, unlearned; honour, untaught;
Civility, not seen in others; knowledge,
That wildly grows in him, but yields a crop
As if it had been sown. What a piece of work!
How noble in faculty! infinite in reason!
A combination and a form indeed,
Where every god did seem to set his seal.
Heaven has him now! Yet let our idolatrous fancy
Still sanctify his relics; and this day
Stand aye distinguished in the kalendar
To the last syllable of recorded time:
For if we take him but for all in all,
We ne'er shall look upon his like again.

English poems of this class are very scarce, and
the exceeding difficulty of their production will be

evident from the examples which follow. "Life" is said to have occupied a year's laborious search among the voluminous writings of thirty-eight leading poets of the past and present times. The compilation first appeared in the "San Francisco Times," and was the work of Mrs. H. A. Deming. The numbers prefixed to the lines refer to the authors from whom they are taken, their names being given at the end:

LIFE.

1. Why all this toil for triumphs of an hour?
2. Life's a short summer, man a flower.
3. By turns we catch the vital breath and die—
4. The cradle and the tomb, alas! so nigh.
5. To be, is better far than not to be,
6. Though all man's life may seen a tragedy;
7. But light cares speak when mighty griefs are dumb,
8. The bottom is but shallow whence they come.
9. Your fate is but the common lot of all:
10. Unmingled joys here to no man befall,
11. Nature to each allots his proper sphere;
12. Fortune makes folly her peculiar care;
13. Custom does often reason overrule,
14. And throw a cruel sunshine on a fool.
15. Live well; how long or short, permit to Heaven;
16. They who forgive most, shall be most forgiven.
17. Sin may be clasped so close that we cannot see its face—
18. Vile intercourse where virtue has no place.
19. Then keep each passion down, however dear;
20. Thou pendulum bewixt a smile and tear.

21. Her sensual snares, let faithless pleasures lay,
22. With craft and skill, to ruin and betray ;
23. Soar not too high to fall, but stoop to rise,
24. We masters grow of all that we despise.
25. Oh, then, I renounce that impious self-esteem ;
26. Riches have wings, and grandeur is a dream.
27. Think not ambition wise because 'tis brave,
28. The paths of glory lead but to the grave.
29. What is ambition ?—'tis a glorious cheat !—
30. Only destructive to the brave and great.
31. What's all the gaudy glitter of a crown ?
32. The way to bliss lies not on beds of down.
33. How long we live, not years but actions tell ;
34. That man lives twice who lives the first life well.
35. Make, then, while yet we may, your God your friend,
36. Whom Christians worship yet not comprehend.
37. The trust that's given guard, and to yourself be just ;
38. For, live we how we can, yet die we must.

1. Young ; 2. Dr. Johnson; 3. Pope ; 4. Prior ; 5. Sewel ; 6. Spenser ; 7. Daniell; 8. Sir Walter Raleigh ; 9. Longfellow ; 10. Southwell ; 11. Congreve; 12. Churchill; 13. Rochester ; 14. Armstrong ; 15. Milton ; 16. Bailey ; 17. Trench ; 18. Somerville ; 19. Thomson ; 20. Byron ; 21. Smollett ; 22. Crabbe; 23. Massinger ; 24. Cowley ; 25. Beattie ; 26. Cowper ; 27. Sir Walter Davenant ; 28. Gray ; 29. Willis ; 30. Addison ; 31. Dryden ; 32. Francis Quarles ; 33. Watkins ; 34. Herrick ; 35. William Mason ; 36. Hill ; 37. Dana ; 38. Shakespeare.

The next Mosaic poem appeared some years ago in *Notes and Queries*, in a communication signed James Monk, and is entitled—

The Poets' "Essay on Man."

1. What strange infatuation rules mankind,
2. What different spheres to human bliss assigned ;

3. To loftier things your finer pulses burn,
4. If man would but his finer nature learn ;
5. What several ways men to their calling have,
6. And grasp at life though sinking to the grave.

7.   Ask what is human life? the sage replies,
8. Wealth, pomp, and honour are but empty toys ;
9. We trudge, we travel, but from pain to pain,
10. Weak, timid landsmen, on life's stormy main ;
11. We only toil who are the first of things,
12. From labour health, from health contentment springs.
13. Fame runs before us as the morning star,
14. How little do we know that which we are ;
15. Let none then here his certain knowledge boast,
16. Of fleeting joys too certain to be lost ;
17. For over all there hangs a cloud of fear,
18. All is but change and separation here.

19.   To smooth life's passage o'er its stormy way,
20. Sum up at night what thou hast done by day ;
21. Be rich in patience if thou in gudes be poor ;
22. So many men do stoope to sight unsure ;
23. Choose out the man to virtue best inclined,
24. Throw envy, folly, prejudice behind ;
25. Defer not till to-morrow to be wise,
26. Wealth heaped on wealth, nor truth, nor safety buys ;
27. Remembrance worketh with her busy train.
28. Care draws on care, woe comforts woe again ;
29. On high estates huge heaps of care attend,
30. No joy so great but runneth to an end ;
31. No hand applaud what honour shuns to hear,
32. Who casts off shame, should likewise cast off fear ;

33. Grief haunts us down the precipice of years.
34. Virtue alone no dissolution fears ;
35. Time loosely spent will not again be won,
36. What shall I do to be for ever known ?

37.　But now the wane of life comes darkly on,
38. After a thousand mazes overgone ;
39. In this brief state of trouble and unrest,
40. Man never is, but always to be blest.
41. Time is the present hour, the past is fled,
42. O thou Futurity, our hope and dread.
43. How fading are the joys we dote upon,
44. Lo ! while I speak the present moment's gone.

45.　O Thou Eternal Arbiter of things,
46. How awful is the hour when conscience stings !
47. Conscience, stern arbiter in every breast,
48. The fluttering wish on wing that will not rest.
49. This above all,—To thine own self be true,
50. Learn to live well, that thou may'st die so too.
51. To those that list the world's gay scenes I leave,
52. Some ills we wish for, when we wish to live.

1. Chatterton ; 2. Rogers ; 3. Sprague ; 4. Dana ; 5. Ben Jonson ;
6. Falconer ; 7. Cowper ; 8. Ferguson ; 9. Quarles ; 10. Burns ;
11. Tennyson ; 12. Beattie ; 13. Dryden ; 14. Byron ; 15. Pomfret ;
16. Waller ; 17. Hood ; 18. Steele ; 19. Dwight ; 20. Herbert ;
21. Dunbar ; 22. Whitney ; 23. Rowe ; 24. Langhorne ; 25.
Congreve ; 26. Dr. Johnson ; 27. Goldsmith ; 28. Drayton ; 29.
Webster ; 30. Southwell ; 31. Thomson ; 32. Sheridan Knowles ;
33. Landor ; 34. Edward Moore ; 35. Greene ; 36. Cowley ; 37.
Joanna Baillie ; 38. Keats ; 39. B. Barton ; 40. Pope ; 41. Marsden ;
42. Elliot ; 43. Blair ; 44. Oldham ; 45. Akenside ; 46. Percival ;
47. J. A. Hillhouse ; 48. Mallet ; 49. Shakespeare ; 50. Sir J.
Denham ; 51. Spenser ; 52. Young.

The preceding was shortly after supplemented by another, professedly taken from a very scarce work called "The Lonsdale Magazine," and entitled

MARRIAGE.

1. Marriage, if rightly understood,
   Gives to the tender and the good,
2. The eye, where pure affection beams,
   The tear, from tenderness that streams—
3. Whate'er a blooming world contains,
   That wings the air, that skims the plains.

4. Go search among your idle dreams,
   Your busy or your vain extremes,
   And find a life of equal bliss,
   Or own the next begun in this.
5. Cordial of life, thus marriage pours
   Her comfort on our heavier hours.
6. The hour that rolls for ever on,
   Tells us years must soon be gone—
7. Say, dost thou not at evening hour
   Feel some soft and secret power
   Gliding o'er thy yielding mind,
8. Nor leave one wretched thought behind?
9. Come press my lips and lie with me,
10. From avarice and ambition free;
11. Or say, what soft propitious hour,
    I best may choose to hail thy power!
12. Plain innocence, in white arrayed,
    Before us lifts her fearless head;

13. Whose yielding hearts and joining hands
    Find blessings twisted with our bands.

14. If these delights thy mind can move,
    Come live with me and be my love.

1. Cotton; 2. Logan; 3. Ogilvie; 4. Parnell; 5. Graves; 6. Dwight; 7. Langhorne; 8. Montgomery; 9. Kirke White; 10. Cowper; 11. Barbauld; 12. Thomson; 13. Watts; 14. Marlowe.

Laman Blanchard, a number of years ago, in George Cruikshank's "Omnibus" published the following Mosaic pieces as "poems bearing no resemblance to anything ever before offered to the public." They are, to all intents and purposes— at least so far as a train of connected ideas go— utter absurdities, and properly should be classed as Nonsense Verses. Mr. Blanchard sarcastically states that he found these poems among the MSS. of one of Sir Fretful Plagiary's numerous descendants, and thinks that if any reader of the verses should be reminded of poets past and present, it can only be because the profusely-gifted bard has clustered together more remarkable and memorable lines than any of his predecessors. "That poem," Mr. Blanchard goes on to say, "can be of no inferior order of merit, in which Milton would have been proud to have written one line, Pope would have been equally vain of the authorship of

a second, Byron have rejoiced in a third, Campbell
gloried in a fourth, Gray in a fifth, Cowper in a
sixth, and so on to the end of the Ode; which thus
realises the poetical wealth of that well-known line
of Sir Fretful's—

'Infinite riches in a little room.' "

Among these productions of Mr. Blanchard's were
the following three:

ODE TO THE HUMAN HEART.

Blind Thamyris, and blind Mæonides,
    Pursue the triumph and partake the gale !
Drop tears as fast as the Arabian trees,
    To point a moral or adorn a tale.

Full many a gem of purest ray serene,
    Thoughts that do often lie too deep for tears,
Like angels' visits, few and far between,
    Deck the long vista of departed years.

Man never is, but always to be blest ;
    The tenth transmitter of a foolish face,
Like Aaron's serpent, swallows up the rest,
    And makes a sunshine in the shady place.

For man the hermit sighed, till woman smiled,
    To waft a feather or to drown a fly,
(In wit a man, simplicity a child,)
    With silent finger pointing to the sky.

But fools rush in where angels fear to tread,
    Far out amid the melancholy main;
As when a vulture on Imaus bred,
    Dies of a rose in aromatic pain.

Music hath charms to soothe the savage breast,
    Look on her face, and you'll forget them all;
Some mute inglorious Milton here may rest,
    A hero perish, or a sparrow fall.

My way of life is fallen into the sere;
    I stood in Venice on the Bridge of Sighs,
Like a rich jewel in an Ethiop's ear,
    Who sees through all things with his half-shut eyes.

Oh for a lodge in some vast wilderness!
    Full many a flower is born to blush unseen,
Fine by degrees and beautifully less,
    And die ere man can say " Long live the Queen!"

WHATEVER IS, IS RIGHT.

Lives there a man with soul so dead,
Who never to himself has said,
    ' Shoot folly as it flies'?
Oh! more than tears of blood can tell,
Are in that word, farewell, farewell!
    'Tis folly to be wise.

And what is friendship but a name,
That boils on Etna's breast of flame?
    Thus runs the world away.

Sweet is the ship that's under sail
To where yon taper cheers the vale,
        With hospitable ray !

Drink to me only with thine eyes
Through cloudless climes and starry skies !
        My native land, good night !
Adieu, adieu, my native shore ;
'Tis Greece, but living Greece no more—
        Whatever is, is right !

ON LIFE, ET CETERA.

Know then, this truth, enough for man to know :
Be thou as chaste as ice, as pure as snow ;
Who would be free, themselves must strike the blow.
Retreating lightly with a lowly fear
From grave to gay, from lively to severe,
To err is human, to forgive divine,
And wretches hang that jurymen may dine
Like quills upon the fretful porcupine.
All are but parts of one stupendous whole,
The feast of reason and the flow of soul.

We ne'er shall look upon his like again,
For panting time toils after him in vain,
And drags, at each remove, a lengthening chain ;
Allures to brighter worlds, and leads the way
With sweet, reluctant, amorous delay !

Another attempt at this laborious trifling appeared in the *People's Friend* of May 1871, evincing great patience and research :

1. A glorious devil, large in heart and brain,
2.   Doomed for a certain term to walk the night,
3. The world forsaking with a calm disdain,
4.   Majestic rises on the astonished sight.

5. Type of the wise who soar, but never roam,—
6.   Mark how it mounts to man's imperial race !
7. High is his perch, but humble is his home,
8.   Fast anchored in the deep abyss of space.

9. And oft the craggy cliff he loved to climb,
10.   Where Punch and Scaramouch aloft are seen ;
11. Where Science mounts in radiant car sublime,
12.   And twilight fairies tread the circled green.

13. And, borne aloft by the sustaining blast,
14.   Whom no man fully sees, and none can see ;
15. 'Wildered and weary, sits him down at last,
16.   Beneath the shelter of an aged tree.

17. I will not stop to tell how far he fled,
18.   To view the smile of evening on the sea ;
19. He tried to smile, and, half succeeding, said,
20.   ' I smell a loller in the wind,' said he.

21. ' What if the lion in his rage I meet ? '
22.   (The Muse interprets thus his tender thought.)
23. The scourge of Heaven ! what terrors round him wait !
24.   From planet whirled to planet more remote.

25. Thence higher still, by countless steps conveyed,
26.   Remote from towns he ran his godly race ;
27. He lectured every youth that round him played—
28.   The jostling tears ran down his honest face.

29. 'Another spring !' his heart exulting cries.
30.   Vain are his weapons, vainer is his force ;
31. A milk-white lion of tremendous size
32.   Lays him along the snows a stiffened corpse.

33. The hay-cock rises, and the frequent rake
34.   Looks on the bleeding foe that made him bleed ;
35. And the green lizard and the golden snake
36..   Pause at the bold irrevocable deed.

37. Will ye one transient ray of gladness dart,
38.   To bid the genial tear of pity flow ?
39. By Heaven ! I would rather coin my heart,
40.   Or Mr. Miller's, commonly called Joe !

1. Tennyson ; 2. Shakespeare ; 3. Thomson ; 4. Taite ; 5. Words-worth ; 6. Pope ; 7. Grahame ; 8. Cowper ; 9. Beattie ; 10. Rogers ; 11. Hemans ; 12. Collins ; 13. Longfellow ; 14. Prior ; 15. Beattie ; 16. Burns ; 17. Wordsworth ; 18. Hemans ; 19. Crabbe ; 20. Chaucer ;. 21. Collins ; 22. Beattie ; 23. Gray ; 24. Campbell ; 25. Bloomfield ; 26. Rogers ; 27. Goldsmith ; 28. Burns ; 29. Bloomfield ; 30. Byron ; 31. Falconer ; 32. Thomson ; 33. Joanna Baillie ; 34. Byron ; 35. Shelley ; 36. Euripides ; 37. Beattie ;. 38 Hemans ; 39. Shakespeare ; 40. Horace Smith.

We conclude the Centones or Mosaics with the following, gathered from some of the most popular poets :

" The curfew tolls the knell of parting day,
    In every clime from Lapland to Japan ;
To fix one spark of beauty's heavenly ray—
    The proper study of mankind is man.

Tell, for you can, what is it to be wise,
    Sweet Auburn, loveliest village of the plain ;
' The Man of Ross ! ' each lisping babe replies,
    And drags, at each remove, a lengthening chain.

Ah ! who can tell how hard it is to climb,
    Far as the solar walk or milky way ?
Procrastination is the thief of time,
    Let Hercules himself do what he may.

'Tis education forms the common mind,
    The feast of reason and the flow of soul ;
I must be cruel only to be kind,
    And waft a sigh from Indus to the pole.

Syphax ! I joy to meet you thus alone,
    Where'er I roam, whatever lands I see ;
A youth to fortune and to fame unknown,
    In maiden meditation fancy free.

Farewell ! and wheresoe'er thy voice be tried,
    Why to yon mountain turns the gazing eye,
With spectacles on nose, and pouch on side,
    That teach the rustic moralist how to die.

Pity the sorrows of a poor old man,
    Whose beard descending swept his aged breast ;
Laugh where we must, be candid where we can,
    Man never is, but always to be blest."

ANAGRAMS.

N Anagram is formed by the transposition of the component letters of a word or phrase so as to give a new word or sentence, and though anagrams may be of small value in a literary point of view, yet they are not altogether devoid of a certain degree of interest. Originally anagrams signified simply a reversal of the order of the letters in a word, as in *live*, which when reversed becomes *evil*, but they have long borne the sense in which they are now used. Their interest is greatly enhanced when the transposition is such as to give an appropriate signification or association of ideas relative to or consistent with the original or primary word from which the anagram has been formed, and there are words of this description which exhibit coincidences that are truly astonishing and almost incredible until proved by examination. This literary frivolity has at least the merit of antiquity, for we find that among the ancient Jewish cabalists the art of *the-muru,* or transposition of the letters of words, was used by them for the purpose of discovering hidden meanings, and they also thought that the qualities of a man's mind and his future destiny could be guessed at by anagrammatising the letters of his name. The art prevailed, too, among the Greeks and Romans, and has continued through the Middle Ages down to comparatively modern times, chiefly, however, as a pastime.

The French literati have always shown a predilection for anagrams, and the results of their labours in this way would fill volumes. Indeed, such was the estimation in which this "art" was held by them at one period, that it is said their kings were provided with a salaried anagrammatist in the same way that royalty in Britain is provided with a poet-laureate. The popularity of anagrams in France was so great two or three centuries ago, that a man sometimes made his fortune by framing a single happy transposition of the name of a king or other great person. Thus all France was delighted with the anagram on François de Valoys, which was converted into *De façon suis royal,* indicating him to be of regal appearance. One French writer, Gabriel Antoine Joseph Hécart, went the length of composing and publishing a poem of 1200 lines, every line of which contained an anagram, but it so happens that out of the 1200 hardly one is worth quotation.

The anagram was also popular in Britain at an early date, being looked upon as an agreeable and amusing relaxation, as well as a favourable method by which those who sought favour might flatter the great ones whose influence they coveted. So early as 1589 we find Puttenhame in his "Arte of English Poesie" speaking of the anagram thus: "They that use it for pleasure is to breed one word out of another, not altering any letter nor the number of them, but only transposing of the same, whereupon many times is produced some grateful newes or matter to them for whose pleasure and service it was intended; and because there is much difficultie in it, and altogether standeth upon hap-hazard, it is compted for a courtly conceit." Puttenhame himself was the author of two anagrams on the name of Queen Elizabeth, whose portrait adorns the original edition of his work. He uses the following words:—"Elissabet Anglorum Regina," which orthography, he contends, "is true and not mistaken, for the letter *zeta* of the Hebrews and Greeks and of all other toungs

is in truth but a double *s* hardly uttered; and
h is but a note of aspiration onely and no letter,
which therefore is by the Greeks omitted." The
first anagram of these words is—

> " Multa regnabis ense gloria "
> (By the sword shalt thou reign in great renown).

The second—

> " Multa regnabis sene gloria "
> (Aged and in much glory shall ye reign).

These two the author made by the first mar-
shalling of the letters, and although he "tossed
and translaced them five hundreth . times," he
could find no other having reference to her
Majesty.

Later on, we find Elizabeth's successor being
flattered by another courtly writer, who sought
favour for his book by dedicating it to King
James, and discovering in the name of his royal
patron, James Stuart, the anagram *a just master.*
This literary gentleman no doubt thought he had
found in this anagram what has been already
pointed to as the best feature in this kind of
writing, an appropriate signification and relation
to the original words. So also with another on
James I., by which some of his courtiers wished to

prove his right to the British monarchy, as the descendant of King Arthur, from his name Charles James Stuart, which they rendered *Claims Arthur's Seat.*

Anagrams were not only in use among courtiers, however, but even the Puritans found in them a modified worldly pastime, and some writers of that party actually commended their use as being of a good tendency. In New England, among the early Puritans there, puns and conceits of a laborious kind and uncouth fashion were much admired, and the death of any notable person was sure to call forth several elegies, almost certain to contain some curious play upon the deceased's name or other characteristic feature—thus, John Norton, a learned divine, wrote as follows upon the death of Anne Bradstreet :—

> "Her breast was a brave palace, a *broad street*,
>   Where all heroic, ample thoughts did meet."

In a similar manner, Cotton Mather, the well-known writer on Witchcraft, in an elegy upon the death of the above-named John Norton, says of him—

> " His care to guide his flock and feed his lambs,
>   By words, works, prayers, psalms, alms, and *anagrams.*"

Addison gives a somewhat humorous description of an anagrammatist, who shut himself up for some months for the purpose of twisting the name of his mistress into as many of these conceits as he possibly could, but was astonished to find, after all his mental throes, that he had misspelled her name, and that consequently his productions were all faulty and insufficient. Some writers appear to have had a peculiar facility for composing anagrams, as a French poet one day sent his mistress no less than three dozen of them, all written on her name of Magdelaine. These conceits, however, were as frequently sarcastic as complimentary; and thus, though Scaliger may have felt the palpable hit in having his name rendered into *sacrilege*, Sir John Wiat would enjoy the anagram as a compliment which said that Wiat was *a wit*—this latter being a very simple example. The ingenious writer who discovered in Pilate's question, " Quid est veritas ? " (What is truth?) its own answer, *"Est vir qui adest"* (It is the man who is here), found one of the best and neatest anagrams which has yet been written. Of those reckoned among the best of these literary trifles are the one upon the mistress of Charles IX. of France, Marie Touchet, *Ie*

charme tout (I charm all); and another upon a
lady named Eleanor Davies, who belonged to the
court of Charles I., and pretended to supernatural
and prophetic powers.   To substantiate this claim
on her part, she anagrammatised her name,
Eleanor Davies, into *Reveal, O Daniel!* and this,
though faulty in regard to having too much by
a letter *l*, and too little by an *s*, was sufficient
in her mind to justify the assumption.   Arraigned
before the Court of High Commission, the judges
found that reasoning had no effect upon her—all
attempts to disprove by Scripture her claims to
inspiration being of no avail—till at length one of
the deans took a pen and wrote another and more
excellent anagram upon her name—Dame Eleanor
Davies: *Never so mad a ladie!* This had the
desired effect—the engineer being hoist with his
own petard—and put the prophetic lady into so
despondent a state, that she never afterwards
put forth a claim to supernatural gifts.

Authors long ago were occasionally given to

"Torture one poor word a thousand ways,"

as Dryden says, especially with a view to conceal
their authorship from the critics, and thus we find
the names of several anagrammatised—for instance,

Calvinus into *Alcuinus,* and Rabelais spitefully turned Calvin into *jan cul,* somewhat equivalent to the English *jackass;* friends of Calvin, however, adopted other fashions, as *Lucanius* and *Lucianus.* John Taylor, the "Water Poet," turned his into *Thorny Ailo;* and Bunyan, in the conclusion of the "advertisement" to the "Holy War," has these two lines—

> "Witness my name, if anagram'd to thee,
> The letters make, '*Nu hony in a B.*'"

One half the disguises adopted by French anonymous writers are in the shape of anagrams formed from their names, and with some of our own modern authors we find among them that Sydney Dobell used his first name and anagrammatised it for a second, thus—*Sydney Yendys.* So with *Barry Cornwall, poet,* which is, with the omission of the letter *r,* a version of his real name, Bryan Waller Proctor.

An old Latin book has this written upon the fly-leaf—

ANDREAS RIVETUS.

> Veritas res nuda,
> Sed naturâ es vir,
> Vir naturâ sedes,
> E naturâ es rudis,

Sed es vitâ rarus,
Sed rure vanitas,
In terrâ suâ Deus,
Veni, sudas terra.

Taylor's "Suddaine Turne of Fortune's Wheel" contains this—

"Supremus Pontifex Romanus,
O non sum super petram fixus."

The first line is "Supreme Pontiff of Rome;" and the second, "Alas! I am not founded upon a rock."

There are several anagrams upon King Charles II., of which we select the following,—the first being also by Taylor:—

" Charles Steuart,
Calls true hearts,
Brave prince, thy name, thy fame, thy selfe, and all,
With love and service all true hearts doth call;
So royally include with princely parts,
Thy reall virtues alwaies *calls true hearts.*"

The negotiations relative to the match between Charles and the Infanta of Spain (1624) led to this—

"Charles, Prince of Wales,
Will choose France's pearl."

While Charles Peacham's "Compleat Gentleman" contains—

> " Charles, Prince of Wales,
> *All France cries, O help us !*

On a visit to Newton Hall in Derbyshire, Charles II. is said himself to have written on one of the windows—*Cras ero lux* (To-morrow I shall be light), the anagram of Carolus Rex. The next was found written upon a fly-leaf of an old book at Cologne, bearing the date of 1653, supposed to have belonged at one time to one of the English who accompanied Charles II. in his exile—

" Carolus Stuartus, Angliæ, Scotiæ, et Hiberniæ Rex—
Aulâ, statû, regno exueris, ac hostili arte necaberis."

One Mistress Mary Fage, who lived in the time of Charles I., was perhaps the most prolific anagrammatist England ever produced. She published a volume of anagrams combined with acrostics under the title of " Fame's Rowle " (Roll), in which the names of many notable persons in the three kingdoms were dealt with, to the number of no less than four hundred and twenty. One may serve as a specimen of the rest—

> " To the Right Hon. John Earl of Weymes.
> JOHN WEYMES.
> *Shew men joy.*
> *I*n your great honour, free from all alloy,
> *O* truly noble Weymes, you *shew men joy* ;

*H*aving your virtues in their clearer sight,
*N*othing there is can breed them more delight.

*W*ith joy your wisdome, so doth men contente ;
*E*ver we pray it might be permanent ;
*Y*our virtuous life doth breed so great delight ;
*M*en wish you endless joy you to requite ;
*E*ternal joy may unto you succeede,
*S*hewing men joy who do your comfort breede."

Randle Holmes, who wrote an extraordinary book upon Heraldry, was complimented by an expressive anagram on his name—

" *Lo, men's herald !* "

In the "Bengal Mofussil Miscellany," republished in London in 1837 as "Indian Reminiscences," there is the following curious anecdote :— "When young Stanislaus, afterwards King of Poland, returned home from his travels, all the illustrious family of Leczinki assembled at Lissa to congratulate him on his arrival. Festivals, shows, rejoicings of every kind took place ; but the most ingenious compliment that graced the occasion was one paid by the College of Lissa. There appeared on the stage thirteen dancers, dressed as youthful warriors; each held in his hand a shield, on which was engraved in characters of gold one of the thirteen letters which

compose the two words 'Domus Lescinia.' They
then commenced their dance, and so arranged it
that at each turn their row of bucklers formed
different anagrams. At the first pause they
presented them in the natural order—

		"Domus Lescinia
At the second	. .	Ades Incolumis
At the third	. .	Omnis es lucida
At the fourth	. .	Mane Sidus loci
At the fifth	. .	Sis columna Dei
At the last	. .	I, scande Solium."

The following may be accepted as an approach to
the different renderings —:

O (heir to the) House of Lescinius,
Thou art present with us still unimpaired—
Thou art all that is wonderful.
Stay with us, O sun of our land!
Thou art one of God's supporters—
Come, ascend thy regal throne.

Ben Jonson, in a "Masque," has this anagram
on the name of Juno—

"And see where *Juno*, whose great name
Is *Unio* in the anagram,
Displays her glistening state and chaire,
As she enlightened all the ayre."

Throughout the masque there is a continual play

upon the words *Union* and *Juno,* as relating to marriage.

In one of Taylor's poems, " The Life and Death of Virgin Mary," there are these lines—

> " I doe not heere impute this deede of shame
> On Judas, because Judas was his name :
> For of that name there have been men of might
> Who the great battles of the Lord did fight,
> And others more.   But sure this impure blot
> Stickes to him, as he's named *Iskarriott;*
> For in an anagram Iskarriott is,
> By letters transposition, *Traitor kis.*"

Iskarriott, anag. *Traitor kis.*

> Kisse, traytor, kisse, with an intent to kill,
> And cry all haile ! when thou dost mean all ill ;
> And for thy fault no more shall Judas be
> A name of treason and false infamie ; ·
> But all that fault I'll on Iskarriott throw,
> Because the anagram explains it so.
> Iskarriott for a bribe, and with a kisse,
> Betrayed his Master, the blest King of Blisse."

All men have their enemies, and Taylor had his— amongst these there was one who took a pitiful way of showing his dislike by twisting Taylor's name in this fashion—

> " John Talour the poet,
> *Art thou in Hel, O poet ?* "

One Car was an intimate and loving friend of the poet Crawshawe, and on the poet's death Car found some consolation in discovering that Crawshawe could be transposed into the words, *He was Car*, and wrote the following lines accordingly—

" Was Car then Crawshawe, or was Crawshawe Car,
Since both within one name combinèd are ?
Yes, Car's Crawshawe, he Car ; 'tis love alone
Which melts two hearts, of both composing one ;
So Crawshawe's still the same—so much desired
By strongest wits, so honoured, so admired ;
Car was but he that entered as a friend,
With whom he shared his thoughts, and did commend
(While yet he lived) this work ; they loved each other :
Sweet Crawshawe was his friend ; he Crawshawe's brother :
So Car had title then ; 'twas his intent
That what his riches penned poor Car should print ;
Nor fears he check, praising that happy one
Who was beloved by all, dispraised by none.
To wit, being pleased with all things, he pleased all ;
Nor would he give nor take offence ; befall
What might, he would possess himself, and live
As dead (devoid of all int'rest) t'all might give
Disease t'his well-composed mind, forestalled
With heavenly riches, which had wholly called
His thoughts from earth, to live above in th' air,
A very bird of Paradise.   No care
Had he of earthly trash.   What might suffice
To fit his soul to heavenly exercise
Sufficed him ; and, may we guess his heart
By what his lips bring forth, his only part

Is God and godly thoughts.   Leaves doubt to none
But that to whom one God is all, all's one.
What he might eat or wear he took no thought,
His needful food he rather found than sought.
He seeks no downs, no sheets, his bed's still made
If he can find a chair or stool, he's laid ;
When day peeps in, he quits his restless rest,
And still, poor soul, before he's up he's drest.
Thus dying did he live, yet lived to die
In the Virgin's lap, to whom he did apply
His virgin thoughts and words, and thence wast styled
By foes, the chaplain of the Virgin mild,
While yet he lived without : his modesty
Imparted this to some, and they to me.
Live happy then, dear soul ; enjoy thy rest
Eternally by pains thou purchasedst,
While Car must live in care, who was thy friend ;
Nor cares he how he live, so in the end
He may enjoy his dearest Lord and thee,
And sit and sing more skilful songs eternally. '

George Herbert gives several anagrams, among
which is the following :—

" Mary
Army
How well her name an *Army* doth present,
In whom the *Lord of Hosts* did pitch His tent ! "

The Latin language furnishes a number of
anagrams, among which the one subjoined is a
good example—

' Roma dabit oram, Maro,
  Ramo, armo, mora, et amor.
Roma tuum nomen quam non pertransiit *Oram*
  Cum Latium ferrent sæcula prisca jugum ?
Non deerat vel fama tibi, vel carmina famæ,
  Unde *Maro* laudes duxit ad astra tuas.
At nunc exsucco similis tua gloria *Ramo*
  A veteri trunco et nobilitate cadit.
Laus antiqua et honor perierunt, te velut *Armo*
  Jam deturbârunt tempora longa suo.
Quin tibi jam desperatæ *Mora* nulla medetur ;
  Qua Fabio quondam sub duce nata salus.
Hinc te olim gentes miratæ odêre vicissim ;
  Et cum sublata laude recidit *Amor*."

Cleaveland's Works contain the next—

DEFINITION OF A PROTECTOR.

What's a Protector ? He's a stately thing,
That apes it in the non-age of a king.
A tragic actor—Cæsar in a clown,
He's a brass farthing stamped with a crown.
A bladder blown, with other breaths puffed full,
Not the *Perillus*, but *Perillus* Bull.
Æsop's proud ass, veil'd in the lion's skin,
An outward saint lined with a devil within.
An echo whence the royal sound doth come,
But just as barrel-head sounds like a drum.
Fantastic image of the royal head,
The Brewers' with the king's arms quartered ;
He is a counterfeited piece, that shows
Charles his effegies with a copper nose.

In fine, he's one we must Protector call,
From whom the King of kings protect us all.
Protector = *O Portet, C. R.*

Tombstones occasionally in former times gave instances of anagrams, as it was not an uncommon belief that a person's character and fortune were hidden in his name. Of this kind are the two following examples. At Ashby Canons, Northampton, there is one of the date of 1639, on

SARAI GRIME,
Is marriage.

A virgin's death, we say, her marriage is,
Spectators viewe as pregnant proofe in this;
Her suitor's Christ, to Him her troth she plights,
Being both agreed, then to the nuptial's rites.
Virtue's her tire, prudence her wedding ring,
Angels the bridesmen in the heavenly quire;
Her joynture's blisse, what more could she desire?
Noe wonder hence soe soon she sped away,
Her husband call'd, she must not make delay.
Not dead, but married shee, her progenye,
The stem of grace, that lives eternally."

The second of these obituary anagrams is to be found at Bletchley, dated 1657, on—

MRS. FAIETH WALKER
Walke by Faith.

Well did thy life, word, anagram agree,
To will and walke aright was all to thee.

Thy tender years were gracious; all thy life
Was virtuous, while a virgin, when a wife;
Here thou didst walke by faith, but now above
By light with Him thy soul did dearly love.
A happy change, thy life now full of blisse,
Thy Christ thy Husband, Heaven thy jointure is.

The assassin of Henry III. of France had his name rendered in this way—

> "Frère Jacques Clément,
> *C'est l'enfer qui m'a créé.*"

The celebrated Holy Alliance was thus travestied—

> "La Sainte Alliance,
> *La Sainte Canaille.*"

Dr. Burney has the credit of the following excellent anagram, written on receipt of the news of the victory of the Nile :—

> "Horatio Nelson,
> *Honor est a Nilo.*"

The words, "Arthur Wellesley, Duke of Wellington," have been transposed into *Let well-foil'd Gaul sekure thy r(e)nown*—an imperfect but not inappropriate example. One on the lamented Princess Charlotte was thought to be particularly happy—the words, "Princess Charlotte Augusta of Wales," were transposed into *P. C. Her august*

O

race is lost, O fatal news! The following is very apt :—

> "When *I cry that I sin* is transposed, it is clear,
> My resource, *Christianity*, soon will appear."

The celebrated Dr. Abernethy, as much remembered perhaps for his eccentricity and brusqueness as for his skill, had his name of John Abernethy turned into *Johnny the Bear.* The annexed is an excellent instance of this laborious trifling :—

A TELEGRAM ANAGRAMMATISED.

Though but a *late germ*, with a wondrous elation,
Yet like a *great elm* it o'ershadows each station,
Et malgré the office is still a large fee mart,
So joyous the crowd was, you'd thought it a *glee mart;*
But they raged at no news from the nations belligerent,
And I said, *Let 'm rage*, since the air is refrigerant.
I then *met large* numbers, whose drink was not sherbet,
Who scarce could look up when their eyes the gas-*glare met;*
So when I had learned from commercial adviser,
That *mere galt* for sand was the great fertiliser,
I bade *Mr. Eaglet*, although 'twas ideal,
Get some from the clay-pit, and so *get 'm real;*
Then, just as my footstep was leaving the portal,
I met an *elm targe* on a great Highland mortal,
With the maid he had wooed by the loch's flowery *margelet*,
And rowed in his boat, which for rhyme's sake call bargelet,
And blithe to the breeze would have set the sail daily,
But it blew at that rate which our sailors *term gale*, aye ;
I stumbled against the fair bride he had married,
When a *merle gat* at large from a cage that she carried ;

She gave a loud screech ! and I could not well blame her,
But lame as I was, I'd no wish to *get lamer;*
So I made my escape—ne'er an antelope fleeter,
Lest my verse, like the poet, should limp through *lag metre.*

The following appeared in an Edinburgh newspaper some years ago :—

THE LENT OARS.

Illustrating Fifty different Renderings of the Letters composing the Word " Monastery."

I am a boatman on the Lago Maggiore, but, fool that
I am, I lent my oars to the Monks of St. Thomas's, who
used to cross the lake in their own boat, and who, on
my inquiring about them, vowed they never had got
them. I spoke to the mayor of the canton, who trans-
mitted a letter my dear Mary had written, and promised
he would send for an answer himself. Having waited
for some time rather impatiently, I set off to the monastery to inquire if the *mayor sent* or not for the answer to
Mary's note about *my ten oars.* The abbot had gone on
a visit to the adjoining convent, and I was informed that
the letter was sent there, and they thought it likely my
oars were there too. I went thither, and on gaining
admission, I inquired if the answer had been sent for.
" *Ay, monster,*" said she, " though *ten mayors* had sent
they would not have got one." " Come, come, *no
mastery* over me ; *may no rest* be mine here or hereafter
if I do not have my oars ! *Yes, matron,* there is *one St.
Mary* to whom I shall pray for interference." " See
your *stone Mary* there," said she, pointing to an image

of the blessed Virgin set in the wall. I prostrated my-self before it, saying, "O *my one star*, my Mary! look down *on my tears*, and *O try means* to get me back my oars. May my soul, which has *met no rays* of thine for long, *store many* favours now. Oh! Mary, do *so try, amen.*" On rising I was astounded on hearing the matron exclaim, "*My! treason!*" Woman though she was, I could have smitten her to the ground, for here came the abbot angrily and anxiously inquiring, "What treason?" Taking me for a French spy, he approached cautiously, but seeing as *yet no arms* about me, he grew bolder, and caused me to be searched for *army notes* or papers. Though he found nothing, I could scarce prevail upon him to grant a truce *or amnesty* till I could explain my errand. "*Ay, no terms* with the villain," said he, threatening to *tan my sore* hide for me. I remonstrated, "*Stay, Ermon*, be not hasty; I trump you no *mean story* in showing you this;" and here I showed him my *torn, seamy* coat, as evidence that no government had favoured me with a degree in *money arts.* "*Yet Romans*," said he, "call *Rome nasty*, and I was suspicious you were one of that kind." "No, *my senator*, I am nothing great, but I am not so bad as that." I was glad to get off without further mentioning my oars, and so left the place.

I was terribly vexed, however, at the way affairs had turned out, so that I could not help telling my care to an old woman I met not far off, and whom I knew. "Do you see *yon stream* on this side of the lake?" said I; "*many tears* have I shed there; I never refused to lend an oar when asked, but no one *sent my oar* back, till now I have lost them all." "Dear me, that's scandalous; take *a rest on my* bundle for a short time; I am sure I saw *Tom N. Sayer* with some of them, and I'll just run over and see." I did as she said, and had not long to wait for her return. " *Ye ran most* nimbly, but how sped you?" At no great *rate, my son;* he has some, but he ran away." "Ran away!" I exclaimed. " *Yes, Tom ran,* though I told him you meant to *say no term* of payment for the bother you had been put to." "May he rot—*yes, man, rot*—for his roguery; by all the bloody heroes, from *Mars to Ney,* were I a tailor I would *try no seam* till I found him; and then—. But I am no tailor, I am but a boatman; so I see no way to make up my loss but by laying a little *on my rates* of passage or smuggling a trifle of *Morny's tea.*" "If a *tear, my son,* would avail thee anything, I would shed plenty; but you *may rest on* my doing what I can for you, so neither hinder *nor stay me* just now, as I must away." "Good-bye," said I; "but may Old Davy *tar my nose* for me if I don't watch that chap. Fine way for a poor *tar's money* to go, always buying oars. Yes, Tom, I'll be down *smart on ye* some of these days."

Thoroughly disgusted, I turned *my toes, ran* swiftly home, and vowed myself *a snore at my* ease, unless my *mentor say* me nay.

We conclude with the following selection of these conceits :—

Florence Nightingale,	Penitentiary,	French Revolution,
Flit on, cheering angel.	*Nay, I repent it,*	*Violence run forth.*
Revolution,	Presbyterian,	Masquerade,
Love to ruin.	*Best in prayer.*	*Queer as Mad.*
Parliament,	Midshipman,	Sweetheart,
Partial men.	*Mind his map.*	*There we sat.*

Catalogues,
Got as a clue.
Lawyers,
Sly ware.
Punishment,
Nine thumps.
Old England,
Golden land.

Paradise lost,
Reap sad toils.
Paradise regained,
Dead respire again.
Telegraph,
Great help.
Astronomers,
Moon starers.

Parishioners,
I hire parsons.
Democratical,
Comical trade.
Gallantries,
All great sin.
Impatient,
Tim in a pet.

THE PALINDROME.

PALINDROMIC, or Reciprocal Verses (Gr. *palin*, backwards; *dromos*, a running) is the name given to verses which read the same either backwards or forwards. They are the most difficult of all the literary frivolities we have yet met with—their composition requiring considerable skill and invention, yet having no useful purpose. The English language is not very well adapted for this kind of Jump-Jim-Crowism, and only a few examples are to be met with; it is more common, however, in Latin and Greek, and there are a number in these languages. There is, indeed, a curious and rare volume in Greek of this nature, being a poem by "Ambrose Hieromonachus Pamperes, with Scholia and all the Histories contained in it; being of great use to those who study it deeply. Now first published, 1802, at Vienna in Austria, at the Greek printing press of George Bendotes." This work consists of one hundred and sixty pages, the first eight containing the dedication to the Emperor of All the Russias, Alexander I. There is also an Introduction, giving directions how the book is to be read, also an epigram praising the Greek writers, affirming that in all of them will be found wisdom. Then comes the poem itself, consisting of 416 verses, and an equal number of scholia on these verses—each verse being explained by a commentary, introducing notices of great men, kings, poets, mythological characters, and others. The arrangement of the words is of course frequently forced, the allusions obscure, and the sense difficult to discover, but they are by no means what are called nonsense verses, for by close attention, and with the aid of the notes, every one of them may be construed. The poem, each line of which is a complete palindrome, commences thus—

"Onax es o, ethete te Theos ex ano,"
signifying—

" O King, who was thus placed by God from above."

This poem by Pamperes was written on the words the Empress Catherine uttered when some of her chief officers were put to death, and her troops destroyed by the Poles. On hearing the unexpected news she was in the deepest grief and could not rest. She immediately called together her counsellors, and began her speech—

"Rypara, anomata, ata mona, ara pyr," &c.

"How cruel, mean, and unlawful are these things that I have heard. How full of impiety is this unexpected and unlawful loss. Nothing else is required for revenge except fire," &c.

Of the few palindromes in the English language, one represents our first parent introducing himself to Eve in these words—

"Madam, I'm Adam."

Taylor, the Water Poet, made several attempts at constructing palindromes, but could arrive at nothing better than—

"Lewd did I live, & evil did I dwel"—

not altogether perfect, however, inasmuch as if the last word was properly written, the reciprocity would fail. Something similar is this other—

"Live was I ere I saw evil."

Another English one has reference to Napoleon, who is supposed to say—

"Able was I ere I saw Elba."

These last two are very complete, as each word remains intact, which in palindromic verses is not always the case—the component letters frequently running into different words in the reverse reading. The following Latin example preserves this kind of completeness :—

"Sator arepo tenet opera rotas."

There are a number of names which are palindromic in the English language, and it is somewhat curious that they are mostly feminine, as— Eve, Anna, Hannah, Ada, Madam, and others. The following enigma is founded on like words :—

"First find out a word that doth silence proclaim,
  And backwards and forwards is always the same ;
Then, next, you must find out a feminine name,
  That backwards and forwards is always the same ;
An act, or writing, or parchment, whose name
  Both backwards and forwards is always the same ;
A fruit that is rare, whose botanical name
  Read backwards and forwards is always the same ;
A note used in music, which time doth proclaim,
  And backwards and forwards is always the same ;
The initials or terminals equally frame
A title that's due to the fair married dame,
  Which backwards and forwards is always the same."

The words sought for are—Mum, Anna, Deed, Anana, Minim, whose initials and endings equally form Madam, "the title that's due to the fair married dame."

A Roman lawyer chose this for his motto—

"Si nummi immunis"—

which has been freely translated—

"Give me my fee, and I warrant you free."

A Latin elegiac verse gives in every line a complete palindrome:—

"Salta, tu levis es ; summus se si velut Atlas,
   (Omina ne sinimus,) suminis es animo.
Sin, oro, caret arcanâ cratera coronis
   Unam arcas, animes semina sacra manu.
Angere regnato, mutatum, o tangere regna,
   Sana tero, tauris si ruat oret anas :
Milo subi rivis, summus si viribus olim,
   Muta sedes ; animal lamina sede satum.
Tangeret, i videas, illisae divite regnat ;
   Aut atros ubinam manibus orta tua !
O tu casurus, rem non mersurus acuto
   Telo, sis-ne, tenet ? non tenet ensis, olet."

In the time of Queen Elizabeth, a lady who had been forbidden to appear at court on account of some suspicions against her, the truth of which she denied, took for the device on her seal, the moon, partly obscured,.with the motto—

" Ablata at alba."
(*Retired but pure.*)

The following is supposed to be written to a young man detained at Rome on a love affair, and is founded upon an older and unproducible verse, which gave a dreadful picture of the state of morals at Rome in ancient times :—

"Roma, ibi tibi sedes— ibi tibi Amor ;
  Româ etsi te terret et iste Amor,
  Ibi etsi vis te non esse—sed es ibi,
  Roma te tenet et Amor."

Thus rendered into English—

"At Rome you live—at Rome you love ;
  From Rome that love may you affright,
  Although you'd leave—you never move,
  For love and Rome both bar your flight."

The older and unproducible verse referred to as the origin of the preceding example, was the work of Sotades, a Roman poet who lived 250 years B.C., and has the credit of having invented this kind of literary folly. Sotades having degraded his muse by devoting his verse to obscenity, *Sotadea Carmina* became the general name for verse of that character. The few of his lines which are cited by Quintilian are well known.

In various churches in the East this line is to be seen engraved on baptismal fonts—

" Νίχον ἀνομήμα, μή μόναν ὄχιν "
" Wash away my sins, not my face only."

There is one which is applied to the " Witches' Sabbath," which runs thus—

" In girum imus noctu, non ut consumimur igni "—
" We go round in a circle at night, not to be consumed by fire."

The following surrounds a figure of the sun in the mosaic pavement at Sa Maria del Fiori at Florence :—

" En giro torte sol ciclos et rotor igne."

Camden gives us this example—

" Odo tenet mulum, madidam mappam tenet Anna.
Anna tenet mappam, madidam, mulum tenet Odo.' '

The following, in which the *words* only read backwards, is said to express, in the first form, the sentiments of a Roman Catholic :—

" Patrum dicta probo, nec sacris belligerabo ; "

read backwards, we have the sentiments of a Protestant :—

" Belligerabo sacris, nec probo dicta patrum."

Another of this kind is one which refers to the sacrifice of Abel—

"Sacrum pingue dabo, nec macrum sacrificabo ; "

and in the second way is applicable to that of Cain :

"Sacrificabo macrum nec dabo pingue sacrum."

The following Latin verse also affords two opposite meanings :—

"Prospicimus modo, quod durabunt tempore longo
    Fœdera, nec patriæ pax cito diffugiet."

"Diffugiet cito pax patriæ, nec fœdera longo
    Tempore durabunt, quod modo prospicimus."

Another Latin poem of about sixty lines begins in this way—

"Sumere tironem si vis, me norit eremus :
    Jurem non animo nomina non merui.
Aspice : nam raro mittet timor arma, nec ipsa
    Si se mente reget, non tegeret Nemesis.
Me tum animat recte, me dem, et certamina mutem,
    Si res ana velit utile, vanus eris."

A German example runs—

"Bei Leid lieh stets Heil die Lieb."
    (In trouble, comfort is lent by love.)

Those which follow are also good examples—

"Si bene te tua laus taxat sua lautè tenebis."

"Acide me malo, sed non desola me, medica."

Mr. H. Campkin some years ago sent the following piece to "Notes and Queries," and stated that it was written to please a youthful group, and, though nonsensical enough, the lines serve to show that the English language is capable of being twisted into uncouth ways if any one will take the trouble :—

" One winter's eve around the fire, a cosy group, we sat,
Engaged, as was our custom old, in after-dinner chat :
Small talk it was, no doubt, because the smaller folk were there,
And they, the young monopolists ! absorbed the lion's share.
Conundrums, riddles, rebuses, cross-questions, puns atrocious,
Taxed all their ingenuity, till Peter the precocious—
Old head on shoulders juvenile—cried, 'Now for a new task,
Let's try our hand at *Palindromes !*' 'Agreed! But first,' we ask,
'Pray, Peter, what *are* Palindromes? The forward imp replied,
'A Palindrome's a string of words, of sense or meaning void,
Which reads both ways the same ; and here, with your permission,
I'll cite some half-a-score of samples, lacking all precision,
(But held together by loose rhymes) to test my definition !'

A milksop jilted by his lass, or wandering in his wits,
Might murmur, *Stiff, O dairyman, in a myriad of fits !*
A limner, by photography dead beat in competition,
Thus grumbled : *No, it is opposed, art sees trade's opposition !*
A nonsense-loving nephew might his soldier uncle dun,
With *Now stop, Major-general, are negro jam pots won !*
A supercilious grocer, if inclined that way, might snub
A child with, *But Ragusa store, babe, rots a sugar tub !*
Thy sceptre, Alexander, is a fortress, cried Hephaestion :
Great A. said, *No, it's a bar of gold, a bad log for a bastion !*

A timid creature fearing rodents—mice, and such small fry—
Stop, Syrian, I start at rats in airy spots, might cry.
A simple soul, whose wants are few, might say with hearty zest,
Desserts I desire not, so long no lost one rise distressed.
A stern Canadian parent might—in earnest, not in fun—
Exclaim, *No sot nor Ottawa law at Toronto, son!*
A crazy dentist might declare, as something strange or new,
That *Paget saw an Irish tooth, sir, in a waste-gap!* True!
A surly student, hating sweets, might answer with *élan,*
Name tarts, no, medieval slave, I demonstrate man!
He who in Nature's bitters findeth sweet food every day,
Eureka! till I pull up ill I take rue, well might say."

There is an old legendary story that his Satanic Majesty was an adept at this kind of versification, and the subjoined account of one of his attempts is taken from Hone's "Every-day Book." "St. Martin having given up the profession of a soldier, and being elected Bishop of Tours, when prelates neither kept horses, carriages, nor servants, had occasion to go to Rome to consult His Holiness upon some important ecclesiastical matter. As he was walking gently along the road he met the devil, who politely accosted him, and ventured to observe how fatiguing and indecorous it was to perform so long a journey on foot, like the commonest of cockle-shell chaperoned pilgrims. The saint knew well the drift of Old Nick's address, and commanded him to become immediately a beast of burden or *jumentum;* which the devil did in a twinkling, by assuming the shape of a mule. The saint jumped upon the fiend's back, who at first trotted cheerfully along, but soon slacked his pace. The bishop of course had neither whip nor spurs, but was possessed of a much more powerful stimulus, for, says the legend, he made the sign of the Cross, and the smarting devil instantly galloped away. Soon, however, and naturally enough, the father of sin returned to sloth and obstinacy, and Martin hurried him again with repeated signs of the Cross, till, twitched and stung to the quick by those crossings so hateful to him, the vexed and tired reprobate uttered the following distich in a rage :—

'Signa te, signa ; temere me tangis et angis ;
  Roma tibi subito motibus ibit amor.'

That is—' Cross, cross thyself ; thou plaguest and vexest me without necessity ; for, owing to my exertions, Rome, the object of thy wishes, will soon be near.' "

———

Hardly akin to this palindromic dexterity, but which may be mentioned here, is the attempt to construct a verse which shall contain the whole of

P

the letters in the alphabet. The English version
of the Bible has one passage which does this, with
the exception of the letter *j* (Ezra vii. 21) ; and
here are four lines as an example—

> " God gives the grazing ox his meat,
>   And quickly hears the sheep's low cry,
> But man, who tastes His finest wheat,
>   Should joy to lift His praises high."

The greater feat, however, would be to have a line
containing all the letters, but these only occurring
once. The late Professor De Morgan frequently
relieved the severity of his mathematical studies
by composing puzzles of this kind, but could make
nothing of it, till he made use of the poetical
license of employing *u* for *v* and *i* for *j.* The
result was—

> "I, quartz pyx, who fling muck beds."

The professor's line encouraged others to try
something better, resulting in

> " Quiz my black whigs ; export fund ;"

and another—

> "Dumpy Quiz, whirl back fogs next :"

all alike having the duplication of letters—*u* for *v*,

and *i* for *j*. De Morgan, in sending these oddities
to " Notes and Queries," decided that the nearest
approach to good sense was in the following :—

" Get nymph ; quiz sad brow ; fix luck."

LITERARY MISFORTUNES.

AN old countryman, on the occasion of a recent visit to a printing-offiee for the first time, casually remarked to one of the compositors that he did not understand how they all came to be such good "spellers." Having been told they generally considered it as easy to spell correctly as not, and that from long practice it was unusual to make a mistake, he remarked further that he supposed them conversant with every language they might be called upon to put in type. This fact, for it is one, is quite reconcilable with the idea of another equally verdant visitor—that a phonetic system of spelling would be an advantage, where each compositor would be left to the freedom of his own will. Others, again, even in these enlightened times, are so ignorant of the actual labour and various processes required in the production of books, that they think nothing can be easier. Instance the old lady who called at a bookseller's shop in the North, asking for a "big prent" Bible. After being shown several, none of which appeared of large enough type to satisfy her, she very coolly remarked, "I'm gaun up the toon to buy some bits of things, an' ye can jist pit your stampin' airns in the fire, an' hae ane ready for me as I come back." Poor old lady! her ignorance was manifest enough; but there are plenty of authors nearly as unreasonable in their demands at the hands of the printer—the misspelling of a proper name, or the omission of a comma, throwing them into a state of mental agitation, which may perhaps beget a letter animadverting in strong terms upon the mistake to the publisher or editor of the work in question.

Mistakes will happen in the best works, in spite of all the care which can be taken by the printers in the getting-up of the books, and Dr. Hill Burton, in his "Book-Hunter," would seem to infer that blunders have occasionally subserved a very important purpose. "One curious service of printers' blunders," he says, "of a character quite distinct from their bibliographical influence, is their use in detecting plagiarisms. It may seem strange that there should be any difficulty in critically determining this question, when the plagiarism is so close as to admit of this test; but there are pieces of very hard work in science— tables of reference, and the like—where, if two people go through the same work, they will come to the same conclusion. In such cases, the prior worker has sometimes identified his own by a blunder, as he would a stolen china vase by a crack. Peignot complains that some thirty or forty pages of his ' Dictionnaire Bibliographique' were incorporated in the ' Siècles Littéraires de la France,' ' avec une exactitude si admirable, qu'on y a précieusement conservé toutes les fautes typo-graphiques.' "

The printers are not always in fault, however, as regards the origin of errors, for the author fre-quently leads them astray by carelessly-written "copy," both in punctuation and spelling. One well-known American writer recommended that all authors should work for a time in a printing-offiee, as a means of reforming a diffuse style and incorrect punctuation — compositors becoming critically aware, in the picking up letter by letter of a long and complex sentence, of the best means of curtailing and strengthening sentences, and being quick at detecting repetitions, to say nothing of the art of correct punctuation. It is part of the Proof-Reader's duty to mark a note of interrogation against any passage in a book preparing for press which he does not think is right, or when a sentence is incomplete. Authors profit by these quiet estimates of their meaning, and many a weak point, which might have marred a writer's reputation, has been set right by attention being drawn to it by the unobtrusive (?) of the Proof-Reader. Though not exactly perfect, the Reader generally bestows much time and patience over his work, and the general correctness of the many books now published evidences that their labour is not in vain, though seldom or never is he complimented for his care—freedom from censure may be said to be the only praise he ever gets. And what an amount of knowledge he is supposed to possess in all departments of literature! He should know all about the Constitutions of Clarendon, the Statute of Provisors, Pragmatic Sanctions, Development Theories, the Bangorian Controversy, &c., and besides Latin and French, a knowledge of Greek and Hebrew will not come amiss, though it may not benefit him pecuniarily. He should be able to tell whether the perisome in the Brisingidæ is coriaceous or not, or consists of an ectodern of ciliated cuticle and a mesoderm of calcareous skeletal ossicula with a ciliated epithelium—in fact, he would require to be a walking encyclopædia, a living Dictionary of Phrase and Fable! The Reader is generally attended by a satellite, redolent of ink and paste—the P.D.—who reads over the author's MS. to him while he looks on the proof and notes the errors, and this youthful genius will supply words or travesty them in the most ingenious and outrageous manner. We have known of one who read off the copy, "The Leg end of the Kid" for Legend of the Cid, and another travestied the line—wilfully, we suspect—

" His soul was like a star, and dwelt apart,"

into the burlesque—

" His sole was like a skate, and smelt afar !"

A third boy read "Paul's Epistle to the Caledonians" instead of Corinthians.

Many a good work is sadly disfigured by the negligence of authors in correcting their proofs; while other writers, again, are extremely diligent in making unnecessary alterations. Cases have occurred where one volume has grown into two by means of corrections, and others have had their price considerably heightened in consequence. It is recorded that both Milton and Addison were solicitous regarding the correction of their works while passing through the press. Savage was most scrupulous in correcting his proofs, and the poet Gray would not unfrequently spend weeks over them, revising and re-revising. The satirical poet Churchill expressed himself rather energetically on this point, when he said "that it was like cutting away one's own flesh;" while Julius Scaliger so carefully prepared his MS. that it seldom needed correction, and the print frequently corresponded with it page for page and line for line. "Easy composition, but laborious correcting," was Burns' own description of his work. Ben Jonson was once requested to revise a sermon full of typographical and other errors, but he declined the task, and recommended that it should be sent to the House of Correction. Burke, the celebrated orator, was careless in regard to his MS., and one of his effusions received so many corrections and interlineations that the compositors refused to correct it, but took down the types and reset the whole. Dr. Johnson was most assiduous over his proofs, and between the original publication of his essays in the "Rambler," and their collection and reprint in the form of a book, there were thousands of alterations made.

Errors and misfortunes do not proceed only from the many who write and publish, but the few who occupy the highest position in the literary world are equally to blame, chiefly owing to the hurried way in which much of their MS. is prepared for press. Good penmanship, as a branch of education, in many cases would seem to have been greatly neglected, and we have heard of instances where the signature of a letter has been so completely unintelligible as to involve the necessity of the writer's name being cut from the missive and gummed on to the envelope of the answer. This may be looked upon as an extreme case, perhaps, but that such a necessity may occasionally arise is quite within the experience of many persons whose correspondence is at all extensive. We have seen MS. from a well-known author which could be likened to nothing better than the autograph of a dying spider which had paid a surreptitious visit to an ink-bottle. Lawyers of high standing send their MS. to the printers with technical phrases misspelled and legal terms abbreviated, and expect the compositor to decipher and set it up in a readable condition. Divines of known ability leave their "copy" without points or even "caps" to mark the end or beginning of sentences—thus giving much additional labour, and causing thereby much loss of time and temper. Were their works left in the same state as that in which they are frequently written, no one would attribute the fault to the author—the printer alone would be held responsible. Some writers have asserted, however, by way of excuse for themselves, that printers, when they get extra-bad MS., pay more attention to it, and that therefore there are fewer errors in proofs from that which is ill-written than in that which is well-written. A learned dean —we think it was Dr. Hook—is reported to have said that the worse the penmanship the cleaner the proof! The compositor may well wish to put what Dean Alford calls a shriek (!) after that assertion.

Carelessness in style is another cause of errors, and often, by the misuse of pronouns, renders what might have been intelligible enough, doubtful and false in meaning. As an example of this kind of obscurity, take the following sentence from a scientific work published some years ago :—"When we say, in astronomy, that the earth revolves round the sun, or that the moon revolves round the earth, we do not speak with absolute correctness, for in all such cases both bodies are revolving round the common centre of inertia of the two. In the case of the sun and the earth, as the former is a million times larger than the latter, the common centre of the *two* being so much nearer *its* centre than to the centre of the earth, is really within *its* body or circumference." To which of the nouns do these *its* apply? One of the leading London papers on one occasion produced the following. The "old man" of the statement is old Mr. Fleming of Glasgow, who figured some years ago in a noted criminal case there. "There, after a while, during Mrs. M'Lachlan's temporary absence, the old man murdered her with a cleaver. He then made her swear to tell no one, and gave her the property, that the blame might be laid upon robbers." Having first murdered the woman in her absence, he then makes her swear to tell no one—very extraordinary altogether.

Before adverting to the literary misfortunes peculiar to the newspaper press, we shall notice a few which have occurred in books, some of which may as fairly be attributed to the writer as to the printer. We may premise that the similarity in the spelling of some words, others with the differ-

ence of only a letter, and the comparative resemblance of the written conformation of many words,
are the most fruitful causes—the mistakes often
having a fitness of themselves which, independently
of the amusement they afford, is sometimes superior
to that of mere incongruity.   Thomas Moore, in
the " Fudges in England," happily hits off the
liability of printers to commit errors, when he
makes Fanny say—

> " But a week or two since, in my ' Ode to the Spring,'—
> Which I meant to have made a most beautiful thing,—
> Where I talked of the 'dew-drops from freshly-blown roses,
> The nasty things made it ' freshly-blown noses !'
> And once when, to please my cross aunt, I had tried
> To commem'rate some saint of her clique who had died,
> Having said he ' had taken up in heaven his position,'
> They made it, he ' had taken up to heaven his physician !'"

Mr. H. Martin of Halifax some years ago adverted
to an error which occurred in a communication of
his to one of the journals, and said : " Upwards of
thirty years' experience in connection with the
press has taught me to be very lenient towards
misprints.   The difficulty of detecting typographical errors is much greater that the uninitiated
are inclined to believe.   I have often observed
that, even if the spelling be correct, a wrong word
is very apt to remain undetected."   He then

notices an instance in an edition of Shakespeare's
"Merchant of Venice," where the lines—

> " Young Alcides, when he did redeem
>   The virgin tribute paid by howling Troy "—

were made into nonsense by the conversion of
Troy into *Tory.* Mr. Martin says further: " In a
short biographical notice of Pope which I compiled
for an edition of his poems, I briefly enumerated
his prose works, among which I named his
' Memoirs of a Parish Priest;' when the proof
came before me, I found the compositor had set
it, ' *Memoirs of a Paint Brush.'* "

To which of the two, author or compositor, are
we indebted for this vile misquotation of a line
from Burns? —

> "Now Tam, O Tam ! had they been *queens !* "

Queens never were plentiful in Ayrshire, but it
could turn out many a bevy of

> "Queans,
> A' strapping hizzies in their teens."

In a cheap edition of Burns there is this error—

> " O gin my love were yon red *nose ;* "

And in another edition still—

> " But hark ! I'll tell ye o' a plot,
> Though dinna ye be speakin' o't ;
> I'll nail the self-conceited *Scot*
> As dead's a herrin' ! "

There is a certain association sometimes between the colour of a rose and a nose, and perhaps to some people there is a similar link between a Scot and a *sot*.

A book was published some years ago, in which a modern example of public spirit and good citizenship was brought into comparison with the conduct of Cato and Brutus. This was the end of a paragraph, and no doubt was intended for a good finishing effect, but unfortunately the two Roman names were printed *Cats* and *Brutes !*

Mr. Pyecroft, in his " Ways and Words of Men of Letters," relates the following conversation :—
"' Really,' said a printer to him, ' gentlemen should not place such unlimited confidence in the eyesight of our hard-worked and half-blinded reader of proofs; for I am ashamed to say that we utterly ruined one poet through a ludicrous misprint.' ' Indeed ! And what was the unhappy line ? ' ' Why, sir, the poet intended to say—

> " See the pale martyr in a sheet of fire ! "

instead of which the line appeared—

"See the pale martyr *with his shirt on fire !*"

The reviewers of course made the most of so entertaining a blunder, and the poor poet was never heard of more in the field of literature.'" The same gentleman also notices another singular error, in the passage quoted by Dr. Johnson as an authority under the verb "to sit." "Asses are ye that sit in judgment" (Judg. v. 10). The verse is, "Speak! ye that ride on white asses, ye that sit in judgment, and walk by the way."

In Pope's notes on "Measure for Measure," he says the story was taken from "Cinthio," dec. 8, nov. 5—meaning 8th decade and 5th novel. One of the many emendators of Shakespeare, however, thought fit to fill out these abbreviations, and we therefore read December 8, November 5! Pope has also been misquoted on another occasion by some prosaic compositor, who sought to bring the poet's idea within the limits of his own understanding, thus—

> "Who could take offence,
> When pure description held the place of *sauce ?*"

instead of "the place of *sense.*"

In one of the many Christmas books published

nowadays at that festive season, there was a passage to the effect that, though young ladies sometimes affected through coyness a dislike to be kissed under the misletoe, "they did not object to it under the *nose*"—which we would charitably understand to have been meant for "under the rose!" We forget in what Radcliffian romance the following occurred—the passage was a vigorous one, the scene well wrought up ; the heroine was on the point of being sacrificed to the revenge of the villain of the story, when opportune aid arrived to the rescue of the fair damsel in the person of a knight riding on a *warehouse !* We fancy "war-horse" was here meant. The omission of the letter *y* gave a curious turn to the following line :—

" My *years* flow back, I'm young again."

A monkish writer of a work published in 1561, called the "Anatomy of the Mass," and consisting of 172 pages of text and 15 of errata, attributed the many mistakes in the book to the "artifices of Satan." He "supposes that the devil, to ruin the fruit of this work, employed two very malicious frauds : the first before it was printed, by drench- ing the manuscript in a kennel, and having reduced it to a most pitiable state, rendered several parts

Q

illegible ; the second, in obliging the printers to commit such numerous blunders, never yet equalled in so small a work." The Bible itself has not escaped from these misfortunes. One edition, printed by John Basket at Oxford, is known as the "Vinegar Bible," from the fact that the Parable of the Vineyard is therein styled the Parable of the Vinegar. A printer's wife in Germany, while an edition of the Bible was printing at her house, one night took an opportunity of stealing into the office, to alter that sentence of subjection to her husband pronounced upon Eve in Genesis. She took out the first two letters of the word *Herr* (lord), and substituted *Na* in their place, thus altering the passage from "and he shall be thy lord" (*Herr*) to "and he shall be thy fool" (*Narr*). In a Cambridge Bible publishèd some years back, appears "I shall never *forgive* (forget) thy precepts." John Field, a Cambridge printer, published an edition of the Bible in 1653, containing a great number of errors, of which the following is an example :—"Know ye not that the unrighteous *shall inherit* the kingdom of God ?" (1 Cor. vi. 9), for "shall not inherit." Disraeli, in his "Curiosities," gives an account of a similar scandalous omission of the important negative in the Seventh Commandment. The printers were summoned before the Court of High Commission; and this "*not*" served to bind them in a fine of £3000. A prior circumstance had occurred which induced the Government at that time to be very vigilant regarding the Biblical press: the learned Bishop Usher, going one day to preach at St. Paul's Cross, entered a bookseller's shop on his way and procured a Bible of the London edition. When he came to look for his text, to his astonishment he discovered that the verse was altogether omitted from the copy he had purchased.

Such errors in the Bible cannot easily occur nowadays, as all editions are subjected to severe scrutiny. But there are many curious discrepancies between the English and Scotch Bibles, chiefly in the spelling of various words—all the usual marks of punctuation, however, are employed in both, with the exception of what printers call the "dash" (—), and this is not used at all either in Old or New Testament, with one solitary exception, which the reader will find by turning to Exodus xxxii. 32. Jeremiah xxxi. 15 in Scotch Bibles has " Rachel weeping for her children," in English Bibles it is " *Rahel* weeping." English Bibles have caterpiller, hungred, houshold, &c., Scotch have caterpillar, household, hungered, &c.,

One English Bible spells cheerful in the Old Testament chearful (Prov. xv. 13; Zech. viii. 19, ix. 17, &c.), while in the New Testament it is cheerful throughout—this latter edition comes from the well-known house of Eyre and Spottiswoode.

The similarity of the written conformation of two letters has led occasionally to awkward mistakes, as the author of a temperance novel found to his astonishment when he saw that where he meant to say, "drunkenness is folly," it was rendered "*drunkenness is jolly !*" A very popular authoress, speaking of her heroine as "enjoying more indulgence than usually falls to the lot of her sex," wrote so illegibly that it appeared as "falls to the lot of *horses.*" Audubon's "Ornithology" contains this sentence, which shows that authors occasionally make strange slips—"The earth was rent asunder in several places ; *one or two islands sank for ever,* and the inhabitants fled in dismay towards the *eastern shores.*" And Bulwer somewhere says, "I *hear* the vain shadows *glide.*" One of the most curious blunders made by an author was that of Thackeray, when collecting materials for his "Irish Sketch Book." Driving along a road, he saw at intervals posts set up with the letters G. P. O. upon them. Overtaking a peasant,

he inquired the meaning of the initials, and was
gravely informed that they stood for "God Preserve O'Connell!" Out came the tourist's note-
book, in which a memorandum was jotted down of
the curious statement. In the first edition of the
" Sketch Book " the fact was duly mentioned ; but
it was suppressed in all subsequent issues, owing
to the tardy discovery that the letters represented
" General Post-Offiee," indicating that the highway
was a post-road. During the agitation some years
ago upon the Marriage Affinity Bill, a circular was
prepared by some clerical opponents of the measure
in which a curious error was passed in proof by the
whole of these gentlemen, that "a man should not
be allowed to marry the *"wife of a deceased sister"*
—fortunately the blunder was discovered before
the circulars were issued.

The Dean of Westminster some years ago
presided at the anniversary of the Printers' Pension
Society, and in the course of his address, referring
to the general correctness aimed at by printers,
made the following remarks :—" He thought people
hardly knew how curious was the feeling that
arose in authors when they received back their
proof-sheets. He said a feeling of shame, because
he was sure that authors must feel how great an

infliction they imposed on the ingenuity and on the patience of the printer. They were always conscious of the difficulty which was taken off their hands by the interpretation of the printer, who deciphered that which was committed to him ; and he said, also amusement, because nothing enlivened an author so much, when plodding through the weary pages he had written, as the ingenious conjectures made by the printer to decipher what he (the author) had written. He remembered on one occasion receiving some anonymous correspondence, seeking to know what was meant in a passage in one of his works— namely, 'the horn of the burning beast.' He looked at the passage, and was himself in some perplexity to know what was the meaning of 'the horn of the burning beast.' Perhaps some of them might discover, in the extraordinary sagacity they possessed, that the passage referred to resolved itself into 'the thorn of the burning bush.' He had also heard it asked whether indeed some of those mistakes laid to the charge of authors did· not really proceed from the humour of those who set up the type. Doubtless some of them remembered that famous passage in the 'History of Europe,' where the late Sir Archibald Alison described the funeral of the Duke of Wellington, in which he spoke of the pall-bearers, including among other distinguished officers the name of 'Sir Peregrine Pickle.' He had often heard that quoted as an instance of the extraordinary ignorance of that learned historian. But he confessed that he thought it was not so much an instance of ignorance on the part of Sir Archibald Alison as it was of the humour of some compositor, in whom the memory of Sir Peregrine Pickle was more familiar than the memory of Sir Peregrine Acton."

Even the want of a comma may lead to strange results, as in a bill which was presented to a farmer, which ran—" To hanging two barn-doors and myself seven hours, 4s. 6d." There is also the famous blunder in the contract for lighting the town of Liverpool in 1819, the words of which were—" The lamps to be in number 4050, of two spouts each, composed of twenty threads of cotton." The contractor would have proceeded to furnish each lamp with the said twenty threads, but this being only half the usual quantity, the commissioner discovered that the difference arose from the misplacing of the comma, which should have preceded, instead of followed, the word *each*. The contract was annulled to prevent a lawsuit. A good example of the effect of misplacing a comma is to be found in the ancient oracle—" Thou shalt go thou shalt return never by war shalt thou perish." By one way of placing the commas, the consulter of the oracle was forbidden to go upon the purposed expedition; by reading it his own way, he went and perished. Then there was that unlucky Bishop of Asello, who suffered the loss of his bishopric through the blunder of a stupid painter who was employed to trace an inscription over the gate of the bishop's palace. The legend ran thus—

" Porta patens esto nulli, claudaris honesto."

("Gate, be thou open to nobody, be shut to an honest man.")

The placing of the comma after *esto* would have set it all right, as—

"Gate, be thou open, not shut to an honest man."

A recent critique upon a performance of Othello has the following, showing how much the want of a comma may mar the sense of a passage :—" The Moor, seizing a bolster full of rage and jealousy, smothers her." This reminds us of the very Irish epitaph, which places the brother of the deceased in an awkward position : "Erected to the memory of John Phillips, accidentally shot as a mark of affection by his brother." Another from the sister isle is a remark which appeared in an article in a newspaper upon Robespierre, which said "that he left no children behind him, except a brother, who was killed at the same time." A printer, meddling with the verdict of a coroner's jury, struck out a comma after the word "apoplexy," making it read —"Deceased came to his death by excessive drinking, producing apoplexy in the minds of the jury." A correspondent sent a piece of poetry to a newspaper with the following introduction :—"The following lines were written more than fifty years ago, by one who has for many years slept in his grave merely for his own amusement." There are sometimes words quaintly put together, when the meaning is purposely disguised by forced pointing, as in the nursery rhyme—

> "Every lady in the land
>   Has twenty nails on each hand,
>   Five and twenty on hands and feet ;
>   This is true without deceit."

This is rather puzzling, till a comma is placed after *nails, five,* and *feet,* omitting the one after *hand.*

In all works hurriedly produced, such as newspapers, there is, of course, a greater liability to
commit errors; but, all things considered, newspapers are marvels of correct typography, and it
cannot be doubted that the careful and painstaking
method of reading over the proof slips alone pro-
duces this result.   These proofs frequently contain
curious errors—such as Paper-families for Pater-
familias, or " Eh ! the Brute !" for " Et tu, Brute ! "
But these are generally set right before printing by
the Reader comparing the proof with the author's
MS. — supposing that this is in itself correct,
which is not always the case; and then it is the
duty of the Reader to see that there are no incon-
sistencies in spelling, punctuation, abbreviations,
&c.   In "making-up" newspapers—or the piecing
together of different paragraphs into columns—
the jumbling together of two separate items will
occasionally occur, and a good specimen of this
kind of mixture appeared some time ago in a French
newspaper: "Dr. X. has been appointed head
physician to the Hôpital de la Charité.   Orders
have been issued by the authorities for the immediate extension of the Cimetière de Parnasse."   This
confusion was perhaps better illustrated in the report
of a public meeting in the United States, at which

one of the "strong-minded" females of the day appeared on the same platform with Mr. Train, and the lady wrote as follows to the paper regarding its report :—"By some fantastic trick of your typesetter, my speech in St. James's Hall on Saturday evening, is suddenly terminated, and so linked to that of Mr. Train, that I am made to run off in an entirely new vein of eloquence. Among many other exploits, I am made to boast that I neither smoke, nor chew, nor drink, nor lie, nor steal, nor swear, as if such accomplishments were usual among American women; and wherever I refer to my honoured countrymen as white males, I am reported as having addressed them as 'white mules.' All these are very good jokes if credited to the printer's devil, but not to those who represent an unpopular idea, and carefully weigh their words." The New Haven (U. S.) *Journal and Courier* lately produced a curious jumble in reporting two items which had somehow got mixed. One read—"A large cast-iron wheel, revolving nine hundred times per minute, exploded in that city yesterday, after a long and painful illness. Deceased was a prominent thirty-second degree Mason." The other paragraph detailed how " John Fadden, the well-known florist and real-estate broker, of Newport, R. I., died in Wardner and Russell's sugar-mill at Crystal Lake, Ill., on Saturday, doing $3000 damage to the building, and injuring several workmen and Lorenzo Wilcox fatally."

Of errors of other kinds we give the following. In an article upon the short-time agitation it was stated that "a factory boy had been *shaved* to death" (slaved). George Stephenson, the celebrated engineer, when examined before the Commons' Committee upon Railways, was asked by a member what would happen to the train supposing a cow chanced to stray upon the line. Stephenson's reply was that he did not know what might be the result to the train, but that "it would be unco bad for the coo." An accident of this kind recently occurred, and a local newspaper reported, " As the safest way, the engineer put on full steam, dashed up against the cow, and literally cut it into *calves!* " This rather astonishing statement created some surprise, which was, however, put an end to by the next issue of the paper, which stated that "the cow was cut into halves." Darwin may assert strange things, but the following does not enter into his list of affinities:—that "ants reside in subterranean *taverns;*" or this: "A live *surgeon* was caught in the Thames, and was sold to the inhabitants (!) at sixpence a pound." The "Literary Gazette" once made the following apology:—"By the breaking of the head of an *h*, or the misprint of the letter *n*, a very tempting advertisement to invest in certain lines, was entitled 'Purchase of Railway *Snares.*'" Those who complain of the mismanagement of the great water companies might not be displeased to read that "the scheme proposed by Government is to *bung up* the existing companies,"—what should have been stated was that there was an intention of "buying up" the monopolists. The Directors of the Indigent Old Men's Society of Edinburgh, on looking for the report of one of their annual meetings in the next morning's paper, were no doubt astonished to find it reported as the *Indignant* Old Men's Society. So with a learned bishop, who had been viewing the antiquities of an old church: he was stated to have expressed himself gratified with its *iniquities!* A correspondent of a daily paper recently suggested a remedy for the crowded state of towns by proposing the erection of *submarine* dwellings for the working classes— suburban residences would be quite as comfortable, and freer from damp! The animadversion of a newspaper upon a public officer—some parochial Bumble—which said he had been "tried in the balance and found *panting*," was as likely to be correct as if it had said he had been "found wanting." A child was once reported as having died from eating a large quantity of *piers*—well, stone fruit is said to be rather indigestible. An American paper, describing a political demonstration, averred that the procession was very fine, and nearly two miles long, as was also the prayer of the chaplain. Another American paper reporting the speeches at a Burns' festival, made one of the orators say—

> " O Caledonia ! stern and wild !
> *Wet* nurse for a poetic child."

It must have taxed the ingenuity of the compositor, who set up the paragraph in which we are told "the Christian religion strictly enjoins *mahogany*," instead of "monogamy." A serious fight took place lately in a public-house in the Cowgate of Edinburgh, on the occasion of a painting being disposed of by *Raphael*—"raffle" was the mode adopted. A provincial paper speaks of the excitement caused by a recent highway *bobbery;* and another, in printing the report of a Life Insurance Society, congratulated the members on the low rate of *morality* during the past year. Considerable annoyance was caused at a public meeting by a lady having taken an *historical* fit—"hysteria" was the nature of the attack. In criticising the plan of a public building, the beauty of the edifice was represented as much marred by the number of *acute angels* introduced—"acute angles" being no doubt the object of disapproval. Many *confusions* of the limbs took place at a recent railway accident. In the giving of the surgeon's statement of the post-mortem examination of the body of a lady supposed to have been poisoned, it was incidentally mentioned that a great deal of *anatomy* had been found—it should have been "antimony." This latter word crops up again in another place where it is not wanted—as in a recent criticism of a speech by Mr. Gladstone : "What, then, by way of novelty, does Mr. Gladstone propose ? Simply the extension to the other Christian powers of Turkey of the *antimony* now enjoyed by Roumania." Of course, the word should have been "autonomy." Again, "Mr. Gladstone dwelt on the right which England had earned by expenditure of blood and treasure to interfere in Turkish provinces ; but now, with *a leopard and a hound*, he has formulated a plan for making the Christian provinces practically autonomous"—a "leap and a bound" was meant here. These two last examples are "first-proof" faults, and were corrected before publication.

One or two more, and we have done. In the *Times* report of Disraeli's speech upon the causes of the rebellion in India, that usually exception-ally correct paper made him refer to the law which "permitted Hindoo *windows* to marry." A still more curious instance occurred in the same paper in connection with the Jamaica prosecutions. Mr. Stephens was reported to have said that he had treated Mr. Eyre as he had often treated *obscene* and uninteresting criminals. It was easy to see that this was a misprint for "obscure," but the editor insisted that the error was in the manuscript. Towards the close of the American Civil War, a newspaper contained a strong leader upon the failure of the Southern States to establish their independence, and contained the curious statement that since General Lee had capitulated, the other divisions of the Confederate armies "would, in all likelihood, now commence a *gorilla* warfare"— guerilla, of course, was here meant. About the same time, there appeared a report of the seizure of the goods of a certain refractory gentleman for the non-payment of a local tax which had been the occasion of much trouble in one of our northern cities, and mention was made of one article which had been seized among the rest, and this was characterised as "an *eloquent* chest of drawers." In complimenting a soldier as a "battle-scarred veteran," a paper gave him the character of a "battle-*scared* veteran," and in afterwards inserting an erratum and apology, made matters worse by styling him a "*bottle*-scarred veteran!"

R

SHAPED POEMS.

IGURATE or Shaped Poems have considderable antiquity, and several in Greek, attributed to Theocritus, Simmias of Rhodes, and others, have come down to us; while mediæval Latin poetry also furnishes many of these curious versifications. The minor poets of Dryden's time were much given to this literary folly, though it sometimes required a little aid from the imagination to trace the resemblance to the object indicated, and greater attention was frequently paid to the shape of the verse than to its sense or rhythm. Ben Jonson satirised these early poets for their facility in this pattern-cutting style, saying they could fashion

"A pair of scissors and a comb in verse."

Bottles, glasses, axes, fans, hearts, wings, true-love knots, ladies' gowns, flying angels, trumpets of fame, &c., were all favourite forms; and, with another class of poets, pulpits, altars, and tombstones were the mode; whilst Gabriel Harvey is reputed to have been an adept at verses "in the form of a pair of gloves, a pair of spectacles, and a pair of pot-hooks." Butler also speaks severely regarding this literary folly; referring in the "Character of a Small Poet" to Edward Benlowes, called in his day "the excellently learned," he says of him: "There is no feat of activity, nor gambol of wit, that ever was performed by man, from him that vaults on Pegasus, to him that tumbles through the hoop of an anagram, but Benlowes has got the mastery of it, whether it be high-rope wit or low-rope wit. He has all sorts of echoes, rebuses, chronograms, &c. As for altars and pyramids in poetry, he has outdone all men that way; for he has made a gridiron and a frying-pan in verse, that besides the likeness in shape, the very tone and sound of the words did perfectly represent the noise that is made by these utensils. When he was a captain, he made all the furniture of his horse, from the bit to the crupper, in the beaten poetry, every verse being fitted to the proportion of the thing; as the *bridle of moderation*, the *saddle of content*, and the *crupper of constancy ;* so that the same thing was to the epigram and emblem even as the mule is both horse and ass."

Verses in such fantastic and grotesque shapes
were also common in France at one time—the poet
Pannard (1640) tortured his agreeable vein into
such forms, making his Bacchanalian songs take
the form of bottles and glasses, this being done by
lengthening or shortening the lines as required,
though with sad detriment to the verse. Pannard's
method will be best understood from the following
two examples of his verse :

Nous ne pouvons rien trouver sur la terre
qui soit si bon ni si beau que le verre.
Du tendre amour berceau charmant,
c'est toi, champêtre fougère, .
c'est toi qui sers à faire
l'heureux instrument
où souvent pétille,
mousse, et brille
le jus qui rend
gai, riant,
content.
Quelle douceur
il porte au cœur !
tot
tot
tot
Qu'on m'en donne
vite et comme il faut
tot
tot
tot
qu'on m'en donne
vite et comme il faut
L'on y voit sur ses flots chéris
nager l'allégresse et les ris.

Que mon
fl a c o n
me   semble   bon!
Sans   lui
l' e n n u i
me   nuit,
me   suit;
je   sens
mes   sens
mourants,
pe s a n t s.
Quand   je   le   tiens,
Dieux !   que je   suis bien !
que son   aspect est   agréable !
que je fais cas de ses divins présens !
C'est de son sein fécond, c'est de ses heureux flancs
que   coule   ce   nectar   si   doux,   si   délectable,
qui rend tous les esprits, tous les cœurs satisfaits !
Cher objet de mes vœux, tu fais toute ma gloire.
Tant que mon cœur vivra, de tes charmants bienfaits
il saura conserver la fidèle mémoire.

Both in China and Japan such literary feats are
held in great esteem even in the present day; in
the latter country the poet not unfrequently
arranges his verses in the shape of a man's head—
thus perhaps giving a facial outline of the subject
of his verse; and though the Chinese may not
make so good a choice, taking perhaps a cow or
some other animal for the design, they display
greater ingenuity by so doing.

William Browne, an old English poet, in his

"Britannia's Pastorals," has the following verse
done up in a true-love knot :

> " This is love and worth commending,
>   Still beginning, never ending ;
>   Like a wilie net ensnaring,
>   In a round shuts up all squaring,
>   In and out, whose every angle
>   More and more doth still entangle ;
>   Keeps a measure still in moving,
>   And is never light but loving.
>   Twining arms, exchanging kisses,
>   Each partaking other's blisses ;
>   Laughing, weeping, still together,
>   Bliss in one is mirth in either.
>   Never breaking, ever bending ;
>   This is love and worth commending."

Of Browne it has been said that "to few authors
has it chanced to be so enthusiastically lauded
by one age and so thoroughly neglected by the
next."

Puttenhame, in his "Art of Poesie," has defended
earnestly this species of literary trifling, and gives
specimens of poems in the form of lozenges, pillars,
&c.; one of these being in honour of Queen Elizabeth, in the form of two pillars, each of which
consists of a base of lines of eight syllables, the

shafts of lines of four syllables, the capitals being the same as the bases—one pillar reading up, the other down.

Of these Figurate verses we give only a few examples, as being of little interest, giving the first place to one by George Herbert:

THE ALTAR.

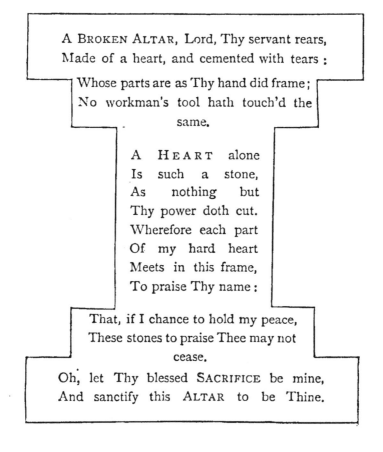

A BROKEN ALTAR, Lord, Thy servant rears,
Made of a heart, and cemented with tears :
Whose parts are as Thy hand did frame;
No workman's tool hath touch'd the same.

A HEART alone
Is   such   a   stone,
As   nothing   but
Thy power doth cut.
Wherefore each part
Of my hard heart
Meets in this frame,
To praise Thy name :

That, if I chance to hold my peace,
These stones to praise Thee may not cease.
Oh, let Thy blessed SACRIFICE be mine,
And sanctify this ALTAR to be Thine.

The next is also from the same author:

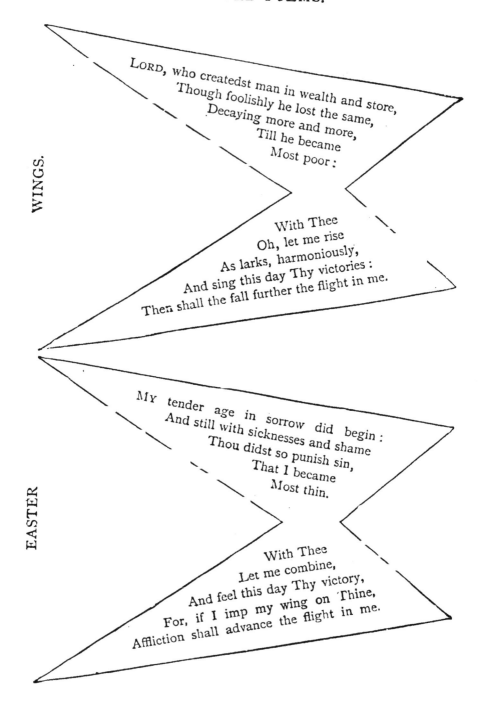

WINGS.

LORD, who createdst man in wealth and store,
Though foolishly he lost the same,
Decaying more and more,
Till he became
Most poor :

With Thee
Oh, let me rise
As larks, harmoniously,
And sing this day Thy victories :
Then shall the fall further the flight in me.

EASTER

MY tender age in sorrow did begin :
And still with sicknesses and shame
Thou didst so punish sin,
That I became
Most thin.

With Thee
Let me combine,
And feel this day Thy victory,
For, if I imp my wing on Thine,
Affliction shall advance the flight in me.

Quaint as may be the construction of the next example, yet never has the story been told with more truthful simplicity:

THE CROSS.

Blest they who seek,
While in their youth,
With spirit meek,
The way of truth;
To them the sacred Scriptures now display
Christ, as the only true and living way.
His precious blood on Calvary was given
To make them heirs of endless bliss in Heaven;
And e'en on earth the child of God can trace
The glorious blessings of his Saviour's grace.
For them He bore
His Father's frown;
For them He wore
The thorny Crown;
Nailed to the Cross,
Endured its pain,
That His life's loss
Might be their gain.
Then haste to choose
That better part,
Nor e'en dare refuse
The Lord thy heart,
Lest He declare,
"I know you not,"
And deep despair
Should be your lot.
Now look to Jesus, who on Calvary died,
And trust on Him alone who there was crucified.

The next couple come appropriately together, and may gratify the disciples of Sir Wilfrid Lawson:

SONG OF THE DECANTER.

There was an old decan-
ter, and its mouth was
gaping wide ;   the
rosy wine had
ebbed away
and left
its crys-
tal side :
and the wind
went humming—
humming
up and
down: the
wind it blew,
and through the
reed-like
hollow neck
· the wildest notes it
blew.   I placed it in the
window, where the blast was
blowing free, and fancied that its
pale mouth sang the queerest strains to
me.   " They tell me—puny conquerors ! the
Plague has slain his ten, and war his hundred
thousand of the very best of men ; but I "—t'was
thus the Bottle spake—" but I have conquered
more than all your famous conquerors, so
feared and famed of yore.   Then come, ye
youths and maidens all, come drink from
out my cup, the beverage that dulls the
brain and burns the spirits up; that puts
to shame your conquerors that slay their
scores below; for this has deluged mil-
lions with the lava tide of woe. Tho'
in the path of battle darkest streams
of blood may roll; yet while I killed
the body, I have damn'd the very
soul. The cholera, the plague,
the sword, such ruin never wro't,
as I in mirth or malice on the
innocent have brought.   And
still I breathe upon them, and
they shrink before my breath,
and year by year my thousands
tread   the   dusty   way of death."

THE WINE-GLASS.

Who hath woe ? Who hath sorrow ? Who
hath contentions ? Who hath wounds
without cause ? Who hath redness
of eyes ? They that tarry long
at the wine ! they that
go to seek mixed wine !
Look not thou upon the
wine when it is red,
when it giveth
its colour
in the
CUP,
when it
moveth itself
aright.
At
the last it
biteth like a serpent,
and stingeth like an adder !

The next is not exactly Figurate :—

EPITAPH.

Earth goes to			As mould to mould,
Earth treads on	}	Earth,	{ Glittering in gold,
Earth as to			Return ne'er should,
Earth shall be			Goe where he would.
Earth upon			Consider may,
Earth goes to	}	Earth	{ Naked away,
Earth though on			Be stout and gay,
Earth shall on			Pass poor away.

Be merciful and charitable,
Relieve the poor as thou art able.
A shroud to thy grave,
Is all thou shalt have.

We have here an—

ODE TO AN OLD VIOLIN.

Torn,
Worn,
Oppress'd, I mourn !
Bad,
Sad,
Three-quarters mad !
Money gone,
Credit none ;
Duns at door,
Half a score ;
Head in pain,
Rack'd again ;
Children ailing,
Mother railing,
Billy whooping,
Betsy crouping,
Besides poor Joe
With festered toe.
Come, then, my fiddle,
Come, my time-worn friend,
With gay and brilliant sounds
Me sweet though transient solace lend.
Thy polished neck in close embrace
I clasp while joy illumes my face.
When o'er thy strings I draw my bow,
My drooping spirit pants to rise ;
A lively strain I touch,—and lo !
I seem to mount above the skies.
There on Fancy's wings I soar,
Heedless of the duns at door.
Oblivious all ! I feel my woes no more ;
But skip o'er the strings,
As my old fiddle sings,
"Cheerily, O merrily go !
Presto ! good master,
You very well know,
I will find music,
If you will find bow,
From E up in alto, to G down below."
Fatigued, I pause to change the time
For some *adagio* solemn and sublime.
With graceful action moves the sinuous arm ;
My heart, responsive to the soothing charm,
Throbs equally, whilst every health-corroding care
Lies prostrate, vanquished, by the mellifluous air.
More and more plaintive grown, my eyes with tears o'erflow,
And Resignation mild soon smooths my wrinkled brow.
Reedy Hautboy may squeak, wailing Flauto may squall,
The Serpent may grunt, and the Trombone may bawl ;
But thou, my old Fiddle, art prince of them all.
Could e'en Dryden return thy praise to rehearse,
His Ode to Cecilia would seem rugged verse,
Now to thy case, in flannel warm to lie,
Till called again to pipe thy master's
eye.

The following is said to be engraved on an old monument in one of the London city churches:

Qu an tris di c vul stra
   os guis ti ro um nere vit.
H san chris mi t mu la

In this verse the last syllable of each word in the top line is the same as that of each corresponding word in the bottom line, and is to be found in the centre. It reads thus:

Quos anguis tristi diro cum vulnere stravit
Hos sanguis christi miro tum munere lavit.

Translated thus:

Those who have felt the serpent's venomed wound
In Christ's miraculous blood have healing found.

The next is by Christopher Harvie, a great friend of George Herbert, and the last is by Herbert himself.

THE SABBATH, OR LORD'S DAY.

Hail	Vail
Holy	Wholly
King of days,	To thy praise,
The Emperor,	For evermore
Or Universal	Must the rehearsal
Monarch of time, the week's	Of all, that honour seeks,
Perpetual Dictator.	Under the World's Creator,
Thy	My
Beauty	Duty
Far exceeds	Yet must needs
The reach of art,	Yield thee mine heart,
To blazon fully ;	And that not dully :

And I thy light eclipse,
When I most strive to raise thee.
What
Nothing
Else can be,
Thou only art ;
Th' extracted spirit
Of all Eternity,
By favour antedated.

Spirits of souls, not lips
Alone, are fit to praise thee,
That
Slow thing
Time by thee
Hath got the start,
And doth inherit
That immortality
Which sin anticipated.

O
That I
Could lay by
This body so,
That my soul might be
Incorporate with thee,
And no more to six days owe.

PARADISE.

I BLESS Thee, Lord, because I GROW
Among Thy trees, which in a ROW
To Thee both fruit and order OW.

What open force, or hidden CHARM,
Can blast my fruit, or bring me HARM,
While the enclosure is Thine ARM?

Enclose me still, for fear I START.
Be to me rather sharp and TART,
Than let me want Thy hand and ART.

When Thou dost greater judgments SPARE,
And with Thy knife but prune and PARE,
Even fruitful trees more fruitful ARE.

Such sharpness shows the sweetest FRIEND:
Such cuttings rather heal than REND:
And such beginnings touch their END.

PROSE POEMS.

IN many of the prose works of our modern authors there are to be found specimens of accidental versification and unintentionally measured strains, as well as passages of such a nature as to lead to the supposition that a certain degree of rhythmical writing and rugged blank verse had been sought after. It would be difficult, however, to collect examples of this; but in the writings of Charles Dickens we find two excellent illustrations. The first is from the "Old Curiosity Shop," where the funeral of Little Nell is described:

" And now the bell—
The bell she had so often heard by night
And day, and listened to with solemn
Pleasure, almost as a living voice—
Rung its remorseful toll for her, so young,
So beautiful, so good. Decrepit age,
And vigorous life, and blooming youth, and
Helpless infancy, poured forth—on crutches, ·
In the pride of strength and health, in the full

Blush of promise, in the mere dawn of life—
To gather round her tomb.   Old men were there,
Whose eyes were dim and senses failing;
Grandmothers, who might have died ten years ago
And still been old; the deaf, the blind, the lame,
The palsied, the living dead in many
Shapes and forms; to see the closing of that
Early grave.   What was the death it would shut
In, to that which still could crawl and creep
Above it?   Along the crowded path they
Bore her now; pure as the newly-fallen
Snow that covered it, whose days on earth had
Been as fleeting.   Under that porch where she
Had sat when Heaven in its mercy brought
Her to that peaceful spot, she passed again,
And the old church received her in its quiet shade."

Again, some will no doubt be surprised to recognise in the next example the Song of the Kettle from the " Cricket on the Hearth "—evidently an unintentional outburst on the part of the author, in which the lines not only preserve their symmetry, but also rhyme with each other:

" It's a dark night, sang the kettle, and the rotten leaves are lying
        by the way;
  And above, all is mist and darkness, and below, all is mire and clay;
  And there is only one relief in all the sad and murky air,
  And I don't know that it is one, for it's nothing but a glare
  Of deep and angry crimson, where the sun and wind together
  Set a brand upon the clouds for being guilty of such weather;
  And the widest open country is a long dull streak of black;
  And there's hoarfrost on the finger-post, and thaw upon the track;

And the ice it isn't water, and the water isn't free ;
And you couldn't say that anything is what it ought to be ;
But he's coming, coming, coming ! "——

Our friends across the Atlantic, however, have
a peculiar way of their own in regard to poetical
prose, in which they travesty some of the best
poems in the English language in a very amusing
way. Yankee philology has been a source of much
discussion in many periodicals—their peculiar go-
ahead idiosyncrasies finding vent in the concoction
of new phrases and words which are not only apt
but very expressive. This is not the place to enter
into any lengthened discussion on the point, but
by way of introduction to the peculiar prose poems
which have been produced in the States, we may
refer shortly to the "high-falutin'" style of their
metaphors and similes. This tendency has often
been noticed in respect to American literature,
and readers of Mark Twain, Artemus Ward, and
other writers, will easily remember many instances
of these curiosities, in which are produced the
effects of wit by twisting a phrase from its figura-
tive to its literal meaning. For example, we are
told of a man who made a hat for the head of a
discourse, and a shoe for the foot of a mountain.
We learn of a gentleman who sat down on the

spur of the moment; of a young lady who fainted at a bare idea, who wore spectacles over her naked eyes, who refused to sit in the lap of luxury, blushing at the mention of the lapse of ages (forgetting that *lapse* is not the plural of *lap*), and who would not sit on the sea-shore lest her waist might· be encircled by an arm of the sea.   Among others may be noted "the hook and line with which a fisherman caught a cold; the hammer which broke up a meeting; a fluke from the anchor of hope; one of the spurs of the Rocky Mountains; a hinge from the gates of death; a story which melted a heart of oak; buttons from a coat of paint; spectacles for the eyes of a potato; braces for a shoulder of mutton; dye for the beard of an oyster; ear-rings for an ear of corn; cheese from the milk of human kindness; butter from the cream of a joke, and eggs from a nest of thieves."

Of these Prose Poems we limit ourselves to the following selection :—

A RAVENING REVERIE.

Once upon a midnight stormy a lone bachelor attorney pondered many a curious volume of his heart's forgotten lore ; while he nodded, nearly napping, suddenly there came a tapping, as of some one gently rapping—rapping at his chamber-door.   " 'Tis the spirits," and he started,

"rapping at my chamber-door. Oh, for help! I am
frightened sore!" Then into his chamber flitting (not
even one permitting him to fly into the closet or to get
behind the door), came the ghosts of fond hearts broken
(with many a ring and other token), and they sat them
down beside him, on the dusty, book-strewn floor—sat
amidst the volumes of most venerable lore. Quoth the
lawyer, "What a bore! It must be something serious;
this is certainly mysterious, quite an advent of the spirits
—resurrection *con amore.* But I understand them
mostly!"—here there came a rap so ghostly, that he could
no more dissemble as he had done heretofore, and his
face grew pale and paler, as he started for the door—
down he fell upon the floor. Then there came a clatter,
clatter, and his teeth began to chatter, as the spirits
gathered round him, and accused him very sore, how
with gladsome face all smiling. and with winning words
beguiling, he had charmed away the senses of fair
maidens by the score; and each lass had fondly fancied
'twas her he did adore. Quoth the lawyer, "Never
more!" Startled at the stillness broken by reply so
aptly spoken, for the answer, strange enough, quite a
relevancy bore; they began a noisy rapping—sort of
spiritual clapping, which the lawyer thought would be
but a fashionable encore—and again, as if his soul in
that word he would outpour, did he groan out, "Never
more!" Presently his soul grew stronger; hesitating
then no longer—"Oh, oh!" said he, "sweet spirits,
your forgiveness I implore; on my knees to every ghostess,
who to love has played the hostess, I will recant the
many faithless things I swore! Will you promise then to
leave me?" here he pointed to the door. Rapped the

spirits, " Never more ! " " Be that word our sign of
parting," said the hapless wight upstarting, " hie ye hence
into the darkness, seek ye out some distant shore.   In
the noisy camp or forum, in the lonely *sanc sanctorum*—
such ghastly, grim, ungainly guests were never seen before.
Leave my loneliness unbroken," here he opened wide the
door.   Rapped the spirits, " Never more ! "   So these
vixen spirits of evil—spirits still, though most uncivil—
they will never leave the lawyer, though in tears he may
implore.   At his false heart they are tapping, they are
rapping, rapping, and he wishes, oh, how vainly ! that
his haunted life were o'er ; and he often sighs : " Oh,
could I but recall the days of yore, I would flirt—oh,
never more ! "

A Maiden's " Psalm of Life."

Tell us not in idle jingle " marriage is an empty
dream ! " for the girl is dead that's single, and things are
not what they seem.   Life is real ! life is earnest ! single
blessedness a fib ; " Man thou art, to man returnest ! "
has been spoken of the rib.   Not enjoyment, and not
sorrow, is our destined end or way, but to act that each
to-morrow finds us nearer marriage day.   Life is long
and youth is fleeting, and our hearts, though light and gay,
still like pleasant drums are beating wedding marches
all the way.   In the world's broad field of battle, in the
bivouac of life, be not like dumb driven cattle !—be a
heroine—a wife !   Trust no future, howe'er pleasant,
let the dead Past bury its dead ! act—act to the living
Present ! heart within and hope ahead ! Lives of married
folks remind us we can live our lives as well, and,
departing, leave behind us such examples as shall " tell ! "

Such examples, that another, wasting time in idle sport, a forlorn unmarried brother, seeing, shall take heart and court. Let us, then, be up and doing, with a heart on triumph set; still contriving, still pursuing, and each one a husband get.

AFTER KINGSLEY—A LONG WAY.

Three women went shopping out in the west, out into the West End of London town. Each had on the bonnet she kept for her best; and they ordered things wholesale, and had 'em put down. For men must work, and women must waste; and what's earned at leisure is spent in haste, though the husbands all are moaning. Three men sat up at a latesome hour, and trimmed their accounts as the sun went down. They looked for a squall, and they looked sad and sour, and their coat sleeves were rolled up all ragged and brown. For men must work, and women must waste, and be dressed in the height of the fashion and taste, though the husbands all are moaning. Three writs they are out in the bailiff's hands, on the suing of one who wants money down. But the debtors, poor devils, can't meet their demands; so they go to a sponging-house kept in the town. For men must work, and women must waste; and the parents are beggared, the children disgraced, and good-bye to papa and his moaning.

THE SONG OF THE "REB."

'Neath a ragged Palmetto a Southerner sat, a-twisting the band of his Panama hat, and trying to lighten his mind of a load, by humming the words of the following ode:—Oh! for a darkey, oh! for a whip, oh! for a cocktail, and oh! for a nip; oh! for a shot at old Greeley and Beecher, oh! for a crack at a Yankee school-teacher; oh! for a captain, and oh! for a ship, oh! for a cargo of darkies each trip. And so he kept ohing for what he had not, not content with owing for all that he'd got.

A LITTLE MORE.

(*At thirty.*) Five hundred guineas I have saved—a rather moderate store. No matter; I shall be content when I've a little more. (*At forty.*) Well, I can count ten thousand now—that's better than before; and I may well be satisfied when I've a little more. (*At fifty.*) Some fifty thousand—pretty well; but I have earned it sore. However, I shall not complain when I've a little more. (*At sixty.*) One hundred thousand—sick and old; ah! life is half a bore, yet I can be content to live when I've a little more. (*At seventy.*) He dies—and to his greedy heirs he leaves a countless store. His wealth has purchased him a tomb, and very little more!

A TALE OF A DOG.

A lady with a crinoline was walking down a street—her feathers fluttered in the air, her hoops stuck out some feet. She walked the earth as if she felt of it she was no part, and proudly did she step along, for pride was in her heart. She did not see a curly dog which walked close by her side, all save the curly tail of which her crinoline did hide. His tail the dog with pleasure shook—it fluttered in the wind, and from the lady's crinoline stuck out a foot behind. A crowd the tail did soon espy as it waved to and fro, and like a rudder seemed to point the way the maid must go. The curly dog right pleased was he the quarters he had got, and walked beside the lady in a kind of doggish trot. Each step the lady now did take served to increase her train, while those who followed in her wake roared out with might and main. Some held their sides, they laughed so hard, and others fairly cried, while many even still confess that they'd "like to died." But still the lady sailed along in crinoline and pride, unmindful of the crowd behind or dog close by her side. But soon another dog espied the tail which fluttered free, it so provoked the doggish ire he could not let it be. But with a deep ferocious growl, for battle straight he went, and 'neath the lady's crinoline both dogs were quickly pent. They fought, 'tis said, one hour or more—the lady nothing knew—but with her head erect sailed on, and did her way pursue. Some say she never would have known at all about the fight, had not one dog mistook and gave her "limb" an awful bite. But since that day, I've heard it said, that lady ne'er was seen upon the street with so much pride and *such* a crinoline.

THE EDITOR.

With fingers blackened with ink, with eyelids heavy and red, the local editor sat in his chair, writing for daily bread. The small boy was by his side, the foreman grumbled and swore, and the office boy, like an " Oliver Twist," constantly cried for "more." He had told of a broken leg that had never been broken at all, he had killed off the nearest friend he had, and torn up a house in a squall. And now he was at an end, he hadn't an item left; and he bowed his head to the small boy's scorn like a fellow of hope bereft. They found him a corpse that night in streets so drear and sloppy, with the foreman whispering into his ear and the small boy waiting for copy.

A NOVELETTE.

Sweet Margaret Fane came up the lane from picking the ripe-red berries, and met young Paul, comely and tall, going to market with cherries. Stopping, she blushed, and he looked flushed, perhaps 'twas the burdens they carried; when they passed on, their burdens were one, and at Christmas they were married.

"MY PRETTY JANE."

It is many years since I fell in love with Jane Jerusha Skeggs, the handsomest country girl by far that ever went on legs. By meadow, creek, and wood, and dell, so often we did walk, and the moonlight smiled on her melting lips, and the night winds learned our talk. Jane Jerusha was all to me, for my heart was young and true, and loved with a double and twisted love, and a love that was honest, too. I roamed all over the neighbours' farms, and I robbed the wildwood bowers, and tore my trousers and scratched my hands in search of choicest flowers. In my joyous love I brought all these to my Jerusha Jane; but I wouldn't be so foolish now, if I were a boy again. A city chap then came along, all dressed up in fine clothes, with a shiny hat and shiny vest and a moustache under his nose. He talked to her of singing-schools (for her father owned a farm), and she left me, the country love, and took the new chap's arm.

And all that night I never slept, nor could I eat next day, for I loved that girl with a fervent love that nought could drive away. I strove to win her back to me, but it was all in vain; the city chap with the hairy lip married Jerusha Jane. And my poor heart was sick and sore until the thought struck me, that just as good fish still remained as ever was caught in the sea. So I went to the Methodist church one night, and saw a dark brown curl peeping from under a gipsy hat, and I married that very girl. And many years have passed and gone, and I think my loss my gain; and I often bless that hairy chap that stole Jerusha Jane.

THE OLD OAK.

Old Mr. Fuddle fell down in a puddle, just as a runaway horse and shay came dashing and splashing and tearing that way. In helpless plight he roared with fright ; the horse came quick, all gallop and kick, when the old man raised his old oak stick ; the horse then shied a little aside, for sticks were no friends to his well-fed hide. Within a foot of Fuddle's toes, within an inch of his ruby nose, the wheel comes whizzing, and on it goes. Up rises Fuddle from out the puddle, and stands on the road with a staggering stride, then wheeling away from the scene of the fray, he flourished his stick with a hero's pride.

NORAH O'NEIL.

You say you are lonely without me, that you sigh for one glance of my eye; you're blarneying always about me—Oh ! why don't you to papa apply ? You men are so very deceiving, I can't believe aught that you say; your love I will only believe in when my jointure is made out *au fait.*　This trash about eyes, voice, and glances may do for a miss in her teens; but he who to me makes advances must talk of his bank-stock and means.　You beg me to go galavanting, to meet you at the foot of the lane—with a kiss, too! why, man, you're ranting! do you think that I'm wholly insane?　When you meet a young lady of sense, sir, don't whine about sorrow and tears; it's a matter of shillings and pence, sir; no tale of romance interferes.　Oh, poverty's not at all funny (my style I will never conceal); if I can't get a husband with money, then I'll live and die Norah O'Neil.

A Moonlight Walk.

On a quiet day, in leafy June, when bees and birds were all in tune, two lovers walked beneath the moon. The night was fair—so was the maid; they walked and talked beneath the shade, with none to harm or make afraid.　Her name was Sue, and his was Jim; and he was fat and she was slim; he took to her and she to him. Says Jim to Sue, "By all the snakes that squirm among the bush and brakes, I love you better than oatmeal cakes."　Says Sue to Jim, "Since you've begun it, and been and come and gone and done it, I like you next to a new bonnet."　Says Jim to Sue, "My heart you've busted; but I have always girls mistrusted."　Says Sue to Jim, "I will be true; if you love me as I love you, no knife can cut our love in two."　Says Jim to Sue, "Through thick and thin, for your true love count me in; I'll court no other girl ag'in."　Jim leaned to Sue; Sue leaned to Jim; his nose just touched her straw hat brim: four lips met—went ahem! ahem!　And then—

and then—and then—then! Oh girls, beware of men in June, and underneath the silver moon, when frogs and crickets are in tune, lest you get your names in the papers soon.

The Gingham Gown.

I met her in the sunset bright, her gingham gown was blue; her eyes, that danced with pure delight, were of the same dear hue. And always, when the sun goes down, I think of the girl in the gingham gown.

An Editorial.

'Tis sweet, on winter's night, at home to sit by fire and taper; but ah, it is a wiser thing, by far, to read our paper. Won't you take our paper? Can't you take our paper? The joys of earth are little worth unless you take our paper. Maidens waiting lovers true, you must take our paper. Swains, who would not idle woo, you must take our paper. Won't you take our paper? Can't you take our paper? Love's joys below you'll never know, unless you take our paper.

"Good-bye, Sweetheart, Good-bye!"

"Farewell, farewell!" I cried. "When I return thou'lt be my bride—till then be faithful—sweet, adieu—in silence oft I'll think of you." The glistening tears strained her bright eyes—her thickening breath is choked with sighs—her tongue denies her bosom's sway—"Farewell!" —I tore myself away. "One moment stay," she stammered out; as quick as thought I wheeled about. "My angel, speak! can aught be done to comfort thee when I am gone? I'll send thee specimens of art from every European mart; I'll sketch for thee each Alpine scene, to let thee see where I have been. A stone from Simplon's dreadful height shall gratify thy curious sight. I'll climb the fiery Ætna's side to bring home treasures for my bride; and oh! my life, each ship shall bear a double letter for my fair!" "Ah, George!" the weeping angel said, and on my shoulder fell her head, "for constancy, my tears are hostage—but when you write, please pay the postage!"

SOMETHING LIKE POETRY.

Tennyson claims to be a great poet, and yet he may fret and study and tear about for a week, and then can't yank an ode to a sawmill, while the sweet singer of Michigan only gave two minutes to whacking up one beginning: "All hail to thee, most terrible invention, Which chews up trees to any wished dimension, And when something distracts a man's attention, Will break him up so that a gov'ment pension Won't do him any good. Oh, fierce devourer thou of men and wood!"

A PRINTER'S LITANY.

From want of gold, from wives that scold, from maidens old, by sharpers "sold"—preserve us!

From foppish sneers, mock auctioneers, and woman's tears—deliver us!

From stinging flies, from coal-black eyes, and babies' cries—deliver us!

From seedy coats, protested notes, and leaky boats—protect us!

From creaking doors, a wife that snores, confounded bores, and dry-goods stores—protect us!

Fom shabby hats, and torn cravats, and flying brick-bats—save us!

INDEX.

ABERNETHY, Dr., 210
Acrostic verses on writing, 48
Addison on chronograms, 119; echo song by, 131
Address to my Sweetheart, 147
Address to one of the Brethren, 80
Address to Queen Mary, 30
Advertisement, macaronic, 103
Æstivation, 114
After Kingsley, 277
Albury church, chronogram at, 119
Alexander I. of Russia, 216
Alliteration, 17
Alphabetic curiosities, 48
Altar, the, 263
American rivers, names of, 168
Amphigourie, 158
Anacreon, the Odes of, 24
Anacreon, the Scottish, 30
Anagram by Herbert, 206
Anagrams, selection of, 213
Andreas Rivetus, 199
An editorial, 283
Ane New Year's gift, 30
Anne, Queen, portrait of, 14
Anstruther Musomanik Society, 74
Approach of Evening, 65
Arte of English Poesie, 194
Aurora, alliterative address to, 43
Authors' names, anagrams on, 199
Autocrat of the Breakfast Table, the, 133
Autumn days, 171

BALES, Peter, 12
Beedell, Mr., 13
Benlowes, Edward, 259
Bible, a miniature, 12
Bible, errors in the, 242
Birthday of Shakespeare, on the, 178
Blanchard, Laman, 185
Bogart, an American poet, 84
Bolton, Cuthbert, 67
Bonaparte and the Echo, 130
Bonn, chronogram from, 118

Book-titles, alliterative, 33
Bradstreet, Anne, 196
Breitmann Ballads, the, 111
Bridget Brady, 165
Britannia's Pastorals, 131
Browne, William, 131, 261
Buggiados, the, 90, 91
Burns, 39
Burton, Dr. Hill, 229
Butler on echo verses, 122
Byron, Lord, 39

CALL, the, 154
Camden, palindromic lines from, 221
Campkin, Mr. H., palindromes by, 223
Cannon, Rev. Edward, 164
Car, 205
Caxton, William, 62
Celtic verse, 19
Cento from popular poets, 191
Cento-Virgilianus, the, 176
Charles I., portrait of, 14
Charles II., King, anagrams on, 200, 201
Charlotte, Princess, anagram on, 209
Chartier, Allain, verses by, 67
Cherry and the Slae, the, 31
Chinese versification, 261
Christian and his Echo, the, 137
Christianity, anagram on the word, 210
Christine of Pisa, Moral Proverbs of, 61
Christ's Victory and Triumph, lines from, 153
Christus ascendit ad cœlos, 177
Christus Cruxifixus, 47
Chronicle, a, 161
Churchill, 150
Clement, Jacques, 209
Coins and medals, chronographic, 119
Coleridge, 38, 157
Collins, Mortimer, 40; single-rhymed alphabet by, 55
Cologne, church at, chronogram from, 118

Combinations of Latin words, 9, 10
Comedie of Supposes, the, 63
Commentary, Trapp's, 33
Come, love, come, a lipogrammatic song, 60
Cotton Mather, 196
Crawshawe, anagram on, 205
Cross, the, 265
Curiosities, alphabetic, 48
Curious advertisement, 37
Curse of Minerva, the, 39

DAME Life and Dame Death, 21
Dance of the Seven Deadly Sins, 30
Davies, Dame Eleanor, 198
Dean of Westminster, the, 245
Delany, Mrs., lines by, 73
Delepierre, M. Octave, 89, 178
Deming, Mrs. H. A., 180
De Morgan, Professor, 226
Dialogue between Glutton and Echo, 127
Dickens, Charles, 271
Diploma, macaronic, 91–96
Dishington, Tom, macaronic, 98
Disraeli, Isaac, 59
Dobell, Sydney, 199
Double-faced Creed, the, 144
Drummond of Hawthornden, 89, 90
Duchess of Northumberland, lines by, 73
Dulot, a French poetaster, 70
Dunbar, 19, 29, 30, 88

EASTER Wings, 264
Echo, the, 124
Ecloga de Calvis, 46
Edinburgh, snowball riot at, 104
Editor, the, 279
Ego and Echo, 134
Elegy, an, 51
Elizabeth, Queen, chronogram on, 120; anagram on, 194
Epigram from Scaliger, 166
Epitaph on a dog, 102
Epitaphs, curious, 64, 267
Equivocal verses, 143
Essay on man, the poets', 181
Euphue's Golden Legacy, 155
Exercise on the Alphabet, 44
Expulsio Adami et Evæ, 177

FAERIE Queene, the, 62
Fage, Mistress Mary, 201
Fall of Eve, the, 65
Fame's Rowle, 201
Field, the Cambridge printer, 242
Fitzgerald, Dr., lines on, 172
Fletcher, the brothers, 152
Flodden Field, ballad of, 26, 27
Florence Huntingdon, lines to Miss, 169

Folengo, Teofilo, 87, 88
Fontenelle, 159
Fortune, lines on, 68
Francillon, R. E., echo verse by, 135
François de Valoys, anagram on, 193
Frosteïdos, 106

GEDDES, a macaronic writer, 101
Gee, Mrs., to, 46
German palindrome, 222
Gilchrist, Octavius, 87
Gingham Gown, the, 283
Golden Age, the, 79
Good-bye, Sweetheart, Good-bye, 283
Gray, 29
Grime, Sarai, anagram on, 208

HAILES, Lord, 89
Hall, 157
Harvie, Christopher, 269
Heaven, 136
Hécart, Gabriel, A. J., 193
Herbert, George, 136, 142, 154, 206, 263, 265, 270
Holmes, Randle, 202
Holmes, Wendell, 113
Holy Alliance, the, anagram on, 209
Homero-Centones, the, 176
Hone's Every-day Book, 224
Horace, chronogram from, 116
Hubibras, extract from, 122
Huet, 11
Hugbald's Ecloga, 46
Human Heart, ode to the, 186

ICELANDIC verse, 18
Ignoramus, comedy of, 100
Iliad of Homer, the, in a nutshell, 11
Impromptu, 164
Incontrovertible Facts, 66
Inscription, monumental, 269
Invitation, the, 148
Iskarriot, anagram on, 204

JAMES, King, anagram on, 195
Jingling rhymes, 167
Johnnie Dowie's, 82
Jonson, Ben, 203

KETTLE, Song of the, 272

LADIES, Panegyric on the, 148
Lalla Rookh, lines from, 151
Last Day, the, 81
Lasus, the Greek poet, 58
Latin anagrams, 199, 207
Latin combinations, 9, 10
Latin palindromes, 220–223
Leland, Charles G., 111
Lent Oars, the, 211
Lessius, Leonard, 127

Leti, Gregorio, 59
Life, 180
Life's Alphabet, 49
Lines by a medium, 163
Lines to Miss Florence Huntingdon, 169
Lingo drawn for the Militia, 97
Little Jack Horner, 111
Little John Nobody, 22, 23
Little More, a, 278
Lipograms, 58
Llanover, Lady, 73
Lodge, Thomas, 155
Lord Duff's Toast, 51
Lord's Prayer, the, 138
Love, 83
Love letter, alliterative, 45
Love song, a, 101, 112
Lydia Kane, acrostic to, 85, 86

MADRIGAL, 156
Marie Touchet, anagram on, 197
Marriage, 184
Martin, Mr. H., of Halifax, 237
Martin, St., anecdote of, 224
Meston, William, 91
Microscopic writing, 11-15
Miller of Batheaston, Sir John and Lady, 71
Mi Molle Anni, 109
Miniature writing, 11-15
Moll, 101
Monastery, anagrams on, 211
Monk, James, 181
Montgomery, Alexander, 31
Moonlight Walk, a, 282
Moore, Thomas, 151
Moral Proverbs of Christine of Pisa, 61
Morning on Arthur's Seat, 81
" My boast is in the Cross of Christ," 140
My Molly and I, 110
My Pretty Jane, 280
Myself, 164

NAMES, palindromic, 218
Napoleon, libel on, 129
Nelson, anagram on, 209
Neuile, Alexander, 63
Newcastle *burr*, the, 36
Newspaper errors, 253-257
Nora O'Neil, 281
North, Lord, 33
Norton, John, 196
Novelette, a, 280

ODE to an Old Violin, 268
Ode to the Human Heart, 136
O'Keefe, song by, 103
O'd Oak, the, 281
On Life, et cetera, 188

" Our life is hid with Christ," 142

PALINDROMIC names, 218
Palm, bookseller of Nuremberg, 129
Pamperes, Ambrose, 215
Panegyric on the Ladies, 148
Pannard, a French poet, 260
Paradise, 270
Peacock, Dean, 34
Peignot, 230
Peleg Wale's machine, lines by, 171
Pen and ink portraits, 14, 15
Penmanship, good, 234
People's Friend, cento from the, 189
Percy's Reliques, 19, 22
Persian " Gazel," a, 59
Piers Plowman's Visions, 19
Pinkerton, 115
Platform, the, 146
Poets' Essay on Man, the, 181
Pope, portrait of, 14 ; on alliteration, 24, 34 ; on monosyllables, 150 ; song by, 159
Porson, Professor, macaronic by, 97
Portraits, miniature, 14, 15
Prideaux, Bishop, chronogram on, 120
Printer's Litany, a, 284
Proba Falconia, 176, 177
Proctor, Bryan Waller, 199
Protector, Definition of a, 207
Proverbs, alliterative, 47
Psalm of Life, a Maiden's, 276
Pugna Porcorum, the, 46
Punctuation, 230, 247, 249
Puritans, the, 196
Purple Island, the, lines from, 152
Puttenhame, 194, 262
Puzzles, alphabetic, 226
Puzzles, chronographic, 116
Pyecroft, Mr., 239

QUARLES' Emblems, 28

RAVENING Reverie, a, 274
Reader, the Press, 231
Reciprocal verses, 215
Revolutionary lines, 145
Richelieu, Cardinal, portrait of, 15
Rivers, American, names of, 168
Rivers, Earl, 61
Rogers, the poet, 23
Ross, Alexander, 178
Russo-Turkish war, the, 65

SABBATH, the, 269
Scaliger, 197 ; epigram by, 166
Scissors, ways of spelling, 16
Scot, Alexander, 30
Scott, Sir Walter, 39
Serenade in M flat, 34, 35
Seven Deadly Sins, Dance of the, 30

Shakespeare, alliterative lines from, 32 ;
  monosyllabic lines from, 115
Shakespeare's Birthday, on, 178
Siege of Belgrade, the, 41
Single-rhymed alphabets, 53–57
Skoodoowabskooksis, the, 169
Snowball riot at Edinburgh, 104
Society, address to the, 84
Something like Poetry, 284
Song by a Person of Quality, 159
Song, echo, by Addison, 131
Song of the Decanter, 266
Song of the " Reb," 277
" Songs of Singularity," 34
Sotades, 220
Spanish Armada, lines on defeat of, 98
Spanker, 37
Spenser, 29
Stanislaus, King, anecdote of, 202
Stifelius, Michael, anecdote of, 121
Stonihurst, lines by, 163
Stuart, James, anagram on, 195
Sweetheart, Address to my, 147
Swift, Dean, 101

Tale of a dog, a, 278
Taylor, John, 200, 204, 217
Telegram, a, anagrammatised, 210
Tencin, Madame, 159
Testament of Andro Kennedy, 89
Teutonic verse, 19
Thackeray, anecdote of, 244
Thaddeus, Ruddy, lines by, 165
Themuru, the art of, 193
Tipperary, rhymes for, 172
Titles of books, alliterative, 33
Tombstones, anagrams on, 208
To my Mistress, 101
To my Nose, 165

Tony's Address to Mary, 102
To the Leading Periodical, 111
Trapp, the commentator, 33
Tryphiodorus, a Greek poet, 58
Turkish Alphabet, the, 50
Tusser's Husbandry, 36
" Twa Maryit Wemen," the, 21

Univocalic trifling, 64

Vega, Lope de, 59
Villiers, George, chronogram upon, 117
Virgil, 25, 26
Virgilius Evangelizans, 178
Virtue, 154
Vision of Mirza, the, 115

Walker, Mrs. Faieth, 208
Wallis, Dr., 67
Walpole, Horace, 71
Weber's ballad of Flodden Field, 26, 27
Wellington, Duke of, 209
Weymes, Earl of, anagram on, 201
Whatever is, is right, 187
Wheatley, Mr., 121
Wiat, Sir John, anagram on, 197
Wild Sports of the East, macaronic
  from, 99
William III., Latin poem on, 47
Wine-glass, the, 267
Witches' Sabbath, the, 221
Word of Welcome, a, 165
Workard, Mr. J. B., 54
Writing, acrostic verses on, 48]

Xtravaganza xtraordinary, 45

Yankee philology, 273
Young's Night Thoughts, 157

PRINTED BY BALLANTYNE, HANSON AND CO.
EDINBURGH AND LONDON

CHATTO & WINDUS'S
LIST OF BOOKS.

* * * * * * * * * * * * * *

About.—The Fellah: An Egyptian Novel. By EDMOND ABOUT. Translated by Sir RANDAL ROBERTS. Post 8vo, illustrated boards, 2s. ; cloth limp, 2s. 6d.

Adams (W. Davenport), Works by:

A Dictionary of the Drama. Being a comprehensive Guide to the Plays, Playwrights, Players, and Playhouses of the United Kingdom and America, from the Earliest to the Present Times. Crown 8vo, half-bound, 12s. 6d. [*Preparing*.

Latter-Day Lyrics. Edited by W. DAVENPORT ADAMS. Post 8vo, cloth limp, 2s. 6d.

Quips and Quiddities. Selected by W. DAVENPORT ADAMS. Post 8vo, cloth limp, 2s. 6d.

Advertising, A History of, from the Earliest Times. Illustrated by Anecdotes, Curious Specimens, and Notices of Successful Advertisers. By HENRY SAMPSON. Crown 8vo, with Coloured Frontispiece and Illustrations, cloth gilt, 7s. 6d.

Agony Column (The) of "The Times," from 1800 to 1870. Edited, with an Introduction, by ALICE CLAY. Post 8vo, cloth limp, 2s. 6d.

Aide (Hamilton), Works by:

Carr of Carrlyon. Post 8vo, illustrated boards, 2s.

Confidences. Post 8vo, illustrated boards, 2s.

Alexander (Mrs.).—Maid, Wife, or Widow? A Romance. By Mrs ALEXANDER. Post 8vo, illustrated boards, 2s. ; cr. 8vo, cloth extra, 3s. 6d.

Allen (Grant), Works by:

The Evolutionist at Large. Second Edition, revised. Cr. 8vo, cl. extra, 6s.

Vignettes from Nature. Crown 8vo, cloth extra, 6s.

Colin Clout's Calendar. Crown 8vo, cloth extra, 6s.

Architectural Styles, A Handbook of. Translated from the German of A. ROSENGARTEN, by W. COLLETT-SANDARS. Crown 8vo, cloth extra, with 639 Illustrations, 7s. 6d.

Art (The) of Amusing: A Collection of Graceful Arts, Games, Tricks, Puzzles, and Charades. By FRANK BELLEW. With 300 Illustrations. Cr. 8vo, cloth extra, 4s. 6d.

Artemus Ward:

Artemus Ward's Works: The Works of CHARLES FARRER BROWNE, better known as ARTEMUS WARD. With Portrait and Facsimile. Crown 8vo, cloth extra, 7s. 6d.

Artemus Ward's Lecture on the Mormons. With 32 Illustrations. Edited, with Preface, by EDWARD P. HINGSTON. Crown 8vo, 6d.

The Genial Showman: Life and Adventures of Artemus Ward. By EDWARD P. HINGSTON. With a Frontispiece. Crown 8vo, cloth extra, 3s. 6d.

Ashton (John), Works by:
A History of the Chap-Books of the Eighteenth Century. With nearly 400 Illusts., engraved in facsimile of the originals. Cr. 8vo, cl. ex., 7s. 6d.
Social Life in the Reign of Queen Anne. From Original Sources. With nearly 100 Illusts. Cr.8vo,cl.ex.,7s.6d.
Humour, Wit, and Satire of the Seventeenth Century. With nearly 100 Illusts. Cr. 8vo, cl. extra, 7s. 6d.
English Caricature and Satire on Napoleon the First. 120 Illusts. from Originals. Two Vols., demy 8vo, 28s.

Bacteria.—A Synopsis of the Bacteria and Yeast Fungi and Allied Species. By W. B. GROVE, B.A. With 87 Illusts. Crown 8vo, cl. extra, 3s. 6d.

Balzac's "Comedie Humaine" and its Author. With Translations by H. H. WALKER. Post 8vo, cl.limp,2s. 6d.

Bankers, A Handbook of London; together with Lists of Bankers from 1677. By F. G. HILTON PRICE. Crown 8vo, cloth extra, 7s. 6d.

Bardsley (Rev. C.W.),Works by:
English Surnames: Their Sources and Significations. Third Ed., revised. Cr. 8vo, cl. extra, 7s. 6d. [Preparing.
Curiosities of Puritan Nomenclature. Crown 8vo, cloth extra, 7s. 6d.

Bartholomew Fair, Memoirs of. By HENRY MORLEY. With 100 Illusts. Crown 8vo, cloth extra, 7s. 6d.

Basil, Novels by:
A Drawn Game. Three Vols., cr. 8vo.
The Wearing of the Green. Three Vols., crown 8vo.   [Shortly.

Beaconsfield, Lord: A Biography. By T. P. O'CONNOR, M.P. Sixth Edit., New Preface. Cr.8vo, cl.ex.7s.6d.

Beauchamp. — Grantley Grange: A Novel. By SHELSLEY BEAUCHAMP. Post 8vo, illust. bds., 2s.

Beautiful Pictures by British Artists: A Gathering of Favourites from our Picture Galleries. In Two Series. All engraved on Steel in the highest style of Art. Edited, with Notices of the Artists, by SYDNEY ARMYTAGE, M.A. Imperial 4to, cloth extra, gilt and gilt edges, 21s. per Vol.

Bechstein. — As Pretty as Seven, and other German Stories. Collected by LUDWIG BECHSTEIN. With Additional Tales by the Brothers GRIMM, and 100 Illusts. by RICHTER. Small 4to, green and gold, 6s. 6d.; gilt edges, 7s. 6d.

Beerbohm. — Wanderings i Patagonia; or, Life among the Ostric Hunters. By JULIUS BEERBOHM. Wit Illusts. Crown 8vo, cloth extra, 3s. 6d

Belgravia for 1884. On Shilling Monthly, Illustrated by P MACNAB.—Two Serial Stories are no appearing in this Magazine: "Th Lover's Creed," by Mrs. CASHE HOEY; and "The Wearing of th Green," by the Author of "Love th Debt."
. Now ready, the Volume for MARC to JUNE, 1884, cloth extra, gilt edge 7s. 6d.; Cases for binding Vols., 2s. each

Belgravia Annual. With Storie by F. W. ROBINSON, J. ARBUTHNO WILSON, JUSTIN H. McCARTHY, E MONTGOMERIE RANKING, and others Demy 8vo, with Illusts., 1s. [Preparing

Bennett (W.C.,LL.D.),Works by
A Ballad History of England. Pos 8vo, cloth limp, 2s.
Songs for Sailors. Post 8vo, clot limp, 2s.

Besant (Walter) and Jame Rice, Novels by. Post 8vo, illust boards, 2s. each; cloth limp, 2s. 6d each; or crown 8vo, cloth extra 3s. 6d. each.
Ready-Money Mortiboy.
With Harp and Crown.
This Son of Vulcan.
My Little Girl.
The Case of Mr. Lucraft.
The Golden Butterfly.
By Celia's Arbour.
The Monks of Thelema.
'Twas in Trafalgar's Bay.
The Seamy Side.
The Ten Years' Tenant.
The Chaplain of the Fleet.

Besant (Walter), Novels by:
All Sorts and Conditions of Men An Impossible Story. With Illustra tions by FRED. BARNARD. Crow 8vo, cloth extra, 3s. 6d.; post 8v illust. boards, 2s.; cloth limp, 2s. 6d
The Captains' Room, &c. Wit Frontispiece by E. J. WHEELER Crown 8vo, cloth extra, 3s. 6d.; pos 8vo, illust. bds., 2s.; cl. limp, 2s. 6d.
All in a Garden Fair. With 6 Illusts by H. FURNISS. New and Cheape Edition. Cr. 8vo, cl. extra, 3s. 6d.
Dorothy Forster. New and Cheape Edition. With Illustrations by CH GREEN. Crown 8vo, cloth extra 3s. 6d.   [Preparing

The Art of Fiction. Demy 8vo, 1s.

Betham-Edwards (M.), Novels
by. Crown 8vo, cloth extra, 3s. 6d.
each.; post 8vo, illust. bds., 2s. each.

Felicia. | Kitty.

Bewick (Thos.) and his Pupils.
By AUSTIN DOBSON. With 95 Illustrations. Square 8vo, cloth extra, 10s. 6d.

Birthday Books:—
The Starry Heavens: A Poetical
Birthday Book. Square 8vo, handsomely bound in cloth, 2s. 6d.

Birthday Flowers: Their Language
and Legends. By W. J. GORDON.
Beautifully Illustrated in Colours by
VIOLA BOUGHTON. In illuminated
cover, crown 4to, 6s.

The Lowell Birthday Book. With
Illusts., small 8vo, cloth extra, 4s. 6d.

Blackburn's (Henry) Art Handbooks. Demy 8vo, Illustrated, uniform in size for binding.
Academy Notes, separate years, from
1875 to 1883, each 1s.

Academy Notes, 1884. With 152 Illustrations. 1s.

Academy Notes, 1875-79. Complete
in One Vol.,with nearly 600 Illusts. in
Facsimile. Demy 8vo, cloth limp, 6s.

Academy Notes, 1880-84. Complete
in One Volume, with about 700 Facsimile Illustrations. Cloth limp, 6s.

Grosvenor Notes, 1877. 6d.

Grosvenor Notes, separate years, from
1878 to 1883, each 1s.

Grosvenor Notes, 1884. With 78
Illustrations. 1s.

Grosvenor Notes, 1877-82. With
upwards of 300 Illustrations. Demy
8vo, cloth limp, 6s.

Pictures at South Kensington. With
70 Illustrations. 1s.

The English Pictures at the National
Gallery. 114 Illustrations. 1s.

The Old Masters at the National
Gallery. 128 Illustrations. 1s. 6d.

A Complete Illustrated Catalogue
to the National Gallery. With
Notes by. H. BLACKBURN, and 242
Illusts. Demy 8vo, cloth limp, 3s.

Illustrated Catalogue of the Luxembourg Gallery. Containing about
250 Reproductions after the Original
Drawings of the Artists. Edited by
F. G. DUMAS. Demy 8vo, 3s. 6d.

The Paris Salon, 1884. With over 300
Illusts. Edited by F. G. DUMAS.
Demy 8vo, 3s.

ART HANDBOOKS, continued—
The Art Annual, 1883-4. Edited by
F. G. DUMAS. With 300 full-page
Illustrations. Demy 8vo, 5s.

Boccaccio's Decameron ; or,
Ten Days' Entertainment. Translated
into English, with an Introduction by
THOMAS WRIGHT, F.S.A. With Portrait,
and STOTHARD'S beautiful Copperplates. Cr. 8vo, cloth extra, gilt, 7s. 6d.

Blake (William): Etchings from
his Works. By W. B. SCOTT. With
descriptive Text. Folio, half-bound
boards, India Proofs, 21s.

Bowers'(G.) Hunting Sketches:
Canters in Crampshire. Oblong 4to,
half-bound boards, 21s.

Leaves from a Hunting Journal.
Coloured in facsimile of the originals.
Oblong 4to, half-bound, 21s.

Boyle (Frederick), Works by :
Camp Notes: Stories of Sport and
Adventure in Asia, Africa, and
America. Crown 8vo, cloth extra,
3s. 6d.; post 8vo, illustrated bds., 2s.

Savage Life. Crown 8vo, cloth extra,
3s. 6d.; post 8vo, illustrated bds., 2s.

Brand's Observations on Popular Antiquities, chiefly Illustrating
the Origin of our Vulgar Customs,
Ceremonies, and Superstitions. With
the Additions of Sir HENRY ELLIS.
Crown 8vo, cloth extra, gilt, with
numerous Illustrations, 7s. 6d.

Bret Harte, Works by :
Bret Harte's Collected Works. Arranged and Revised by the Author.
Complete in Five Vols., crown 8vo,
cloth extra, 6s. each.
Vol. I. COMPLETE POETICAL AND
DRAMATIC WORKS. With Steel Portrait, and Introduction by Author.
Vol. II. EARLIER PAPERS—LUCK OF
ROARING CAMP, and other Sketches
—BOHEMIAN PAPERS — SPANISH
AND AMERICAN LEGENDS.
Vol. III. TALES OF THE ARGONAUTS
—EASTERN SKETCHES.
Vol. IV. GABRIEL CONROY.
Vol. V. STORIES — CONDENSED
NOVELS, &c.

The Select Works of Bret Harte, in
Prose and Poetry. With Introductory Essay by J. M. BELLEW, Portrait
of the Author, and 50 Illustrations.
Crown 8vo, cloth extra, 7s. 6d.

Gabriel Conroy: A Novel. Post 8vo,
illustrated boards, 2s.

BRET HARTE'S WORKS, *continued—*

An Heiress of Red Dog, and other Stories. Post 8vo, illustrated boards, 2s. ; cloth limp, 2s. 6d.

The Twins of Table Mountain. Fcap. 8vo, picture cover, 1s. ; crown 8vo, cloth extra, 3s. 6d.

Luck of Roaring Camp, and other Sketches. Post 8vo, illust. bds., 2s.

Jeff Briggs's Love Story. Fcap. 8vo, picture cover, 1s. ; cloth extra, 2s. 6d.

Flip. Post 8vo, illustrated boards, 2s. ; cloth limp, 2s. 6d.

Californian Stories (including THE TWINS OF TABLE MOUNTAIN, JEFF BRIGGS'S LOVE STORY, &c.) Post 8vo, illustrated boards, 2s.

Brewer (Rev. Dr.), Works by :

The Reader's Handbook of Allusions, References, Plots, and Stories. Fourth Edition, revised throughout, with a New Appendix, containing a COMPLETE ENGLISH BIBLIOGRAPHY. Cr. 8vo, 1,400 pp., cloth extra, 7s. 6d.

Authors and their Works, with the Dates: Being the Appendices to "The Reader's Handbook," separately printed. Cr. 8vo, cloth limp, 2s.

A Dictionary of Miracles: Imitative, Realistic, and Dogmatic. Crown 8vo, cloth extra, 7s. 6d. ; half-bound, 9s.

Brewster (Sir David), Works by:

More Worlds than One: The Creed of the Philosopher and the Hope of the Christian. With Plates. Post 8vo, cloth extra, 4s. 6d.

The Martyrs of Science: Lives of GALILEO, TYCHO BRAHE, and KEPLER. With Portraits. Post 8vo, cloth extra, 4s. 6d.

Letters on Natural Magic. A New Edition, with numerous Illustrations, and Chapters on the Being and Faculties of Man, and Additional Phenomena of Natural Magic, by J. A. SMITH. Post 8vo, cloth extra, 4s. 6d.

Brillat-Savarin.—Gastronomy

as a Fine Art. By BRILLAT-SAVARIN. Translated by R. E. ANDERSON, M.A. Post 8vo, cloth limp, 2s. 6d.

Burnett (Mrs.), Novels by :

Surly Tim, and other Stories. Post 8vo, illustrated boards, 2s.

Kathleen Mavourneen. Fcap. 8vo, picture cover, 1s.

Lindsay's Luck. Fcap. 8vo, picture cover, 1s.

Pretty Polly Pemberton. Fcap. 8vo,

Buchanan's (Robert) Work

Ballads of Life, Love, and Humo With a Frontispiece by ART HUGHES. Crown 8vo, cloth extra,

Selected Poems of Robert Buchan With Frontispiece by T. DALZ1 Crown 8vo, cloth extra, 6s.

Undertones. Cr. 8vo, cloth extra,

London Poems. Cr. 8vo, cl. extra,

The Book of Orm. Crown 8vo, cl extra, 6s.

White Rose and Red: A Love St Crown 8vo, cloth extra, 6s.

Idylls and Legends of Inverbu Crown 8vo, cloth extra, 6s.

St. Abe and his Seven Wives: A of Salt Lake City. With a Fror piece by A. B. HOUGHTON. Cr 8vo, cloth extra, 5s.

Robert Buchanan's Complete Po cal Works. With Steel-plate trait. Crown 8vo, cloth ex 7s. 6d. [*In the p*r

The Hebrid Isles: Wanderings in Land of Lorne and the Outer brides. With Frontispiece by SMALL. Crown 8vo, cloth extra,

A Poet's Sketch-Book: Selecti from the Prose Writings of ROB BUCHANAN. Crown 8vo, cl. extra

The Shadow of the Sword: A mance. Crown 8vo, cloth ex 3s. 6d. ; post 8vo, illust. boards, 2

A Child of Nature: A Romance. W a Frontispiece. Crown 8vo, c extra, 3s. 6d. ; post 8vo, illust. bds

God and the Man: A Romance. Illustrations by FRED. BARN/ Crown 8vo, cloth extra, 3s. 6d. ; 8vo, illustrated boards, 2s.

The Martyrdom of Madeline: Romance. With Frontispiece by A COOPER. Cr. 8vo, cloth extra, 3s. post 8vo, illustrated boards, 2s.

Love Me for Ever. With a Fro piece by P. MACNAB. Crown cloth extra, 3s. 6d. ; post 8vo, il trated boards, 2s.

Annan Water: A Romance. Cr 8vo, cloth extra, 3s. 6d.

The New Abelard: A Romance. Cr 8vo, cloth extra, 3s. 6d.

Foxglove Manor: A Novel. Tl Vols., crown 8vo.

Burton (Robert) :

The Anatomy of Melancholy. New Edition, complete, correc and enriched by Translations of Classical Extracts. Demy 8vo, cl extra, 7s. 6d.

Melancholy Anatomised : Being Abridgment, for popular use, of B TON'S ANATOMY OF MELANCHO

Burton (Captain), Works by:
To the Gold Coast for Gold: A Personal Narrative. By RICHARD F. BURTON and VERNEY LOVETT CAMERON. With Maps and Frontispiece. Two Vols., crown 8vo, cloth extra, 21s.

The Book of the Sword: Being a History of the Sword and its Use in all Countries, from the Earliest Times. By RICHARD F. BURTON. With over 400 Illustrations. Square 8vo, cloth extra, 32s.

Bunyan's Pilgrim's Progress.
Edited by Rev. T. SCOTT. With 17 Steel Plates by STOTHARD, engraved by GOODALL, and numerous Woodcuts. Crown 8vo, cloth extra, gilt, 7s. 6d.

Byron (Lord):
Byron's Letters and Journals. With Notices of his Life. By THOMAS MOORE. A Reprint of the Original Edition, newly revised, with Twelve full-page Plates. Crown 8vo, cloth extra, gilt, 7s. 6d.

Byron's Don Juan. Complete in One Vol., post 8vo, cloth limp, 2s.

Cameron (Commander) and
Captain Burton.—To the Gold Coast for Gold: A Personal Narrative. By RICHARD F. BURTON and VERNEY LOVETT CAMERON. With Frontispiece and Maps. Two Vols., crown 8vo, cloth extra, 21s.

Cameron (Mrs. H. Lovett),
Novels by:
Crown 8vo, cloth extra, 3s. 6d. each; post 8vo, illustrated boards, 2s. each.
Juliet's Guardian.
Deceivers Ever.

Campbell.—White and Black:
Travels in the United States. By Sir GEORGE CAMPBELL, M.P. Demy 8vo, cloth extra, 14s.

Carlyle (Thomas):
Thomas Carlyle: Letters and Recollections. By MONCURE D. CONWAY, M.A. Crown 8vo, cloth extra, with Illustrations, 6s.

On the Choice of Books. By THOMAS CARLYLE. With a Life of the Author by R. H. SHEPHERD. New and Revised Edition, post 8vo, cloth extra, Illustrated, 1s. 6d.

The Correspondence of Thomas Carlyle and Ralph Waldo Emerson, 1834 to 1872. Edited by CHARLES ELIOT NORTON. With Portraits. Two Vols., crown 8vo, cloth extra, 24s.

Chapman's (George) Works:
Vol. I. contains the Plays complete, including the doubtful ones. Vol. II., the Poems and Minor Translations, with an Introductory Essay by ALGERNON CHARLES SWINBURNE. Vol. III., the Translations of the Iliad and Odyssey. Three Vols., crown 8vo, cloth extra, 18s.; or separately, 6s. each.

Chatto & Jackson.—A Treatise
on Wood Engraving, Historical and Practical. By WM. ANDREW CHATTO and JOHN JACKSON. With an Additional Chapter by HENRY G. BOHN; and 450 fine Illustrations. A Reprint of the last Revised Edition. Large 4to, half-bound, 28s.

Chaucer:
Chaucer for Children: A Golden Key. By Mrs. H. R. HAWEIS. With Eight Coloured Pictures and numerous Woodcuts by the Author. New Ed., small 4to, cloth extra, 6s.

Chaucer for Schools. By Mrs. H. R. HAWEIS. Demy 8vo, cloth limp, 2s.6d.

City (The) of Dream: A Poem.
Fcap. 8vo, cloth extra, 6s. [*In the press.*

Cobban.—The Cure of Souls:
A Story. By J. MACLAREN COBBAN. Post 8vo, illustrated boards, 2s.

Collins (C. Allston).—The Bar
Sinister: A Story. By C. ALLSTON COLLINS. Post 8vo, illustrated bds., 2s.

Collins (Mortimer & Frances),
Novels by:
Sweet and Twenty. Post 8vo, illustrated boards, 2s.

Frances. Post 8vo, illust. bds., 2s.

Blacksmith and Scholar. Post 8vo, illustrated boards, 2s.; crown 8vo, cloth extra, 3s. 6d.

The Village Comedy. Post 8vo, illust. boards, 2s.; cr. 8vo, cloth extra, 3s. 6d.

You Play Me False. Post 8vo, illust. boards, 2s.; cr. 8vo, cloth extra, 3s. 6d.

Collins (Mortimer), Novels by:
Sweet Anne Page. Post 8vo, illustrated boards, 2s.; crown 8vo, cloth extra, 3s. 6d.

Transmigration. Post 8vo, illustrated boards, 2s.; crown 8vo, cloth extra, 3s. 6d.

From Midnight to Midnight. Post 8vo, illustrated boards, 2s.; crown 8vo, cloth extra, 3s. 6d.

A Fight with Fortune. Post 8vo, illustrated boards, 2s.

Collins (Wilkie), Novels by.

Each post 8vo, illustrated boards, 2s; cloth limp, 2s. 6d.; or crown 8vo, cloth extra, Illustrated, 3s. 6d.

Antonina. Illust. by A. CONCANEN.

Basil. Illustrated by Sir JOHN GILBERT and J. MAHONEY.

Hide and Seek. Illustrated by Sir JOHN GILBERT and J. MAHONEY.

The Dead Secret. Illustrated by Sir JOHN GILBERT and A. CONCANEN.

Queen of Hearts Illustrated by Sir JOHN GILBERT and A. CONCANEN.

My Miscellanies. With Illustrations by A. CONCANEN, and a Steel-plate Portrait of WILKIE COLLINS.

The Woman in White. With Illustrations by Sir JOHN GILBERT and F. A. FRASER.

The Moonstone. With Illustrations by G. DU MAURIER and F. A. FRASER.

Man and Wife. Illust. by W. SMALL.

Poor Miss Finch. Illustrated by G. DU MAURIER and EDWARD HUGHES.

Miss or Mrs.? With Illustrations by S. L. FILDES and HENRY WOODS.

The New Magdalen. Illustrated by G. DU MAURIER and C. S. RANDS.

The Frozen Deep. Illustrated by G. DU MAURIER and J. MAHONEY.

The Law and the Lady. Illustrated by S. L. FILDES and SYDNEY HALL.

The Two Destinies.

The Haunted Hotel. Illustrated by ARTHUR HOPKINS.

The Fallen Leaves.

Jezebel's Daughter.

The Black Robe.

Heart and Science: A Story of the Present Time. Crown 8vo, cloth extra, 3s. 6d.

"I Say No." Three Vols., crown 8vo. [*Shortly.*

Colman's Humorous Works:

"Broad Grins," "My Nightgown and Slippers," and other Humorous Works, Prose and Poetical, of GEORGE COLMAN. With Life by G. B. BUCKSTONE, and Frontispiece by HOGARTH. Crown 8vo, cloth extra, gilt, 7s. 6d.

Convalescent Cookery: A

Family Handbook. By CATHERINE RYAN. Post 8vo, cloth limp, 2s. 6d.

Conway (Moncure D.), Works by:

Demonology and Devil-Lore. Two Vols., royal 8vo with 65 Illusts., 28s.

CONWAY'S (M. D.) WORKS, *continued*—

A Necklace of Stories. Illustrated by W. J. HENNESSY. Square 8vo, cloth extra, 6s.

The Wandering Jew. Crown 8vo, cloth extra, 6s.

Thomas Carlyle: Letters and Recollections. With Illustrations. Crown 8vo, cloth extra, 6s.

Cook (Dutton), Works by:

Hours with the Players. With a Steel Plate Frontispiece. New and Cheaper Edit., cr. 8vo, cloth extra, 6s.

Nights at the Play: A View of the English Stage. New and Cheaper Edition. Crown 8vo, cloth extra, 6s.

Leo: A Novel. Post 8vo, illustrated boards, 2s.

Paul Foster's Daughter. Post 8vo, illustrated boards, 2s.; crown 8vo, cloth extra, 3s. 6d.

Cooper.—Heart Salvage, by

Sea and Land. Stories by Mrs. COOPER (KATHARINE SAUNDERS). Three Vols., crown 8vo.

Copyright. — A Handbook of

English and Foreign Copyright in Literary and Dramatic Works. By SIDNEY JERROLD, of the Middle Temple, Esq., Barrister-at-Law. Post 8vo, cloth limp, 2s. 6d.

Cornwall.—Popular Romances

of the West of England; or, The Drolls, Traditions, and Superstitions of Old Cornwall. Collected and Edited by ROBERT HUNT, F.R.S. New and Revised Edition, with Additions, and Two Steel-plate Illustrations by GEORGE CRUIKSHANK. Crown 8vo, cloth extra, 7s. 6d.

Creasy.—Memoirs of Eminent

Etonians: with Notices of the Early History of Eton College. By Sir EDWARD CREASY, Author of "The Fifteen Decisive Battles of the World." Crown 8vo, cloth extra, gilt, with 13 Portraits, 7s. 6d.

Cruikshank (George):

The Comic Almanack. Complete in Two SERIES: The FIRST from 1835 to 1843; the SECOND from 1844 to 1853. A Gathering of the BEST HUMOUR of THACKERAY, HOOD, MAYHEW, ALBERT SMITH, A'BECKETT, ROBERT BROUGH, &c. With 2,000 Woodcuts and Steel Engravings by CRUIKSHANK, HINE, LANDELLS, &c. Crown 8vo, cloth gilt, two very thick volumes, 7s. 6d. each.

CRUIKSHANK (G.), *continued—*

The Life of George Cruikshank. By BLANCHARD JERROLD, Author of "The Life of Napoleon III.," &c. With 84 Illustrations. New and Cheaper Edition, enlarged, with Additional Plates, and a very carefully compiled Bibliography. Crown 8vo, cloth extra, 7s. 6d.

Robinson Crusoe. A beautiful reproduction of Major's Edition, with 37 Woodcuts and Two Steel Plates by GEORGE CRUIKSHANK, choicely printed. Crown 8vo, cloth extra, 7s. 6d. A few Large-Paper copies, printed on hand-made paper, with India proofs of the Illustrations, 36s.

Cussans.—Handbook of Heraldry; with Instructions for Tracing Pedigrees and Deciphering Ancient MSS., &c. By JOHN E. CUSSANS. Entirely New and Revised Edition, illustrated with over 400 Woodcuts and Coloured Plates. Crown 8vo, cloth extra, 7s. 6d.

Cyples.—Hearts of Gold : A Novel. By WILLIAM CYPLES. Crown 8vo, cloth extra, 3s. 6d.

Daniel. — Merrie England in the Olden Time. By GEORGE DANIEL. With Illustrations by ROBT. CRUIKSHANK. Crown 8vo, cloth extra, 3s. 6d.

Daudet.—Port Salvation; or, The Evangelist. By ALPHONSE DAUDET. Translated by C. HARRY MELTZER. With Portrait of the Author. Crown 8vo, cloth extra, 3s. 6d.

Davenant. — What shall my Son be ? Hints for Parents on the Choice of a Profession or Trade for their Sons. By FRANCIS DAVENANT, M.A. Post 8vo, cloth limp, 2s. 6d.

Davies (Dr. N. E.), Works by :

One Thousand Medical Maxims. Crown 8vo, 1s.; cloth, 1s. 6d.

Nursery Hints: A Mother's Guide. Crown 8vo, 1s.; cloth, 1s. 6d.

Aids to Long Life. Crown 8vo, 2s.; cloth limp, 2s. 6d.   [*Shortly.*

Davies' (Sir John) Complete Poetical Works, including Psalms I. to L. in Verse, and other hitherto Unpublished MSS., for the first time Collected and Edited, with Memorial-Introduction and Notes, by the Rev. A. B. GROSART, D.D. Two Vols., crown 8vo, cloth boards, 12s.

De Maistre.—A Journey Round My Room. By XAVIER DE MAISTRE. Translated by HENRY ATTWELL. Post 8vo, cloth limp, 2s. 6d.

De Mille.—A Castle in Spain. A Novel. By JAMES DE MILLE. With a Frontispiece. Crown 8vo, cloth extra, 3s. 6d.

Derwent (Leith), Novels by :

Our Lady of Tears. Cr. 8vo, cloth extra, 3s. 6d.; post 8vo, illust. bds., 2s.

Circe's Lovers. Crown 8vo, cloth extra, 3s. 6d.

Dickens (Charles), Novels by : Post 8vo, illustrated boards, 2s. each.

Sketches by Boz. | Nicholas Nickleby.
Pickwick Papers. | Oliver Twist.

The Speeches of Charles Dickens. (*Mayfair Library.*) Post 8vo, cloth limp, 2s. 6d.

The Speeches of Charles Dickens, 1841-1870. With a New Bibliography, revised and enlarged. Edited and Prefaced by RICHARD HERNE SHEPHERD. Crown 8vo, cloth extra, 6s.

About England with Dickens. By ALFRED RIMMER. With 57 Illustrations by C. A. VANDERHOOF, ALFRED RIMMER, and others. Sq. 8vo, cloth extra, 10s. 6d.

Dictionaries :

A Dictionary of Miracles : Imitative, Realistic, and Dogmatic. By the Rev. E. C. BREWER, LL.D. Crown 8vo, cloth extra, 7s. 6d.; hf.-bound, 9s.

The Reader's Handbook of Allusions, References, Plots, and Stories. By the Rev. E. C. BREWER, LL.D. Fourth Edition, revised throughout, with a New Appendix containing a Complete English Bibliography. Crown 8vo, 1,400 pages, cloth extra, 7s. 6d.

Authors and their Works, with the Dates. Being the Appendices to "The Reader's Handbook," separately printed. By the Rev. E. C. BREWER, LL.D. Crown 8vo, cloth limp, 2s.

Familiar Allusions : A Handbook of Miscellaneous Information ; including the Names of Celebrated Statues, Paintings, Palaces, Country Seats, Ruins, Churches, Ships Streets, Clubs, Natural Curiosities, and the like. By WM. A. WHEELER and CHARLES G. WHEELER. Demy 8vo cloth extra, 7s. 6d.

DICTIONARIES, *continued—*

Short Sayings of Great Men. With Historical and Explanatory Notes. By SAMUEL A. BENT, M.A. Demy 8vo, cloth extra, 7s. 6d.

A Dictionary of the Drama: Being a comprehensive Guide to the Plays, Playwrights, Players, and Playhouses of the United Kingdom and America, from the Earliest to the Present Times. By W. DAVENPORT ADAMS. A thick volume, crown 8vo, half-bound, 12s. 6d.   [*In preparation.*

The Slang Dictionary: Etymological, Historical, and Anecdotal. Crown 8vo, cloth extra, 6s. 6d.

Words, Facts, and Phrases: A Dictionary of Curious, Quaint, and Out-of-the-Way Matters. By ELIEZER EDWARDS. New and Cheaper Issue. Cr. 8vo, cl. ex., 7s. 6d.; hf.-bd., 9s.

Diderot.—The Paradox of Acting. Translated, with Annotations, from Diderot's "Le Paradoxe sur le Comédien," by WALTER HERRIES POLLOCK. With a Preface by HENRY IRVING. Cr. 8vo, in parchment, 4s. 6d.

Dobson (W. T.), Works by:

Literary Frivolities, Fancies, Follies, and Frolics. Post 8vo, cl. lp., 2s. 6d.

Poetical Ingenuities and Eccentricities. Post 8vo, cloth limp, 2s. 6d.

Doran. — Memories of our Great Towns; with Anecdotic Gleanings concerning their Worthies and their Oddities. By Dr. JOHN DORAN, F.S.A. With 38 Illustrations. New and Cheaper Ed., cr. 8vo, cl. ex., 7s. 6d.

Drama, A Dictionary of the. Being a comprehensive Guide to the Plays, Playwrights, Players, and Playhouses of the United Kingdom and America, from the Earliest to the Present Times. By W. DAVENPORT ADAMS. (Uniform with BREWER'S "Reader's Handbook.") Crown 8vo, half-bound, 12s. 6d.   [*In preparation.*

Dramatists, The Old. Crown 8vo, cloth extra, with Vignette Portraits, 6s. per Vol.

Ben Jonson's Works. With Notes Critical and Explanatory, and a Biographical Memoir by WM. GIFFORD. Edited by Colonel CUNNINGHAM. Three Vols.

Chapman's Works. Complete in Three Vols. Vol. I. contains the Plays complete, including the doubtful ones; Vol. II., the Poems and Minor Translations, with an Introductory Essay by ALGERNON CHAS. SWINBURNE; Vol. III., the Transla-e Iliad and Od sse .

DRAMATISTS, THE OLD, *continued—*

Marlowe's Works. Including Translations. Edited, with N and Introduction, by Col. CUNNI HAM. One Vol.

Massinger's Plays. From the Tex WILLIAM GIFFORD. Edited by CUNNINGHAM. One Vol.

Dyer. — The Folk-Plants. By T. F. THISE M.A., &c. Crown 8vo, 7s. 6d.   [*In*

Early English Poets. Edit with Introductions and Annotati by Rev. A. B. GROSART, D.D. Cr 8vo, cloth boards, 6s. per Volum

Fletcher's (Giles, B.D.) Comp Poems. One Vol.

Davies' (Sir John) Comp Poetical Works. Two Vols.

Herrick's (Robert) Comp lected Poems. Three Vols.

Sidney's (Sir Philip) Compl Poetical Works. Three Vols.

Herbert (Lord) of Cherbury's Poe Edited, with Introduction, by CHURTON COLLINS. Crown parchment, 8s.

Edwardes (Mrs. A.), Novels

A Point of Honour. Post 8vo, i trated boards, 2s.

Archie Lovell. Post 8vo, illust. b 2s.; crown 8vo, cloth extra, 3s. 6

Eggleston.—Roxy: A Nov EDWARD EGGLESTON. Post 8v boards, 2s.; cr. 8vo, cloth extr

Emanuel.—On Diamonds a Precious Stones: their History, Va and Properties; with Simple Tests ascertaining their Reality. By HA EMANUEL, F.R.G.S. With numer Illustrations, tinted and plain. Cr 8vo, cloth extra, gilt, 6s.

Englishman's House, The Practical Guide to all intereste Selecting or Building a House, full Estimates of Cost, Quantities, By C. J. RICHARDSON. Third Edit Nearly 600 Illusts. Cr. 8vo, cl. ex., 7s

Ewald (Alex. Charles, F.S. Works by:

Stories from the State Pap With an Autotype Facsimile. Cr 8vo, cloth extra, 6s.

The Life and Times of Pri Charles Stuart, Count of Albe commonly called the Young tender. From the State Papers other Sources. New and Chea Edition, with a Portrait. Crown 8 lo t 7 6d.

Eyes, The.—How to Use our Eyes, and How to Preserve Them. By JOHN BROWNING, F.R.A.S., &c. With 37 Illustrations. Crown 8vo, 1s.; cloth, 1s. 6d.

Fairholt.—Tobacco: Its History and Associations; with an Account of the Plant and its Manufacture, and its Modes of Use in all Ages and Countries. By F. W. FAIRHOLT, F.S.A. With Coloured Frontispiece and upwards of 100 Illustrations by the Author. Crown 8vo, cloth extra, 6s.

Familiar Allusions: A Handbook of Miscellaneous Information; including the Names of Celebrated Statues, Paintings, Palaces, Country Seats, Ruins, Churches, Ships, Streets, Clubs, Natural Curiosities, and the like. By WILLIAM A. WHEELER, Author of " Noted Names of Fiction ; " and CHARLES G. WHEELER. Demy 8vo, cloth extra, 7s. 6d.

Faraday (Michael), Works by:
The Chemical History of a Candle: Lectures delivered before a Juvenile Audience at the Royal Institution. Edited by WILLIAM CROOKES, F.C.S. Post 8vo, cloth extra, with numerous Illustrations, 4s. 6d.

On the Various Forces of Nature, and their Relations to each other: Lectures delivered before a Juvenile Audience at the Royal Institution. Edited by WILLIAM CROOKES, F.C.S. Post 8vo, cloth extra, with numerous Illustrations, 4s. 6d.

Fin-Bec. — The Cupboard Papers: Observations on the Art of Living and Dining. By FIN-BEC. Post 8vo, cloth limp, 2s. 6d.

Fitzgerald (Percy), Works by:
The Recreations of a Literary Man; or, Does Writing Pay? With Recollections of some Literary Men, and a View of a Literary Man's Working Life. Cr. 8vo, cloth extra, 6s.
The World Behind the Scenes. Crown 8vo, cloth extra, 3s. 6d.
Little Essays: Passages from the Letters of CHARLES LAMB. Post 8vo, cloth limp, 2s. 6d.

Post 8vo, illustrated boards, 2s. each.
Bella Donna. | Never Forgotten.
The Second Mrs. Tillotson.
Polly.
Seventy-five Brooke Street.

Fletcher's (Giles, B.D.) Complete Poems: Christ's Victorie in Heaven, Christ's Victorie on Earth, Christ's Triumph over Death, and Minor Poems. With Memorial-Introduction and Notes by the Rev. A. B. GROSART, D.D. Cr. 8vo, cloth bds., 6s.

Fonblanque.—Filthy Lucre: A Novel. By ALBANY DE FONBLANQUE. Post 8vo, illustrated boards, 2s.

Francillon (R. E.), Novels by: Crown 8vo, cloth extra, 3s. 6d. each ; post 8vo, illust. boards, 2s. each.
Olympia. | Queen Cophetua.
One by One.
Esther's Glove. Fcap. 8vo, picture cover, 1s.
A Real Queen. Cr. 8vo, cl. extra, 3s. 6d.

French Literature, History of. By HENRY VAN LAUN. Complete in 3 Vols., demy 8vo, cl. bds., 7s. 6d. each.

Frere.—Pandurang Hari ; or, Memoirs of a Hindoo. With a Preface by Sir H. BARTLE FRERE, G.C.S.I., &c. Crown 8vo, cloth extra, 3s. 6d. ; post 8vo, illustrated boards, 2s.

Friswell.—One of Two: A Novel. By HAIN FRISWELL. Post 8vo, illustrated boards, 2s.

Frost (Thomas), Works by: Crown 8vo, cloth extra, 3s. 6d. each.
Circus Life and Circus Celebrities.
The Lives of the Conjurers.
The Old Showmen and the Old London Fairs.

Fry.—Royal Guide to the London Charities, 1884-5. By HERBERT FRY. Showing, in alphabetical order, their Name, Date of Foundation, Address, Objects, Annual Income, Chief Officials, &c. Published Annually. Crown 8vo, cloth, 1s. 6d.

Gardening Books:
A Year's Work in Garden and Greenhouse: Practical Advice to Amateur Gardeners as to the Management of the Flower, Fruit, and Frame Garden. By GEORGE GLENNY. Post 8vo, cloth limp, 2s. 6d.
Our Kitchen Garden: The Plants we Grow, and How we Cook Them. By TOM JERROLD, Author of " The Garden that Paid the Rent," &c. Post 8vo, cloth limp, 2s. 6d.
Household Horticulture: A Gossip about Flowers. By TOM and JANE JERROLD. Illust. Post 8vo, cl. lp., 2s. 6d.
The Garden that Paid the Rent. By TOM JERROLD. Fcap. 8vo, illus-

Garrett.—The Capel Girls : A Novel. By EDWARD GARRETT. Post 8vo,illust.bds., 2s.; cr.8vo, cl.ex., 3s. 6d.

Gentleman's Magazine (The) for 1884. One Shilling Monthly. A New Serial Story, entitled "Philistia," by CECIL POWER, is now appearing. "Science Notes," by W. MATTIEU WILLIAMS, F.R.A.S., and "Table Talk," by SYLVANUS URBAN, are also continued monthly.

*** *Now ready, the Volume for* JANUARY *to* JUNE, 1884, *cloth extra, price* 8s. 6d. ; *Cases for binding,* 2s. *each.*

German Popular Stories. Collected by the Brothers GRIMM, and Translated by EDGAR TAYLOR. Edited, with an Introduction, by JOHN RUSKIN. With 22 Illustrations on Steel by GEORGE CRUIKSHANK. Square 8vo, cloth extra, 6s. 6d. ; gilt edges, 7s. 6d.

Gibbon (Charles), Novels by : Crown 8vo, cloth extra, 3s. 6d. each ; post 8vo, illustrated boards, 2s. each.

Robin Gray.	Queen of the Meadow.
For Lack of Gold.	
What will the World Say ?	In Pastures Green
	Braes of Yarrow.
In Honour Bound.	The Flower of the Forest. [lem.
In Love and War.	
For the King.	A Heart's Problem

Post 8vo, illustrated boards, 2s.
The Dead Heart.

Crown 8vo, cloth extra, 3s. 6d. each.
The Golden Shaft.
Of High Degree.
Fancy Free.
Loving a Dream.

By Mead and Stream. Three Vols., crown 8vo. [*Shortly.*

Gilbert (William), Novels by : Post 8vo, illustrated boards, 2s. each.
Dr. Austin's Guests.
The Wizard of the Mountain.
James Duke, Costermonger.

Gilbert (W. S.), Original Plays by: In Two Series, each complete in itself, price 2s. 6d. each.

The FIRST SERIES contains—The Wicked World—Pygmalion and Galatea — Charity — The Princess — The Palace of Truth—Trial by Jury.

The SECOND SERIES contains—Broken Hearts—Engaged—Sweethearts—Gretchen—Dan'l Druce—Tom Cobb—H.M.S. Pinafore—The Sorcerer—The Pirates of Penzance.

Glenny.—A Year's Work in Garden and Greenhouse: Practical Advice to Amateur Gardeners as to the Management of the Flower, Fruit and Frame Garden. By GEORGE GLENNY. Post 8vo, cloth limp, 2s. 6d

Godwin.—Lives of the Necro mancers. By WILLIAM GODWIN Post 8vo, cloth limp, 2s.

Golden Library, The : Square 16mo (Tauchnitz size), cloth limp, 2s. per volume.

Bayard Taylor's Diversions of th Echo Club.

Bennett's (Dr. W. C.) Ballad History of England.

Bennett's (Dr.) Songs for Sailors.

Byron's Don Juan.

Godwin's (William) Lives of th Necromancers.

Holmes's Autocrat of the Break fast Table. With an Introductio by G. A. SALA.

Holmes's Professor at the Break fast Table.

Hood's Whims and Oddities. Complete. All the original Illustrations.

Irving's (Washington) Tales of Traveller.

Irving's (Washington) Tales of the Alhambra.

Jesse's (Edward) Scenes and Oc cupations of a Country Life.

Lamb's Essays of Elia. Both Series Complete in One Vol.

Leigh Hunt's Essays: A Tale for a Chimney Corner, and other Pieces. With Portrait, and Introduction by EDMUND OLLIER.

Mallory's (Sir Thomas) Mort d'Arthur: The Stories of King Arthur and of the Knights of the Round Table. Edited by B. MONTGOMERIE RANKING.

Pascal's Provincial Letters. A New Translation, with Historical Introduction and Notes,byT.M'CRIE,D.D.

Pope's Poetical Works. Complete.

Rochefoucauld's Maxims and Moral Reflections. With Notes, and Introductory Essay by SAINTE-BEUVE.

St. Pierre's Paul and Virginia, and The Indian Cottage. Edited, with Life, by the Rev. E. CLARKE.

Shelley's Early Poems, and Queen Mab. With Essay by LEIGH HUNT.

Shelley's Later Poems: Laon and Cythna, &c.

Shelley's Posthumous Poems, the Shelley Papers, &c.

GOLDEN LIBRARY, THE, continued—
Shelley's Prose Works, including A Refutation of Deism, Zastrozzi, St. Irvyne, &c.

White's Natural History of Selborne. Edited, with Additions, by THOMAS BROWN, F.L.S.

Golden Treasury of Thought,
The: An ENCYCLOPÆDIA OF QUOTATIONS from Writers of all Times and Countries. Selected and Edited by THEODORE TAYLOR. Crown 8vo, cloth gilt and gilt edges, 7s. 6d.

Gordon Cumming (C. F.), Works by:
In the Hebrides. With Autotype Facsimile and numerous full-page Illustrations. Demy 8vo, cloth extra, 8s. 6d.

In the Himalayas and on the Indian Plains. With numerous Illustrations. Demy 8vo, cloth extra, 8s. 6d.
[Shortly.

Graham. — The Professor's
Wife: A Story. By LEONARD GRAHAM. Fcap. 8vo, picture cover, 1s.; cloth extra, 2s. 6d.

Greeks and Romans, The Life
of the, Described from Antique Monuments. By ERNST GUHL and W. KONER. Translated from the Third German Edition, and Edited by Dr. F. HUEFFER. With 545 Illustrations. New and Cheaper Edition, demy 8vo, cloth extra, 7s. 6d.

Greenwood (James), Works by:
The Wilds of London. Crown 8vo, cloth extra, 3s. 6d.

Low-Life Deeps: An Account of the Strange Fish to be Found There. Crown 8vo, cloth extra, 3s. 6d.

Dick Temple: A Novel. Post 8vo, illustrated boards, 2s.

Guyot.—The Earth and Man;
or, Physical Geography in its relation to the History of Mankind. By ARNOLD GUYOT. With Additions by Professors AGASSIZ, PIERCE, and GRAY; 12 Maps and Engravings on Steel, some Coloured, and copious Index. Crown 8vo, cloth extra, gilt, 4s. 6d.

Hair (The): Its Treatment in
Health, Weakness, and D'sease. Translated from the German of Dr. J. PINCUS. Crown 8vo, 1s.

Hake (Dr. Thomas Gordon),
Poems by:
Maiden Ecstasy. Small 4to, cloth extra, 8s.

HAKE'S (Dr. T. G.) POEMS, continued—
New Symbols. Crown 8vo, cloth extra, 6s.

Legends of the Morrow. Crown 8vo, cloth extra, 6s.

The Serpent Play. Crown 8vo, cloth extra, 6s.

Hall.—Sketches of Irish Cha-
racter. By Mrs. S. C. HALL. With numerous Illustrations on Steel and Wood by MACLISE, GILBERT, HARVEY, and G. CRUIKSHANK. Medium 8vo, cloth extra, gilt, 7s. 6d.

Halliday.—Every-day Papers.
By ANDREW HALLIDAY. Post 8vo, illustrated boards, 2s.

Handwriting, The Philosophy
of. With over 100 Facsimiles and Explanatory Text. By DON FELIX DE SALAMANCA. Post 8vo, cloth limp, 2s. 6d.

Hanky-Panky: A Collection of
Very Easy Tricks, Very Difficult Tricks, White Magic, Sleight of Hand, &c. Edited by W. H. CREMER. With 200 Illusts. Crown 8vo, cloth extra, 4s. 6d.

Hardy (Lady Duffus). — Paul
Wynter's Sacrifice: A Story. By Lady DUFFUS HARDY. Post 8vo, illust. boards, 2s.

Hardy (Thomas).—Under the
Greenwood Tree. By THOMAS HARDY, Author of "Far from the Madding Crowd." Crown 8vo, cloth extra, 3s. 6d.; post 8vo, illustrated bds., 2s.

Haweis (Mrs. H. R.), Works by:
The Art of Dress. With numerous Illustrations. Small 8vo, illustrated cover, 1s.; cloth limp, 1s. 6d.

The Art of Beauty. New and Cheaper Edition. Crown 8vo, cloth extra, with Coloured Frontispiece and Illustrations, 6s.

The Art of Decoration. Square 8vo, handsomely bound and profusely Illustrated, 10s. 6d.

Chaucer for Children: A Golden Key. With Eight Coloured Pictures and numerous Woodcuts. New Edition, small 4to, cloth extra, 6s.

Chaucer for Schools. Demy 8vo, cloth limp, 2s. 6d.

Haweis (Rev. H. R.).—American
Humorists. Including WASHINGTON IRVING, OLIVER WENDELL HOLMES, JAMES RUSSELL LOWELL, ARTEMUS WARD, MARK TWAIN, and BRET HARTE. By the Rev. H. R. HAWEIS, M.A. Crown 8vo, cloth extra, 6s.

Hawthorne (Julian), Novels by.
Crown 8vo, cloth extra, 3s. 6d. each;
post 8vo, illustrated boards, 2s. each.

Garth. | Sebastian Strome.
Ellice Quentin. | Dust.
Prince Saroni's Wife.

Mrs. Gainsborough's Diamonds.
Fcap. 8vo, illustrated cover, 1s.;
cloth extra, 2s. 6d.

Crown 8vo, cloth extra, 3s. 6d. each.
Fortune's Fool.
Beatrix Randolph. With Illustrations
by A. FREDERICKS.

Mercy Holland, and other Stories.
Three Vols., crown 8vo. [Shortly.

IMPORTANT NEW BIOGRAPHY.
Hawthorne (Nathaniel) and
his Wife. By JULIAN HAWTHORNE.
With 6 Steel-plate Portraits. Two
Vols., crown 8vo, cloth extra, 24s.

[Twenty-five copies of an Edition de
Luxe, printed on the best hand-made
paper, large 8vo size, and with India
proofs of the Illustrations, are reserved
for sale in England, price 48s. per set.
Immediate application should be made
by anyone desiring a copy of this
special and very limited Edition.]

Heath (F. G.). — My Garden
Wild, and What I Grew There. By
FRANCIS GEORGE HEATH, Author of
"The Fern World," &c. Crown 8vo,
cl. ex., 5s.; cl. gilt, gilt edges, 6s.

Helps (Sir Arthur), Works by:
Animals and their Masters. Post
8vo, cloth limp, 2s. 6d.
Social Pressure. Post 8vo, cloth limp,
2s. 6d.
Ivan de Biron: A Novel. Crown 8vo,
cloth extra, 3s. 6d.; post 8vo, illustrated boards, 2s.

Heptalogia (The); or, The
Seven against Sense. A Cap with
Seven Bells. Cr. 8vo, cloth extra, 6s.

Herbert.—The Poems of Lord
Herbert of Cherbury. Edited, with
Introduction, by J. CHURTON COLLINS.
Crown 8vo, bound in parchment, 8s.

Herrick's (Robert) Hesperides,
Noble Numbers, and Complete Collected Poems. With Memorial-Introduction and Notes by the Rev. A. B.
GROSART, D.D., Steel Portrait, Index
of First Lines, and Glossarial Index,
&c. Three Vols., crown 8vo, cloth, 18s.

Hesse - Wartegg (Chevalier
Ernst von), Works by:
Tunis: The Land and the People.
With 22 Illustrations. Crown 8vo,
cloth extra, 3s. 6d.
The New South-West: Travelling
Sketches from Kansas, New Mexico,
Arizona, and Northern Mexico.
With 100 fine Illustrations and Three
Maps. Demy 8vo, cloth extra,
14s. [In preparation.

Hindley (Charles), Works by:
Crown 8vo, cloth extra, 3s. 6d. each.
Tavern Anecdotes and Sayings: In-
cluding the Origin of Signs, and
Reminiscences connected with
Taverns, Coffee Houses, Clubs, &c.
With Illustrations.
The Life and Adventures of a Cheap
Jack. By One of the Fraternity.
Edited by CHARLES HINDLEY.

Hoey.—The Lover's Creed.
By Mrs. CASHEL HOEY. With 12 Illustrations by P. MACNAB. Three Vols.,
crown 8vo. [Shortly.

Holmes (O. Wendell), Works by:
The Autocrat of the Breakfast-
Table. Illustrated by J. GORDON
THOMSON. Post 8vo, cloth limp,
2s. 6d.; another Edition in smaller
type, with an Introduction by G. A.
SALA. Post 8vo, cloth limp, 2s.
The Professor at the Breakfast-
Table; with the Story of Iris. Post
8vo, cloth limp, 2s.

Holmes. — The Science of
Voice Production and Voice Preser-
vation: A Popular Manual for the
Use of Speakers and Singers. By
GORDON HOLMES, M.D. Crown 8vo,
cloth limp, with Illustrations, 2s. 6d.

Hood (Thomas):
Hood's Choice Works, in Prose and
Verse. Including the Cream of the
Comic Annuals. With Life of the
Author, Portrait, and 200 Illustra-
tions. Crown 8vo, cloth extra, 7s. 6d.
Hood's Whims and Oddities. Com-
plete. With all the original Illus-
trations. Post 8vo, cloth limp, 2s.

Hood (Tom), Works by:
From Nowhere to the North Pole:
A Noah's Arkæological Narrative.
With 25 Illustrations by W. BRUN-
TON and E. C. BARNES. Square
crown 8vo, cloth extra, gilt edges, 6s.
A Golden Heart: A Novel. Post 8vo,
illustrated boards, 2s.

Hook's (Theodore) Choice Hu-
morous Works, including his Ludi-
crous Adventures, Bons Mots, Puns and
Hoaxes. With a New Life of the
Author, Portraits, Facsimiles, and
Illusts. Cr. 8vo, cl. extra, gilt, 7s. 6d.

Hooper.—The House of Raby :
A Novel. By Mrs. GEORGE HOOPER.
Post 8vo, illustrated boards, 2s.

Horne.—Orion : An Epic Poem,
in Three Books. By RICHARD HEN-
GIST HORNE. With Photographic
Portrait from a Medallion by SUM-
MERS. Tenth Edition, crown 8vo,
cloth extra, 7s.

Howell.—Conflicts of Capital
and Labour, Historically and Eco-
nomically considered : Being a History and Review of the Trade Unions
of Great Britain, showing their origin,
Progress, Constitution, and Objects, in
their Political, Social, Economical,
and Industrial Aspects. By GEORGE
HOWELL. Cr. 8vo, cloth extra, 7s. 6d.

Hugo. — The Hunchback of
Notre Dame. By VICTOR HUGO.
Post 8vo, illustrated boards, 2s.

Hunt.—Essays by Leigh Hunt.
A Tale for a Chimney Corner, and
other Pieces. With Portrait and Introduction by EDMUND OLLIER. Post
8vo, cloth limp, 2s.

Hunt (Mrs. Alfred), Novels by :
Crown 8vo, cloth extra, 3s. 6d. each ;
post 8vo, illustrated boards, 2s. each.
    Thornicroft's Model.
    The Leaden Casket.
    Self-Condemned.

Ingelow.—Fated to be Free : A
Novel. By JEAN INGELOW. Crown
8vo, cloth extra, 3s. 6d. ; post 8vo,
illustrated boards, 2s.

Irish Wit and Humour, Songs
of. Collected and Edited by A. PERCE-
VAL GRAVES. Post 8vo, cl. limp, 2s. 6d.

Irving (Washington), Works by :
Post 8vo, cloth limp, 2s. each.
    Tales of a Traveller.
    Tales of the Alhambra.

Janvier.—Practical Keramics
for Students. By CATHERINE A.
JANVIER. Crown 8vo, cloth extra, 6s.

Jay (Harriett), Novels by. Each
crown 8vo, cloth extra, 3s. 6d. ; or post
8vo, illustrated boards, 2s.
    The Dark Colleen.
    The Queen of Connaught.

Jefferies (Richard), Works by :
Nature near London. Crown 8vo,
cloth extra, 6s.
The Life of the Fields. Crown 8vo,
cloth extra, 6s.

Jennings (H. J.), Works by :
Curiosities of Criticism. Post 8vo,
cloth limp, 2s. 6d.
Lord Tennyson: A Biographical
Sketch. Crown 8vo, cloth extra, 6s.
[In the press.

Jennings (Hargrave). — The
Rosicrucians: Their Rites and Mysteries. With Chapters on the Ancient
Fire and Serpent Worshippers. By
HARGRAVE JENNINGS. With Five full-
page Plates and upwards of 300 Illustrations. A New Edition, crown 8vo,
cloth extra, 7s. 6d.

Jerrold (Tom), Works by :
The Garden that Paid the Rent.
By TOM JERROLD. Fcap. 8vo, illus-
trated cover, 1s. ; cloth limp, 1s. 6d.
Household Horticulture: A Gossip
about Flowers. By TOM and JANE
JERROLD. Illust. Post 8vo,cl.lp.,2s.6d.
Our Kitchen Garden: The Plants
we Grow, and How we Cook Them.
By TOM JERROLD. Post 8vo, cloth
limp, 2s. 6d.

Jesse.—Scenes and Occupa-
tions of a Country Life. By EDWARD
JESSE. Post 8vo, cloth limp, 2s.

Jones (Wm., F.S.A.), Works by :
Finger-Ring Lore: Historical, Legendary, and Anecdotal. With over
200 Illusts. Cr. 8vo, cl. extra, 7s. 6d.
Credulities, Past and Present; including the Sea and Seamen, Miners,
Talismans, Word and Letter Divina-
tion, Exorcising and Blessing of
Animals, Birds, Eggs, Luck, &c.
With an Etched Frontispiece. Crown
8vo, cloth extra, 7s. 6d.
Crowns and Coronations: A History
of Regalia in all Times and Countries. With One Hundred Illustrations. Cr. 8vo, cloth extra, 7s. 6d.

Jonson's (Ben) Works. With
Notes Critical and Explanatory, and
a Biographical Memoir by WILLIAM
GIFFORD. Edited by Colonel CUN-
NINGHAM. Three Vols., crown 8vo,
cloth extra, 18s.; or separately, 6s. each.

Josephus, The Complete Works
of. Translated by WHISTON. Containing both "The Antiquities of the
Jews" and "The Wars of the Jews."
Two Vols., 8vo, with 52 Illustrations
and Maps, cloth extra, gilt, 14s.

Kavanagh.—The Pearl Foun-tain, and other Fairy Stories. By BRIDGET and JULIA KAVANAGH. With Thirty Illustrations by J. MOYR SMITH. Small 8vo, cloth gilt, 6s.

Kempt.—Pencil and Palette: Chapters on Art and Artists. By ROBERT KEMPT. Post 8vo, cloth limp, 2s. 6d.

Kingsley (Henry), Novels by: Each crown 8vo, cloth extra, 3s. 6d.; or post 8vo, illustrated boards, 2s.

Oakshott Castle. | Number Seventeen

Knight.—The Patient's Vade Mecum: How to get most Benefit from Medical Advice. By WILLIAM KNIGHT, M.R.C.S., and EDWARD KNIGHT, L.R.C.P. Crown 8vo, 1s.; cloth, 1s. 6d.

Lamb (Charles):

Mary and Charles Lamb: Their Poems, Letters, and Remains. With Reminiscences and Notes by W. CAREW HAZLITT. With HANCOCK'S Portrait of the Essayist, Facsimiles of the Title-pages of the rare First Editions of Lamb's and Coleridge's Works, and numerous Illustrations. Crown 8vo, cloth extra, 10s. 6d.

Lamb's Complete Works, in Prose and Verse, reprinted from the Original Editions, with many Pieces hitherto unpublished. Edited, with Notes and Introduction, by R. H. SHEPHERD. With Two Portraits and Facsimile of Page of the "Essay on Roast Pig." Cr. 8vo, cloth extra, 7s. 6d.

The Essays of Elia. Complete Edition. Post 8vo, cloth extra, 2s.

Poetry for Children, and Prince Dorus. By CHARLES LAMB. Carefully reprinted from unique copies. Small 8vo, cloth extra, 5s.

Little Essays: Sketches and Characters. By CHARLES LAMB. Selected from his Letters by PERCY FITZGERALD. Post 8vo, cloth limp, 2s. 6d.

Lane's Arabian Nights, &c.:

The Thousand and One Nights: commonly called, in England, "THE ARABIAN NIGHTS' ENTERTAINMENTS." A New Translation from the Arabic, with copious Notes, by EDWARD WILLIAM LANE. Illustrated by many hundred Engravings on Wood, from Original Designs by WM. HARVEY. A New Edition, from a Copy annotated by the Translator, edited by his Nephew, EDWARD STANLEY POOLE. With a Preface by STANLEY LANE-POOLE. Three Vols., demy 8vo, cloth extra, 7s. 6d. each.

LANE'S ARABIAN NIGHTS, *continued*

Arabian Society in the Middle Ag Studies from "The Thousand One Nights." By EDWARD WILL LANE, Author of "The Mod Egyptians," &c. Edited by STAN LANE-POOLE. Cr. 8vo, cloth extra

Lare
Bacl
CAD:

Larwood (Jacob), Works by

The Story of the London Pa With Illustrations. Crown 8vo, c extra, 3s. 6d.

Clerical Anecdotes. Post 8vo, c limp, 2s. 6d.

Forensic Anecdotes Post 8vo, c limp, 2s. 6d.

Theatrical Anecdotes. Post 8vo, c limp, 2s. 6d.

Leigh (Henry S.), Works by

Carols of Cockayne. With numer Illustrations. Post 8vo, cloth li 2s. 6d.

Jeux d'Esprit. Collected and Ed by HENRY S. LEIGH. Post 8vo, c limp, 2s. 6d.

Life in London; or, The Hist of Jerry Hawthorn and Corinth Tom. With the whole of CR shank's Illustrations, in Colours, a the Originals. Crown 8vo, cloth ex 7s. 6d.

Linton (E. Lynn), Works by

Post 8vo, cloth limp, 2s. 6d. each

Witch Stories.

The True Story of Joshua Davids

Ourselves: Essays on Women.

Crown 8vo, cloth extra, 3s. 6d. each; 8vo, illustrated boards, 2s. each.

Patricia Kemball.

The Atonement of Leam Dund

The World Well Lost.

Under which Lord?

With a Silken Thread.

The Rebel of the Family.

"My Love!"

Ione.

Locks and Keys.—On the velopment and Distribution of Pri tive Locks and Keys. By Lieut.-G PITT-RIVERS, F.R.S. With numer Illustrations. Demy 4to, half R burghe, 16s.

Longfellow:

Longfellow's Complete Prose Works. Including "Outre Mer," "Hyperion," "Kavanagh," "The Poets and Poetry of Europe," and "Driftwood." With Portrait and Illustrations by VALENTINE BROMLEY. Crown 8vo, cloth extra, 7s. 6d.

Longfellow's Poetical Works. Carefully Reprinted from the Original Editions. With numerous fine Illustrations on Steel and Wood. Crown 8vo, cloth extra, 7s. 6d.

Long Life, Aids to: A Medical,
Dietetic, and General Guide in Health and Disease. By N. E. DAVIES, L.R.C.P. Crown 8vo, 2s ; cloth limp, 2s. 6d. [*Shortly.*

Lucy.—Gideon Fleyce: A Novel.
By HENRY W. LUCY. Crown 8vo, cl. extra, 3s. 6d.; post 8vo, illust. bds.,2s.

Lusiad (The) of Camoens.
Translated into English Spenserian Verse by ROBERT FFRENCH DUFF. Demy 8vo, with Fourteen full-page Plates, cloth boards, 18s.

McCarthy (Justin, M.P.),Works
by :

A History of Our Own Times, from the Accession of Queen Victoria to the General Election of 1880. Four Vols. demy 8vo, cloth extra, 12s. each.—Also a POPULAR EDITION, in Four Vols. cr. 8vo, cl. extra, 6s. each.

A Short History of Our Own Times. One Vol., crown 8vo, cloth extra, 6s.

History of the Four Georges. Four Vols. demy 8vo, cloth extra, 12s. each. [Vol. I. *in the press.*

Crown 8vo, cloth extra, 3s. 6d. each ; post 8vo, illustrated boards, 2s. each.

Dear Lady Disdain.
The Waterdale Neighbours.
My Enemy's Daughter.
A Fair Saxon.
Linley Rochford
Miss Misanthrope.
Donna Quixote.
The Comet of a Season.

Maid of Athens. With 12 Illustrations by F. BARNARD. Crown 8vo, cloth extra, 3s. 6d.

McCarthy (Justin. H.; M.P.),
Works by :

Serapion, and other Poems. Crown 8vo, cloth extra, 6s.

An Outline of the History of Ireland, from the Earliest Times to the Present Day. Cr. 8vo, 1s. ; cloth, 1s. 6d.

England under Gladstone. Crown 8vo, cloth extra, 6s.

MacDonald (George, LL.D.),
Works by :

The Princess and Curdie. With 11 Illustrations by JAMES ALLEN. Small crown 8vo, cloth extra, 5s.

Gutta-Percha Willie, the Working Genius. With 9 Illustrations by ARTHUR HUGHES. Square 8vo, cloth extra, 3s. 6d.

Paul Faber, Surgeon. With a Frontispiece by J. E. MILLAIS. Crown 8vo, cloth extra, 3s. 6d.; post 8vo, illustrated boards, 2s.

Thomas Wingfold, Curate. With a Frontispiece by C. J. STANILAND. Crown 8vo, cloth extra, 3s. 6d.; post 8vo, illustrated boards, 2s.

Macdonell.—Quaker Cousins:
A Novel. By AGNES MACDONELL. Crown 8vo, cloth extra, 3s. 6d.; post 8vo, illustrated boards, 2s.

Macgregor. — Pastimes and
Players. Notes on Popular Games. By ROBERT MACGREGOR. Post 8vo, cloth limp, 2s. 6d.

Maclise Portrait-Gallery (The)
of Illustrious Literary Characters; with Memoirs—Biographical, Critical, Bibliographical, and Anecdotal—illustrative of the Literature of the former half of the Present Century. By WILLIAM BATES, B.A. With 85 Portraits printed on an India Tint. Crown 8vo, cloth extra, 7s. 6d.

Macquoid (Mrs.), Works by :

In the Ardennes. With 50 fine Illustrations by THOMAS R. MACQUOID. Square 8vo, cloth extra, 10s. 6d.

Pictures and Legends from Normandy and Brittany. With numerous Illustrations by THOMAS R. MACQUOID. Square 8vo, cloth gilt, 10s. 6d.

Through Normandy. With 90 Illustrations by T. R. MACQUOID. Square 8vo, cloth extra, 7s. 6d.

Through Brittany. With numerous Illustrations by T. R. MACQUOID. Square 8vo, cloth extra, 7s. 6d.

About Yorkshire With 67 Illustrations by T. R. MACQUOID, Engraved by SWAIN. Square 8vo, cloth extra, 10s. 6d.

The Evil Eye, and other Stories. Crown 8vo, cloth extra, 3s. 6d.; post 8vo, illustrated boards, 2s.

Lost Rose, and other Stories. Crown 8vo, cloth extra, 3s. 6d. ; post 8vo, illustrated boards, 2s.

Mackay.—Interludes and Un-
dertones: or, Music at Twilight. By
CHARLES MACKAY, LL.D. Crown 8vo,
cloth extra, 6s.

Magician's Own Book (The):
Performances with Cups and Balls,
Eggs, Hats, Handkerchiefs, &c. All
from actual Experience. Edited by
W. H. CREMER. With 200 Illustrations.
Crown 8vo, cloth extra, 4s. 6d.

Magic No Mystery: Tricks with
Cards, Dice, Balls, &c., with fully
descriptive Directions; the Art of
Secret Writing; Training of Perform-
ing Animals, &c. With Coloured
Frontispiece and many Illustrations.
Crown 8vo, cloth extra, 4s. 6d.

Magna Charta. An exact Facsimile of the Original in the British
Museum, printed on fine plate paper,
3 feet by 2 feet, with Arms and Seals
emblazoned in Gold and Colours.
Price 5s.

Mallock (W. H.), Works by:
The New Republic; or, Culture, Faith
and Philosophy in an English Country
House. Post 8vo, cloth limp, 2s. 6d. ;
Cheap Edition, illustrated boards, 2s.
The New Paul and Virginia; or, Posi-
tivism on an Island. Post 8vo, cloth
limp, 2s. 6d.
Poems. Small 4to, bound in parch-
ment, 8s.
Is Life worth Living? Crown 8vo,
cloth extra, 6s.

Mallory's (Sir Thomas) Mort
d'Arthur: The Stories of King Arthur
and of the Knights of the Round Table.
Edited by B. MONTGOMERIE RANKING.
Post 8vo, cloth limp, 2s.

Marlowe's Works. Including
his Translations. Edited, with Notes
and Introduction, by Col. CUNNING-
HAM. Crown 8vo, cloth extra, 6s.

Marryat (Florence), Novels by:
Crown 8vo, cloth extra, 3s. 6d. each ; or,
post 8vo, illustrated boards, 2s.
Open! Sesame!
Written in Fire.

Post 8vo, illustrated boards, 2s. each.
A Harvest of Wild Oats.
A Little Stepson.
Fighting the Air.

Masterman.—Half a Dozen
Daughters: A Novel. By J. MASTER-

Mark Twain, Works by:
The Choice Works of Mark Tw
Revised and Corrected throughou
the Author. With Life, Portrait,
numerous Illustrations. Crown 8
cloth extra, 7s. 6d.
The Adventures of Tom Sawy
Post 8vo, illustrated boards, 2s.
An Idle Excursion, and other Sketch
Post 8vo, illustrated boards, 2s.
The Prince and the Pauper. W
nearly 200 Illustrations. Crown 8
cloth extra, 7s. 6d.
The Innocents Abroad ; or, The N
Pilgrim's Progress: Being some
count of the Steamship " Qua
City's " Pleasure Excursion
Europe and the Holy Land. W
234 Illustrations. Crown 8vo, cl
extra, 7s. 6d. CHEAP EDITION (un
the title of " MARK TWAIN'S PLEASU
TRIP "), post 8vo, illust. boards, 2
A Tramp Abroad. With 314 Illust
tions. Crown 8vo, cloth extra, 7s. 6
Post 8vo, illustrated boards, 2s.
The Stolen White Elephant,
Crown 8vo, cloth extra, 6s. ; post 8
illustrated boards, 2s.
Life on the Mississippi. With ab
300 Original Illustrations. Cro
8vo, cloth extra, 7s. 6d.
The Adventures of Huckleber
Finn. With numerous Illusts.
8vo, cloth extra, 7s. 6d. [Prepari

Mayhew.—London Characte
and the Humorous Side of Lond
Life. By HENRY MAYHEW. W
numerous Illustrations. Crown 8
cloth extra, 3s. 6d.

Mayfair Library, The :
Post 8vo, cloth limp, 2s. 6d. per Volu
A Journey Round My Room.
XAVIER DE MAISTRE. Transla
by HENRY ATTWELL.
Latter-Day Lyrics. Edited by
DAVENPORT ADAMS.
Quips and Quiddities. Selected
W. DAVENPORT ADAMS.
The Agony Column of "The Time
from 1800 to 1870. Edited, with
Introduction, by ALICE CLAY.
Balzac's "Comedie Humaine" a
its Author. With Translations
H. H. WALKER.
Melancholy Anatomised: A Popul
Abridgment of "Burton's Anaton

MAYFAIR LIBRARY, *continued—*

Gastronomy as a Fine Art. By BRILLAT-SAVARIN.

The Speeches of Charles Dickens.

Literary Frivolities, Fancies, Follies, and Frolics. By W. T. DOBSON.

Poetical Ingenuities and Eccentricities. Selected and Edited by W. T. DOBSON.

The Cupboard Papers. By FIN-BEC.

Original Plays by W. S. GILBERT. FIRST SERIES. Containing: The Wicked World — Pygmalion and Galatea—Charity — The Princess—The Palace of Truth—Trial by Jury.

Original Plays by W. S. GILBERT. SECOND SERIES. Containing: Broken Hearts — Engaged — Sweethearts—Gretchen—Dan'l Druce—Tom Cobb —H.M.S. Pinafore — The Sorcerer —The Pirates of Penzance.

Songs of Irish Wit and Humour. Collected and Edited by A. PERCEVAL GRAVES.

Animals and their Masters. By Sir ARTHUR HELPS.

Social Pressure. By Sir A. HELPS.

Curiosities of Criticism. By HENRY J. JENNINGS.

The Autocrat of the Breakfast-Table. By OLIVER WENDELL HOLMES. Illustrated by J. GORDON THOMSON.

Pencil and Palette. By ROBERT KEMPT.

Little Essays : Sketches and Characters. By CHAS. LAMB. Selected from his Letters by PERCY FITZGERALD.

Clerical Anecdotes. By JACOB LARWOOD.

Forensic Anecdotes; or, Humour and Curiosities of the Law and Men of Law. By JACOB LARWOOD.

Theatrical Anecdotes. By JACOB LARWOOD.

Carols of Cockayne. By HENRY S. LEIGH.

Jeux d'Esprit. Edited by HENRY S. LEIGH.

True History of Joshua Davidson. By E. LYNN LINTON.

Witch Stories. By E. LYNN LINTON.

Ourselves: Essays on Women. By E. LYNN LINTON.

Pastimes and Players. By ROBERT MACGREGOR.

The New Paul and Virginia. By W. H. MALLOCK.

The New Republic. By W. H. MALLOCK.

Puck on Pegasus. By H. CHOLMONDELEY-PENNELL.

MAYFAIR LIBRARY, *continued—*

Pegasus Re-Saddled. By H. CHOLMONDELEY-PENNELL. Illustrated by GEORGE DU MAURIER.

Muses of Mayfair. Edited by H. CHOLMONDELEY-PENNELL.

Thoreau: His Life and Aims. By H. A. PAGE.

Puniana. By the Hon. HUGH ROWLEY.

More Puniana. By the Hon. HUGH ROWLEY.

The Philosophy of Handwriting. By DON FELIX DE SALAMANCA.

By Stream and Sea. By WILLIAM SENIOR.

Old Stories Re-told. By WALTER THORNBURY.

Leaves from a Naturalist's Note-Book. By Dr. ANDREW WILSON.

Medicine, Family.—One Thousand Medical Maxims and Surgical Hints, for Infancy, Adult Life, Middle Age, and Old Age. By N. E. DAVIES, L.R.C.P. Lond. Cr. 8vo, 1s.; cl., 1s. 6d.

Merry Circle (The) : A Book of New Intellectual Games and Amusements. By CLARA BELLEW. With numerous Illustrations. Crown 8vo, cloth extra, 4s. 6d.

Mexican Mustang (On a). Through Texas, from the Gulf to the Rio Grande. A New Book of American Humour. By ALEX. E. SWEET and J. ARMOY KNOX, Editors of "Texas Siftings." 400 Illusts. Cr. 8vo, cloth extra, 7s. 6d.

Middlemass (Jean), Novels by:
Touch and Go. Crown 8vo, cloth extra, 3s.6d.; post 8vo, illust. bds., 2s.
Mr. Dorillion. Post 8vo, illust. bds., 2s.

Miller. — Physiology for the Young; or, The House of Life: Human Physiology, with its application to the Preservation of Health. For use in Classes and Popular Reading. With numerous Illustrations. By Mrs. F. FENWICK MILLER. Small 8vo, cloth limp, 2s. 6d.

Milton (J. L.), Works by:
The Hygiene of the Skin. A Concise Set of Rules for the Management of the Skin; with Directions for Diet, Wines, Soaps, Baths, &c. Small 8vo, 1s. ; cloth extra, 1s. 6d.
The Bath in Diseases of the Skin. Small 8vo, 1s. ; cloth extra, 1s. 6d.
The Laws of Life, and their Relation to Diseases of the Skin. Small 8vo, 1s. ; cloth extra, 1s. 6d.

Moncrieff. — The Abdication;
or, Time Tries All. An Historical Drama. By W. D. SCOTT-MONCRIEFF. With Seven Etchings by JOHN PETTIE, R.A., W. Q. ORCHARDSON, R.A., J. MACWHIRTER, A.R.A., COLIN HUNTER, R. MACBETH, and TOM GRAHAM. Large 4to, bound in buckram, 21s.

Murray (D. Christie), Novels
by. Crown 8vo, cloth extra, 3s. 6d. each; post 8vo, illustrated boards, 2s. each.
A Life's Atonement.
A Model Father.
Joseph's Coat.
Coals of Fire.
By the Gate of the Sea.

Crown 8vo, cloth extra, 3s. 6d. each.
Val Strange: A Story of the Primrose Way.
Hearts.
The Way of the World.

North Italian Folk. By Mrs.
COMYNS CARR. Illust. by RANDOLPH CALDECOTT. Square 8vo, cloth extra, 7s. 6d.

Number Nip (Stories about),
the Spirit of the Giant Mountains. Retold for Children by WALTER GRAHAME. With Illustrations by J. MOYR SMITH. Post 8vo, cloth extra, 5s.

Nursery Hints: A Mother's Guide in Health and Disease. By N. E. DAVIES, L.R.C.P. Crown 8vo, 1s.; cloth, 1s. 6d.

Oliphant. — Whiteladies: A Novel. With Illustrations by ARTHUR HOPKINS and HENRY WOODS. Crown 8vo, cloth extra, 3s. 6d.; post 8vo, illustrated boards, 2s.

O'Connor.—Lord Beaconsfield
A Biography. By T. P. O'CONNOR, M.P. Sixth Edition, with a New Preface, bringing the book down to the Death of Lord Beaconsfield. Crown 8vo, cloth extra, 7s. 6d.

O'Reilly.—Phœbe's Fortunes:
A Novel. With Illustrations by HENRY TUCK. Post 8vo, illustrated boards, 2s.

O'Shaughnessy (Arth.), Works
by:
Songs of a Worker. Fcap. 8vo, cloth extra, 7s. 6d.
Music and Moonlight. Fcap. 8vo, cloth extra, 7s. 6d.
Lays of France. Crown 8vo, cloth

Ouida, Novels by. Crown 8
cloth extra, 5s. each; post 8vo, ill trated boards, 2s. each.

Held in Bondage.	A Dog of Flande
Strathmore.	Pascarel.
Chandos.	Signa.
Under Two Flags.	In a Winter Cl
Cecil Castle-maine's Gage.	Ariadne.
Idalia.	Friendship.
Tricotrin.	Moths.
Puck.	Pipistrello.
Folle Farine.	A Village Co mune.
TwoLittleWooden Shoes.	Bimbi.
	In Maremma.

Wanda: A Novel. Crown 8vo, cl extra, 5s.

Frescoes: Dramatic Sketches. Cro 8vo, cloth extra, 5s.   [Shor

Bimbi: PRESENTATION EDITION. 8vo, cloth gilt, cinnamon edg 7s. 6d.

Princess Napraxine. Three Vo crown 8vo.

Wisdom, Wit, and Pathos. Selec from the Works of OUIDA by SYDNEY MORRIS. Small crown 8 cloth extra, 5s.

Page (H. A.), Works by:
Thoreau: His Life and Aims: A Stu With a Portrait. Post 8vo, cl limp, 2s. 6d.
Lights on the Way: Some Tales w: in a Tale. By the late J. H. AL ANDER, B.A. Edited by H. A. PA Crown 8vo, cloth extra, 6s.

Pascal's Provincial Letters.
New Translation, with Historical troduction and Notes, by T. M'CF D.D. Post 8vo, cloth limp, 2s.

Patient's (The) Vade Mecu
How to get most Benefit from Me cal Advice. By WILLIAM KNIG M.R.C.S., and EDWARD KNIG L.R.C.P. Crown 8vo, 1s.; cloth, 1s.

Paul Ferroll:
Post 8vo, illustrated boards, 2s. ea
Paul Ferroll: A Novel.
Why Paul Ferroll Killed his Wif

nd Simple.
PAUL. With
HELEN PATERS
, 3s. 6d.; post 8

ayn (James), Novels by.
Crown 8vo, cloth extra, 3s. 6d. each;
post 8vo, illustrated boards, 2s. each.

Lost Sir Massingberd.
The Best of Husbands.
Walter's Word.
Halves. | Fallen Fortunes.
What He Cost Her.
Less Black than we're Painted.
By Proxy. | High Spirits.
Under One Roof. | Carlyon's Year.
A Confidential Agent.
Some Private Views.
A Grape from a Thorn.
For Cash Only. | From Exile.

Post 8vo, illustrated boards, 2s. each.

A Perfect Treasure.
Bentinck's Tutor.
Murphy's Master.
A County Family. | At Her Mercy.
A Woman's Vengeance.
Cecil's Tryst.
The Clyffards of Clyffe.
The Family Scapegrace
The Foster Brothers.
Found Dead.
Gwendoline's Harvest.
Humorous Stories.
Like Father, Like Son.
A Marine Residence.
Married Beneath Him.
Mirk Abbey.
Not Wooed, but Won.
Two Hundred Pounds Reward.

Kit: A Memory. Crown 8vo, cloth
extra, 3s. 6d.
The Canon's Ward. With Portrait
of Author. Cr. 8vo, cloth extra, 3s. 6d.
In Peril and Privation: A Book for
Boys. With numerous Illustra-
tions. Crown 8vo, cloth extra, 6s.
[In preparation.

ennell (H. Cholmondeley),
Works by: Post 8vo, cloth limp,
2s. 6d. each.
Puck on Pegasus. With Illustrations.
The Muses of Mayfair. Vers de
Société, Selected and Edited by H.
C. Pennell.
Pegasus Re-Saddled. With Ten full-
page Illusts. by G. Du Maurier.

helps.—Beyond the Gates.
By Elizabeth Stuart Phelps,
Author of "The Gates Ajar." Crown
8vo, cloth extra, 2s. 6d.

Pirkis.—Trooping with Crows:
A Story. By Catherine Pirkis. Fcap.
8vo, picture cover, 1s.

Planche (J. R.), Works by:
The Cyclopædia of Costume; or,
A Dictionary of Dress—Regal, Ecclesiastical, Civil, and Military—from
the Earliest Period in England to the
Reign of George the Third. Including Notices of Contemporaneous
Fashions on the Continent, and a
General History of the Costumes of
the Principal Countries of Europe.
Two Vols., demy 4to, half morocco,
profusely Illustrated with Coloured
and Plain Plates and Woodcuts,
£7 7s. The Vols. may also be had
separately (each complete in itself)
at £3 13s. 6d. each: Vol. I. The
Dictionary. Vol. II. A General
History of Costume in Europe.
The Pursuivant of Arms; or, Her-
aldry Founded upon Facts. With
Coloured Frontispiece and 200 Illus-
trations. Cr. 8vo, cloth extra, 7s. 6d.
Songs and Poems, from 1819 to 1879.
Edited, with an Introduction, by his
Daughter, Mrs. Mackarness. Crown
8vo, cloth extra, 6s.

Play-time: Sayings and Doings
of Baby-land. By Edward Stanford.
Large 4to, handsomely printed in
Colours, 5s.

Plutarch's Lives of Illustrious
Men. Translated from the Greek,
with Notes Critical and Historical, and
a Life of Plutarch, by John and
William Langhorne. Two Vols.,
8vo, cloth extra, with Portraits, 10s. 6d.

Poe (Edgar Allan):—
The Choice Works, in Prose and
Poetry, of Edgar Allan Poe. With
an Introductory Essay by Charles
Baudelaire, Portrait and Fac-
similes. Crown 8vo, cl. extra, 7s. 6d.
The Mystery of Marie Roget, and
other Stories. Post 8vo, illust. bds., 2s.

Pope's Poetical Works. Com-
plete in One Vol. Post 8vo, cl. limp, 2s.

Power.—Philistia: A Novel. By
Cecil Power. Three Vols., crown
8vo.   [Shortly.

Price (E. C.), Novels by:
Valentina: A Sketch. With a Frontispiece by Hal Ludlow. Cr. 8vo,
cl. ex., 3s. 6d.; post 8vo, illust. bds., 2s.
The Foreigners. Crown 8vo, cloth
extra, 3s. 6d.

Proctor (Richd. A.), Works by ;

Flowers of the Sky. With 55 Illusts. Small crown 8vo, cloth extra, 4s. 6d.

Easy Star Lessons. With Star Maps for Every Night in the Year, Drawings of the Constellations, &c. Crown 8vo, cloth extra, 6s.

Familiar Science Studies. Crown 8vo, cloth extra, 7s. 6d.

Rough Ways made Smooth: A Series of Familiar Essays on Scientific Subjects. Cr. 8vo, cloth extra, 6s.

Our Place among Infinities: A Series of Essays contrasting our Little Abode in Space and Time with the Infinities Around us. Crown 8vo, cloth extra, 6s.

The Expanse of Heaven: A Series of Essays on the Wonders of the Firmament. Cr. 8vo, cloth extra, 6s.

Saturn and Its System. New and Revised Edition, with 13 Steel Plates. Demy 8vo, cloth extra, 10s. 6d.

The Great Pyramid: Observatory, Tomb, and Temple. With Illustrations. Crown 8vo, cloth extra, 6s.

Mysteries of Time and Space. With Illusts. Cr. 8vo, cloth extra, 7s. 6d.

The Universe of Suns, and other Science Gleanings. With Illusts. Cr. 8vo, cloth extra, 7s. 6d. [*Shortly.*

Wages and Wants of Science Workers. Crown 8vo, 1s. 6d.

Pyrotechnist's Treasury (The);

or, Complete Art of Making Fireworks. By THOMAS KENTISH. With numerous Illustrations. Cr. 8vo, cl. extra, 4s. 6d.

Rabelais' Works. Faithfully

Translated from the French, with variorum Notes, and numerous characteristic Illustrations by GUSTAVE DORÉ. Crown 8vo, cloth extra, 7s. 6d.

Rambosson.—Popular Astro-

nomy. By J. RAMBOSSON, Laureate of the Institute of France. Translated by C. B. PITMAN. Crown 8vo, cloth gilt, with numerous Illustrations, and a beautifully executed Chart of Spectra, 7s. 6d.

Reader's Handbook (The) of

Allusions, References, Plots, and Stories. By the Rev. Dr. BREWER. Fourth Edition, revised throughout, with a New Appendix, containing a COMPLETE ENGLISH BIBLIOGRAPHY. Cr. 8vo, 1,400 pages, cloth extra, 7s. 6d.

Richardson. — A Ministry of

Health, and other Papers. By BENJAMIN WARD RICHARDSON, M.D., &c.

Reade (Charles, D.C.L.), Novel

by. Post 8vo, illustrated boards, 2 each ; or crown 8vo, cloth extra, l lustrated, 3s. 6d. each.

Peg Woffington. Illustrated by S. FILDES, A.R.A.

Christie Johnstone. Illustrated b WILLIAM SMALL.

It Is Never Too Late to Mend. I lustrated by G. J. PINWELL.

The Course of True Love Never di run Smooth. Illustrated by HELE PATERSON.

The Autobiography of a Thief; Jac of all Trades; and James Lamber Illustrated by MATT STRETCH.

Love me Little, Love me Long. I lustrated by M. ELLEN EDWARDS.

The Double Marriage. Illust. by S JOHN GILBERT, R.A., and C. KEEN

The Cloister and the Hearth. I lustrated by CHARLES KEENE.

Hard Cash. Illust. by F. W. LAWSO

Griffith Gaunt. Illustrated by S. FILDES, A.R.A., and WM. SMALL.

Foul Play. Illust. by DU MAURIER

Put Yourself In His Place. Illu trated by ROBERT BARNES.

A Terrible Temptation. Illustrate by EDW. HUGHES and A. W. COOPE

The Wandering Heir. Illustrate by HELEN PATERSON, S. L. FILDE A.R.A., CHARLES GREEN, and HENR WOODS, A.R.A.

A Simpleton. Illustrated by KAT CRAUFORD.

A Woman-Hater. Illustrated b THOS. COULDERY.

Readiana. With a Steel-plate Portra of CHARLES READE.

Singleheart and Doubleface: Matter-of-fact Romance.

Good Stories of Men and othe Animals.

The Jilt, and other Stories.

Riddell (Mrs. J. H.), Novels by

Crown 8vo, cloth extra, 3s. 6d. each post 8vo, illustrated boards, 2s. eac

Her Mother's Darling.

The Prince of Wales's Garden Part

Rimmer (Alfred), Works by :

Our Old Country Towns. With ove 50 Illusts. Sq. 8vo, cloth gilt, 10s. 6

Rambles Round Eton and Harro 50 Illusts. Sq. 8vo, cloth gilt, 10s. 6

About England with Dickens. Wit 58 Illustrations by ALFRED RIMME and C. A. VANDERHOOF. Square 8v

Robinson (F. W.), Novels by:

Women are Strange. Cr. 8vo, cloth extra, 3s. 6d.; post 8vo, illust. bds., 2s.

The Hands of Justice. Crown 8vo, cloth extra, 3s. 6d.

Robinson (Phil), Works by:

The Poets' Birds. Crown 8vo, cloth extra, 7s. 6d.

The Poets' Beasts. Crown 8vo, cloth extra, 7s. 6d. [*In preparation.*]

Robinson Crusoe: A beautiful reproduction of Major's Edition, with 37 Woodcuts and Two Steel Plates by GEORGE CRUIKSHANK, choicely printed. Crown 8vo, cloth extra, 7s. 6d. A few Large-Paper copies, printed on hand-made paper, with India proofs of the Illustrations, price 36s.

Rochefoucauld's Maxims and Moral Reflections. With Notes, and an Introductory Essay by SAINTE-BEUVE. Post 8vo, cloth limp, 2s.

Roll of Battle Abbey, The; or, A List of the Principal Warriors who came over from Normandy with William the Conqueror, and Settled in this Country, A.D. 1066-7. With the principal Arms emblazoned in Gold and Colours. Handsomely printed, price 5s.

Rowley (Hon. Hugh), Works by:

Post 8vo, cloth limp, 2s. 6d. each.

Puniana: Riddles and Jokes. With numerous Illustrations.

More Puniana. Profusely Illustrated.

Russell (Clark).—Round the Galley-Fire. By W. CLARK RUSSELL, Author of "The Wreck of the *Grosvenor.*" Cr. 8vo, cloth extra, 6s.

Sala.—Gaslight and Daylight. By GEORGE AUGUSTUS SALA. Post 8vo, illustrated boards, 2s.

Sanson.—Seven Generations of Executioners: Memoirs of the Sanson Family (1688 to 1847). Edited by HENRY SANSON. Crown 8vo, cloth extra, 3s. 6d.

Saunders (John), Novels by:

Crown 8vo, cloth extra, 3s. 6d. each; post 8vo, illustrated boards, 2s. each.

Bound to the Wheel.

One Against the World.

Guy Waterman.

The Lion in the Path.

Saunders (Katharine), Novels by:

Crown 8vo, cloth extra, 3s. 6d. each.

Joan Merryweather.

Margaret and Elizabeth.

Gideon's Rook.

The High Mills.

Heart Salvage, by Sea and Land. Three Vols., crown 8vo.

Science Gossip: An Illustrated Medium of Interchange for Students and Lovers of Nature. Edited by J. E. TAYLOR, F.L.S., &c. Devoted to Geology, Botany, Physiology, Chemistry, Zoology, Microscopy, Telescopy, Physiography, &c. Price 4d. Monthly; or 5s. per year, post free. Each Number contains a Coloured Plate and numerous Woodcuts. Vols. I. to XIV. may be had at 7s. 6d. each; and Vols. XV. to XIX. (1883), at 5s. each. Cases for Binding, 1s. 6d each.

Scott's (Sir Walter) Marmion. An entirely New Edition of this famous and popular Poem, with over 100 new Illustrations by leading Artists. Elegantly and appropriately bound, small 4to, cloth extra, 16s.

[The immediate success of "The Lady of the Lake," published in 1882, has encouraged Messrs. CHATTO and WINDUS to bring out a Companion Edition of this not less popular and famous poem. Produced in the same style, and with the same careful and elaborate style of illustration, regardless of cost, Mr. Anthony's skilful supervision is sufficient guarantee that the work is elegant and tasteful as well as correct.]

"Secret Out" Series, The: Crown 8vo, cloth extra, profusely Illustrated, 4s. 6d. each.

The Secret Out: One Thousand Tricks with Cards, and other Recreations; with Entertaining Experiments in Drawing-room or "White Magic." By W. H. CREMER. 300 Engravings.

The Pyrotechnist's Treasury; or, Complete Art of Making Fireworks. By THOMAS KENTISH. With numerous Illustrations.

The Art of Amusing: A Collection of Graceful Arts, Games, Tricks, Puzzles, and Charades. By FRANK BELLEW. With 300 Illustrations.

Hanky-Panky: Very Easy Tricks, Very Difficult Tricks, White Magic, Sleight of Hand. Edited by W. H.

"Secret Out" Series, *continued—*

The Merry Circle: A Book of New Intellectual Games and Amusements. By Clara Bellew. With many Illustrations.

Magician's Own Book: Performances with Cups and Balls, Eggs, Hats, Handkerchiefs, &c. All from actual Experience. Edited by W. H. Cremer. 200 Illustrations.

Magic No Mystery: Tricks with Cards, Dice, Balls, &c., with fully descriptive Directions; the Art of Secret Writing; Training of Performing Animals, &c. With Coloured Frontispiece and many Illustrations.

Senior (William), Works by :

Travel and Trout in the Antipodes. Crown 8vo, cloth extra, 6s.

By Stream and Sea. Post 8vo, cloth limp, 2s. 6d.

Seven Sagas (The) of Prehistoric Man. By James H. Stoddart, Author of "The Village Life." Crown 8vo, cloth extra, 6s.

Shakespeare :

The First Folio Shakespeare.—Mr. William Shakespeare's Comedies, Histories, and Tragedies. Published according to the true Originall Copies. London, Printed by Isaac Iaggard and Ed. Blount. 1623.—A Reproduction of the extremely rare original, in reduced facsimile, by a photographic process—ensuring the strictest accuracy in every detail. Small 8vo, half-Roxburghe, 7s. 6d.

The Lansdowne Shakespeare. Beautifully printed in red and black, in small but very clear type. With engraved facsimile of Droeshout's Portrait. Post 8vo, cloth extra, 7s. 6d.

Shakespeare for Children: Tales from Shakespeare. By Charles and Mary Lamb. With numerous Illustrations, coloured and plain, by J. Moyr Smith. Crown 4to, cloth gilt, 6s.

The Handbook of Shakespeare Music. Being an Account of 350 Pieces of Music, set to Words taken from the Plays and Poems of Shakespeare, the compositions ranging from the Elizabethan Age to the Present Time. By Alfred Roffe. 4to, half-Roxburghe, 7s.

A Study of Shakespeare. By Algernon Charles Swinburne. Crown 8vo, cloth extra, 8s.

Shelley's Complete Works, i Four Vols., post 8vo, cloth limp, 8s or separately, 2s. each. Vol. I. co tains his Early Poems, Queen Ma &c., with an Introduction by Leig Hunt; Vol. II., his Later Poem Laon and Cythna, &c.; Vol. III Posthumous Poems, the Shelley Paper &c.: Vol. IV., his Prose Works, i cluding A Refutation of Deism, Za trozzi, St. Irvyne, &c.

Sheridan :—

Sheridan's Complete Works, wi Life and Anecdotes. Including h Dramatic Writings, printed from tl Original Editions, his Works i Prose and Poetry, Translation Speeches, Jokes, Puns, &c. With Collection of Sheridaniana. Crow 8vo, cloth extra, gilt, with 10 ful page Tinted Illustrations, 7s. 6d.

Sheridan's Comedies: The Rival and The School for Scand Edited, with an Introduction ar Notes to each Play, and a Bi graphical Sketch of Sheridan, t Brander Matthews. With Decor tive Vignettes and 10 full-page Illu trations. Demy 8vo, cl. bds., 12s. 6

Sidney's (Sir Philip) Complet Poetical Works, including all those "Arcadia." With Portrait, Memoria Introduction, Essay on the Poetry Sidney, and Notes, by the Rev. A. Grosart, D.D. Three Vols., crov 8vo, cloth boards, 18s.

Signboards: Their Histor With Anecdotes of Famous Tavern and Remarkable Characters. I Jacob Larwood and John Camde Hotten. Crown 8vo, cloth extr with 100 Illustrations, 7s. 6d.

Slang Dictionary, The : Et mological, Historical, and Anecdota Crown 8vo, cloth extra, gilt, 6s. 6d.

Smith (J. Moyr), Works by :
The Prince of Argolis: A Story of tl Old Greek Fairy Time. By J. Moy Smith. Small 8vo, cloth extra, wi 130 Illustrations, 3s. 6d.

Smith's (J. Moyr) Works, *continued—*
Tales of Old Thule. Collected and Illustrated by J. Moyr Smith. Cr. 8vo, cloth gilt, profusely Illust., 6s.
The Wooing of the Water Witch: A Northern Oddity. By Evan Daldorne. Illustrated by J. Moyr Smith. Small 8vo, cloth extra, 6s.

Spalding.–Elizabethan Demonology: An Essay in Illustration of the Belief in the Existence of Devils, and the Powers possessed by Them. By T. Alfred Spalding, LL.B. Crown 8vo, cloth extra, 5s.

Speight. — The Mysteries of Heron Dyke. By T. W. Speight. With a Frontispiece by M. Ellen Edwards. Crown 8vo, cloth extra, 3s. 6d. ; post 8vo, illustrated boards, 2s.

Spenser for Children. By M. H. Towry. With Illustrations by Walter J. Morgan. Crown 4to, with Coloured Illustrations, cloth gilt, 6s.

Staunton.—Laws and Practice of Chess; Together with an Analysis of the Openings, and a Treatise on End Games. By Howard Staunton. Edited by Robert B. Wormald. New Edition, small cr. 8vo, cloth extra, 5s.

Sterndale.—The Afghan Knife: A Novel. By Robert Armitage Sterndale. Cr. 8vo, cloth extra, 3s. 6d.; post 8vo, illustrated boards, 2s.

Stevenson (R. Louis), Works by:
Travels with a Donkey In the Cevennes. Frontispiece by Walter Crane. Post 8vo, cloth limp, 2s. 6d.
An Inland Voyage. With Front. by W. Crane. Post 8vo, cl. lp., 2s. 6d.
Virginibus Puerisque, and other Papers. Crown 8vo, cloth extra, 6s.
Familiar Studies of Men and Books. Crown 8vo, cloth extra, 6s.
New Arabian Nights. Crown 8vo, cl. extra, 6s.; post 8vo, illust. bds., 2s.
The Silverado Squatters. With Frontispiece. Cr. 8vo, cloth extra, 6s.

St. John.—A Levantine Family. By Bayle St. John. Post 8vo, illustrated boards, 2s.

Stoddard.—Summer Cruising In the South Seas. By Charles Warren Stoddard. Illust. by Wallis Mackay. Crown 8vo, cl. extra, 3s. 6d.

St. Pierre.—Paul and Virginia, and The Indian Cottage. By Bernardin de St. Pierre. Edited, with Life, by the Rev. E. Clarke. Post 8vo, cloth limp, 2s.

Stories from Foreign Novelists. With Notices of their Lives and Writings. By Helen and Alice Zimmern; and a Frontispiece. Crown 8vo cloth extra, 3s. 6d.

Strutt's Sports and Pastimes of the People of England; including the Rural and Domestic Recreations, May Games, Mummeries, Shows, Processions, Pageants, and Pompous Spectacles, from the Earliest Period to the Present Time. With 140 Illustrations. Edited by William Hone. Crown 8vo, cloth extra, 7s. 6d.

Suburban Homes (The) of London: A Residential Guide to Favourite London Localities, their Society, Celebrities, and Associations. With Notes on their Rental, Rates, and House Accommodation. With Map of Suburban London. Cr.8vo,cl.ex.,7s.6d.

Swift's Choice Works, in Prose and Verse. With Memoir, Portrait, and Facsimiles of the Maps in the Original Edition of "Gulliver's Travels." Cr. 8vo, cloth extra, 7s. 6d.

Swinburne (Algernon C.), Works by:
The Queen Mother and Rosamond. Fcap. 8vo, 5s.
Atalanta In Calydon. Crown 8vo, 6s.
Chastelard. A Tragedy. Cr. 8vo, 7s.
Poems and Ballads. First Series. Fcap. 8vo, 9s. Also in crown 8vo, at same price.
Poems and Ballads. Second Series. Fcap. 8vo, 9s. Also in crown 8vo, at same price.
Notes on Poems and Reviews. 8vo,1s.
William Blake: A Critical Essay. With Facsimile Paintings. Demy 8vo, 16s.
Songs before Sunrise. Cr. 8vo, 10s.6d.
Bothwell: A Tragedy. Crown 8vo, 12s. 6d.
George Chapman: An Essay. Crown 8vo, 7s.
Songs of Two Nations. Cr. 8vo, 6s.
Essays and Studies. Crown 8vo, 12s.
Erechtheus: A Tragedy. Cr. 8vo, 6s.
Note of an English Republican on the Muscovite Crusade. 8vo, 1s.
A Note on Charlotte Bronte. Crown 8vo, 6s.
A Study of Shakespeare. Cr. 8vo, 8s.
Songs of the Springtides. Crown 8vo, 6s.
Studies In Song. Crown 8vo, 7s.
Mary Stuart: A Tragedy. Cr. 8vo, 8s.
Tristram of Lyonesse, and other Poems. Crown 8vo, 9s.
A Century of Roundels. Small 4to, cloth extra. 8s.

Symonds.—Wine, Women and
Song: Mediæval Latin Students'
Songs. Now first translated into English Verse, with an Essay by J. AD-
DINGTON SYMONDS. Small 8vo, parchment, 6s. A few LARGE PAPER COPIES,
carefully printed on hand-made paper,
price 21s. [*Preparing.*

Syntax's (Dr.) Three Tours:
In Search of the Picturesque, in Search
of Consolation, and in Search of a
Wife. With the whole of ROWLAND-
SON'S droll page Illustrations in Colours
and a Life of the Author by J. C.
HOTTEN. Medium 8vo, cl. extra, 7s. 6d.

Taine's History of English
Literature. Translated by HENRY
VAN LAUN. Four Vols., small 8vo,
cloth boards, 30s.—POPULAR EDITION,
Two Vols., crown 8vo, cloth extra, 15s.

Taylor (Dr. J. E., F.L.S.), Works
by:
The Sagacity and Morality of
Plants: A Sketch of the Life and
Conduct of the Vegetable Kingdom.
With Coloured Frontispiece and 100
Illusts. Crown 8vo, cl. extra, 7s. 6d.
Our Common British Fossils: A
Complete Handbook. With nu-
merous Illustrations. Crown 8vo,
cloth extra, 7s. 6d. [*Preparing.*

Taylor's (Bayard) Diversions
of the Echo Club: Burlesques of
Modern Writers. Post 8vo, cl. limp, 2s.

Taylor's (Tom) Historical
Dramas: "Clancarty," "Jeanne
Darc," "'Twixt Axe and Crown,"
"The Fool's Revenge," "Arkwright's
Wife," "Anne Boleyn," "Plot and
Passion." One Vol., crown 8vo, cloth
extra, 7s. 6d.
⁎ The Plays may also be had sepa-
rately, at 1s. each.

Tennyson (Lord): A Biogra-
phical Sketch. By H. J. JENNINGS.
Crown 8vo, cloth extra, 6s.

Thackerayana: Notes and Anec-
dotes. Illustrated by Hundreds of
Sketches by WILLIAM MAKEPEACE
THACKERAY, depicting Humorous
Incidents in his School-life, and
Favourite Characters in the books of
his every-day reading. With Coloured
Frontispiece. Cr. 8vo, cl. extra, 7s. 6d.

Thomas (Bertha), Novels by.
Crown 8vo, cloth extra, 3s. 6d. each;
post 8vo, illustrated boards, 2s. each.
   Cressida.
   Proud Maisie.
   The Violin-Player.

Thomas (M.).—A Fight for
A Novel. By W. MOY THOMAS
8vo, illustrated boards, 2s.

Thomson's Seasons and Cas
of Indolence. With a Biograph
and Critical Introduction by AL
CUNNINGHAM, and over 50 fine Illus
tions on Steel and Wood. Crown 8
cloth extra, gilt edges, 7s. 6d.

Thornbury (Walter), Works
Haunted London. Edited by
WARD WALFORD, M.A. With Il
trations by F. W. FAIRHOLT, F.
Crown 8vo, cloth extra, 7s. 6d.
The Life and Correspondence
J. M. W. Turner. Founded u
Letters and Papers furnished by
Friends and fellow Academici
With numerous Illusts. in Colo
facsimiled from Turner's Orig
Drawings. Cr. 8vo, cl. extra, 7s.
Old Stories Re-told. Post 8vo, cl
limp, 2s. 6d.
Tales for the Marines. Post 8
illustrated boards, 2s.

Timbs (John), Works by:
The History of Clubs and Club
in London. With Anecdotes of
Famous Coffee-houses, Hostelr
and Taverns. With numerous Il
trations. Cr. 8vo, cloth extra, 7s.
English Eccentrics and Ecc
tricities: Stories of Wealth
Fashion, Delusions, Impostures,
Fanatic Missions, Strange Sig
and Sporting Scenes, Eccen
Artists, Theatrical Folks, Men
Letters, &c. With nearly 50 Illu
Crown 8vo, cloth extra, 7s. 6d.

Torrens. — The Marqu
Wellesley, Architect of Empire.
Historic Portrait. By W. M. T
RENS, M.P. Demy 8vo, cloth extra,

Trollope (Anthony), Novels
Crown 8vo, cloth extra, 3s. 6d. ea
post 8vo, illustrated boards, 2s. eac
   The Way We Live Now.
   The American Senator.
   Kept in the Dark.
   Frau Frohmann.
   Marion Fay.

Crown 8vo, cloth extra, 3s. 6d. eac
   Mr. Scarborough's Family.
   The Land-Leaguers.

Trollope (Frances E.), Novels
Like Ships upon the Sea. Cro
8vo, cloth extra, 3s. 6d.; post 8
illustrated boards, 2s.
Mabel's Progress. Crown 8vo, cl
extra, 3s. 6d.
Anne Furness. Cr. 8vo, cl. ex., 3s.

Trollope (T. A.).—Diamond Cut Diamond, and other Stories. By THOMAS ADOLPHUS TROLLOPE. Crown 8vo, cloth extra, 3s. 6d.; post 8vo, illustrated boards, 2s.

Tytler (Sarah), Novels by: Crown 8vo, cloth extra, 3s. 6d. each; post 8vo, illustrated boards, 2s. each. **What She Came Through. The Bride's Pass.**

Saint Mungo's City. Three Vols., crown 8vo.

Beauty and the Beast. Three Vols., crown 8vo. [*Shortly.*]

Tytler (C. C. Fraser-). — Mistress Judith: A Novel. By C. C. FRASER-TYTLER. Crown 8vo, cloth extra, 3s. 6d.

Van Laun.—History of French Literature. By HENRY VAN LAUN. Complete in Three Vols., demy 8vo, cloth boards, 7s. 6d. each.

Villari.— A Double Bond: A Story. By LINDA VILLARI. Fcap. 8vo, picture cover, 1s.

Walcott.— Church Work and Life in English Minsters; and the English Student's Monasticon. By the Rev. MACKENZIE E. C. WALCOTT, B.D. Two Vols., crown 8vo, cloth extra, with Map and Ground-Plans, 14s.

Walford (Edw., M.A.),Works by: The County Families of the United Kingdom. Containing Notices of the Descent, Birth, Marriage, Education, &c., of more than 12,000 distinguished Heads of Families, their Heirs Apparent or Presumptive, the Offices they hold or have held, their Town and Country Addresses, Clubs, &c. Twenty-fourth Annual Edition, for 1884, cloth, full gilt, 50s.

The Shilling Peerage (1884). Containing an Alphabetical List of the House of Lords, Dates of Creation, Lists of Scotch and Irish Peers, Addresses, &c. 32mo, cloth, 1s. Published annually.

The Shilling Baronetage (1884). Containing an Alphabetical List of the Baronets of the United Kingdom, short Biographical Notices, Dates of Creation, Addresses, &c. 32mo, cloth, 1s. Published annually.

The Shilling Knightage (1884). Containing an Alphabetical List of the Knights of the United Kingdom, short Biographical Notices, Dates of Creation, Addresses, &c. 32mo, cloth, 1s. Published annually.

WALFORD'S (EDW., M.A.) WORKS, *con.*—
The Shilling House of Commons (1884). Containing a List of all the Members of the British Parliament, their Town and Country Addresses, &c. 32mo, cloth, 1s. Published annually.

The Complete Peerage, Baronetage, Knightage, and House of Commons (1884). In One Volume, royal 32mo, cloth extra, gilt edges, 5s. Published annually.

Haunted London. By WALTER THORNBURY. Edited by EDWARD WALFORD, M.A. With Illustrations by F. W. FAIRHOLT, F.S.A. Crown 8vo, cloth extra, 7s. 6d.

Walton and Cotton's Complete Angler; or, The Contemplative Man's Recreation; being a Discourse of Rivers, Fishponds, Fish and Fishing, written by IZAAK WALTON; and Instructions how to Angle for a Trout or Grayling in a clear Stream, by CHARLES COTTON. With Original Memoirs and Notes by Sir HARRIS NICOLAS, and 61 Copperplate Illustrations. Large crown 8vo, cloth antique, 7s. 6d.

Wanderer's Library, The: Crown 8vo, cloth extra, 3s. 6d. each. Wanderings In Patagonia; or, Life among the Ostrich Hunters. By JULIUS BEERBOHM. Illustrated.
Camp Notes: Stories of Sport and Adventure in Asia, Africa, and America. By FREDERICK BOYLE.
Savage Life. By FREDERICK BOYLE.
Merrie England In the Olden Time. By GEORGE DANIEL. With Illustrations by ROBT. CRUIKSHANK.
Circus Life and Circus Celebrities. By THOMAS FROST.
The Lives of the Conjurers. By THOMAS FROST.
The Old Showmen and the Old London Fairs. By THOMAS FROST.
Low-Life Deeps. An Account of the Strange Fish to be found there. By JAMES GREENWOOD.
The Wilds of London. By JAMES GREENWOOD.
Tunis: The Land and the People. By the Chevalier de HESSE-WARTEGG. With 22 Illustrations.
The Life and Adventures of a Cheap Jack. By One of the Fraternity. Edited by CHARLES HINDLEY.
The World Behind the Scenes. By PERCY FITZGERALD.
Tavern Anecdotes and Sayings; Including the Origin of Signs, and Reminiscences connected with Taverns, Coffee Houses, Clubs, &c. By CHARLES HINDLEY. With Illusts.

WANDERER'S LIBRARY, THE, *continued—*

The Genial Showman: Life and Adventures of Artemus Ward. By E. P. HINGSTON. With a Frontispiece.

The Story of the London Parks. By JACOB LARWOOD. With Illustrations.

London Characters. By HENRY MAYHEW. Illustrated.

Seven Generations of Executioners: Memoirs of the Sanson Family (1688 to 1847). Edited by HENRY SANSON.

Summer Cruising in the South Seas. By CHARLES WARREN STODDARD. Illustrated by WALLIS MACKAY.

Warner.—A Roundabout Journey. By CHARLES DUDLEY WARNER, Author of "My Summer in a Garden." Crown 8vo, cloth extra, 6s.

Warrants, &c. :—

Warrant to Execute Charles I. An exact Facsimile, with the Fifty-nine Signatures, and corresponding Seals. Carefully printed on paper to imitate the Original, 22 in. by 14 in. Price 2s.

Warrant to Execute Mary Queen of Scots. An exact Facsimile, including the Signature of Queen Elizabeth, and a Facsimile of the Great Seal. Beautifully printed on paper to imitate the Original MS. Price 2s.

Magna Charta. An exact Facsimile of the Original Document in the British Museum, printed on fine plate paper, nearly 3 feet long by 2 feet wide, with the Arms and Seals emblazoned in Gold and Colours. Price 5s.

The Roll of Battle Abbey; or, A List of the Principal Warriors who came over from Normandy with William the Conqueror, and Settled in this Country, A.D. 1066-7. With the principal Arms emblazoned in Gold and Colours. Price 5s.

Weather, How to Foretell the, with the Pocket Spectroscope. By F. W. CORY, M.R.C.S. Eng., F.R.Met. Soc., &c. With 10 Illustrations. Crown 8vo, 1s.; cloth, 1s. 6d.

Westropp.—Handbook of Pottery and Porcelain; or, History of those Arts from the Earliest Period. By HODDER M. WESTROFF. With numerous Illustrations, and a List of

Whistler v. Ruskin: Art a Art Critics. By J. A. MACNEI WHISTLER. Seventh Edition, squa 8vo, 1s.

White's Natural History Selborne. Edited, with Additions, THOMAS BROWN, F.L.S. Post 8 cloth limp, 2s.

Williams (W. Mattieu, F.R.A.S Works by:

Science Notes. See the GENTLEMA MAGAZINE. 1s. Monthly.

Science in Short Chapters. Cro 8vo, cloth extra, 7s. 6d.

A Simple Treatise on Heat. Cro 8vo, cloth limp, with Illusts., 2s. 6

The Chemistry of Cookery. Cro 8vo, cloth extra, 6s. *[In the pre*

Wilson (Dr. Andrew, F.R.S.E Works by:

Chapters on Evolution: A Popu History of the Darwinian a Allied Theories of Developme Second Edition. Crown 8vo, clc extra, with 259 Illustrations, 7s. 6d

Leaves from a Naturalist's No book. Post 8vo, cloth limp, 2s. 6d

Leisure-Time Studies, chiefly B logical. Third Edition, with a N Preface. Crown 8vo, cloth ext with Illustrations, 6s.

Winter (J. S.), Stories by : Crown 8vo, cloth extra, 3s. 6d. eac post 8vo, illustrated boards, 2s. ea

Cavalry Life. | Regimental Legen

Wood.—Sabina: A Novel. Lady WOOD. Post 8vo, illust. bd

Words, Facts, and Phrase A Dictionary of Curious, Quaint, a Out-of-the-Way Matters. By ELIEZ EDWARDS. New and cheaper iss cr. 8vo, cl ex., 7s. 6d. ; half-bound, 9

Wright (Thomas), Works by Caricature History of the Georg (The House of Hanover.) With Pictures, Caricatures, Squibs, Bro sides, Window Pictures, &c. Cro 8vo, cloth extra, 7s. 6d.

History of Caricature and of t Grotesque in Art, Literatu Sculpture, and Painting. Profus Illustrated by F. W. FAIRHO F.S.A. Large post 8vo, cl. ex., 7s.

Yat   d), Novels by
Po   ted boards, 2s. eac
C   The Forlorn Ho

NOVELS BY THE BEST AUTHORS.

Now in the press.

WILKIE COLLINS'S NEW NOVEL.

"I Say No." By WILKIE COLLINS. Three Vols., crown 8vo.

Mrs. CASHEL HOEY'S NEW NOVEL

The Lover's Creed. By Mrs. CASHEL HOEY, Author of "The Blossoming of an Aloe," &c. With 12 Illustrations by P. MACNAB. Three Vols., crown 8vo.

SARAH TYTLER'S NEW NOVEL.

Beauty and the Beast. By SARAH TYTLER, Author of "The Bride's Pass," "Saint Mungo's City," "Citoyenne Jacqueline," &c. Three Vols., cr. 8vo.

CHARLES GIBBON'S NEW NOVEL.

By Mead and Stream. By CHARLES GIBBON, Author of "Robin Gray," "The Golden Shaft," "Queen of the Meadow," &c. Three Vols., cr. 8vo.

ROBT. BUCHANAN'S NEW NOVE

Foxglove Manor. By ROBT. BUCHANA uthor of "The Shadow of the Sword, AGod and the Man," &c. Three Vols crown 8vo.

BASIL'S NEW NOVEL.

"The Wearing of the Green." B BASIL, Author of "Love the Debt, "A Drawn Game," &c. Three Vols crown 8vo.

JULIAN HAWTHORNE'S NEW STORIES.

Mercy Holland, and other Stories. B J. HAWTHORNE, Author of "Garth, "Beatrix Randolph," &c. Three Vols crown 8vo.

NEW NOVEL BY CECIL POWER

Philistia. By CECIL POWER. Thre Vols., crown 8vo.

THE PICCADILLY NOVELS.

Popular Stories by the Best Authors. LIBRARY EDITIONS, many Illustrated, crown 8vo, cloth extra, 3s. 6d. each.

BY MRS. ALEXANDER.

Maid, Wife, or Widow?

BY W. BESANT & JAMES RICE.

Ready-Money Mortiboy.
My Little Girl.
The Case of Mr. Lucraft.
This Son of Vulcan.
With Harp and Crown.
The Golden Butterfly.
By Celia's Arbour.
The Monks of Thelema.
'Twas in Trafalgar's Bay.
The Seamy Side.
The Ten Years' Tenant.
The Chaplain of the Fleet.

BY WALTER BESANT.

All Sorts and Conditions of Men.
The Captains' Room.
All in a Garden Fair.

BY ROBERT BUCHANAN.

A Child of Nature.
God and the Man.
The Shadow of the Sword.
The Martyrdom of Madeline.
Love Me for Ever.
Annan Water.
The New Abelard.

BY MRS. H. LOVETT CAMERON.

Deceivers Ever.

BY MORTIMER COLLINS.

Sweet Anne Page.
Transmigration.
From Midnight to Midnight.

MORTIMER & FRANCES COLLIN

Blacksmith and Scholar.
The Village Comedy.
You Play me False.

BY WILKIE COLLINS.

Antonina.	New Magdalen.
Basil.	The Frozen Dee
Hide and Seek.	The Law and th
The Dead Secret.	Lady.
Queen of Hearts.	TheTwo Destinie
My Miscellanies.	Haunted Hotel.
Woman in White.	The Fallen Leave
The Moonstone.	Jezebel'sDaughte
Man and Wife.	The Black Robe,
Poor Miss Finch.	Heart and Scienc
Miss or Mrs.?	

BY DUTTON COOK.

Paul Foster's Daughter

BY WILLIAM CYPLES.

Hearts of Gold.

BY ALPHONSE DAUDET.

Port Salvation.

BY JAMES DE MILLE.

A Castle in Spain.

BY J. LEITH DERWENT.

PICCADILLY NOVELS, *continued—*
BY E. C. PRICE.
Valentina. | The Foreigners.

BY CHARLES READE, D.C.L.
It is Never Too Late to Mend.
Hard Cash. | Peg Woffington.
Christie Johnstone.
Griffith Gaunt.
The Double Marriage.
Love Me Little, Love Me Long.
Foul Play.
The Cloister and the Hearth.
The Course of True Love.
The Autobiography of a Thief.
Put Yourself in His Place.
A Terrible Temptation.
The Wandering Heir. | A Simpleton.
A Woman-Hater. | Readiana.

BY MRS. J. H. RIDDELL.
Her Mother's Darling.
Prince of Wales's Garden-Party.

BY F. W. ROBINSON.
Women are Strange.
The Hands of Justice.

BY JOHN SAUNDERS.
Bound to the Wheel.
Guy Waterman.
One Against the World.
The Lion in the Path.
The Two Dreamers.

BY KATHARINE SAUNDERS.
Joan Merryweather
Margaret and Elizabeth.
Gideon's Rock. | The High Mills.

PICCADILLY NOVELS, *continued—*
BY T. W. SPEIGHT.
The Mysteries of Heron Dyke.

BY R. A. STERNDALE.
The Afghan Knife.

BY BERTHA THOMAS.
Proud Maisie. | Cressida.
The Violin-Player.

BY ANTHONY TROLLOPE.
The Way we Live Now.
The American Senator.
Frau Frohmann.
Marion Fay.
Kept in the Dark.
Mr. Scarborough's Family.
The Land-Leaguers.

BY FRANCES E. TROLLOPE.
Like Ships upon the Sea.
Anne Furness.
Mabel's Progress.

BY T. A. TROLLOPE.
Diamond Cut Diamond.

By IVAN TURGENIEFF and Others
Stories from Foreign Novelists.

BY SARAH TYTLER.
What She Came Through.
The Bride's Pass.

BY C. C. FRASER-TYTLER.
Mistress Judith.

BY J. S. WINTER.
Cavalry Life.
Regimental Legends.

CHEAP EDITIONS OF POPULAR NOVELS.
Post 8vo, illustrated boards, 2s. each.

BY EDMOND ABOUT.
The Fellah.

BY HAMILTON AÏDÉ.
Carr of Carrlyon. | Confidences.

BY MRS. ALEXANDER.
Maid, Wife, or Widow?

BY SHELSLEY BEAUCHAMP.
Grantley Grange.

BY W. BESANT & JAMES RICE.
Ready-Money Mortiboy.
With Harp and Crown.
This Son of Vulcan. | My Little Girl.
The Case of Mr. Lucraft.
The Golden Butterfly.

By BESANT AND RICE, *continued—*
The Monks of Thelema.
'Twas in Trafalgar's Bay.
The Seamy Side.
The Ten Years' Tenant.
The Chaplain of the Fleet.

BY WALTER BESANT.
All Sorts and Conditions of Men.
The Captains' Room.

BY FREDERICK BOYLE.
Camp Notes. | Savage Life.

BY BRET HARTE.
An Heiress of Red Dog.
The Luck of Roaring Camp.
Californian Stories.

CHEAP POPULAR NOVELS, *continued—*

BY ROBERT BUCHANAN.
The Shadow of the Sword.
A Child of Nature.
God and the Man.
The Martyrdom of Madeline.
Love Me for Ever.

BY MRS. BURNETT.
Surly Tim.

BY MRS. LOVETT CAMERON.
Deceivers Ever. | Juliet's Guardian.

BY MACLAREN COBBAN.
The Cure of Souls.

BY C. ALLSTON COLLINS.
The Bar Sinister.

BY WILKIE COLLINS.

Antonina.	Miss or Mrs.?
Basil.	The New Magda-
Hide and Seek.	len.
The Dead Secret.	The Frozen Deep.
Queen of Hearts.	Law and the Lady.
My Miscellanies.	The Two Destinies
Woman In. White.	Haunted Hotel.
The Moonstone.	The Fallen Leaves.
Man and Wife.	Jezebel's Daughter
Poor Miss Finch.	The Black Robe.

BY MORTIMER COLLINS.
Sweet Anne Page.
Transmigration.
From Midnight to Midnight.
A Fight with Fortune.

MORTIMER & FRANCES COLLINS.
Sweet and Twenty. | Frances.
Blacksmith and Scholar.
The Village Comedy.
You Play me False.

BY DUTTON COOK.
Leo. | Paul Foster's Daughter.

BY J. LEITH DERWENT.
Our Lady of Tears.

BY CHARLES DICKENS.
Sketches by Boz.
The Pickwick Papers.
Oliver Twist.
Nicholas Nickleby.

BY MRS. ANNIE EDWARDES.
A Point of Honour. | Archie Lovell.

BY M. BETHAM-EDWARDS.
Felicia. | Kitty.

BY EDWARD EGGLESTON.
Roxy.

CHEAP POPULAR NOVELS, *continued*

BY PERCY FITZGERALD.
Bella Donna. | Never Forgotte
The Second Mrs. Tillotson.
Polly.
Seventy-five Brooke Street.
The Lady of Brantome.

BY ALBANY DE FONBLANQ
Filthy Lucre.

BY R. E. FRANCILLON.
Olympia. | Queen Cophe
One by One.

Prefaced by Sir H. BARTLE FRE
Pandurang Hari.

BY HAIN FRISWELL.
One of Two.

BY EDWARD GARRETT.
The Capel Girls.

BY CHARLES GIBBON.

Robin Gray.	Queen of the
For Lack of Gold.	dow.
What will the	In Pastures G
World Say?	The Flower of
In Honour Bound.	Forest.
The Dead Heart.	A Heart's Prob
In Love and War.	The Braes of
For the King.	row.

BY WILLIAM GILBERT.
Dr. Austin's Guests.
The Wizard of the Mountain.
James Duke.

BY JAMES GREENWOOD.
Dick Temple.

BY ANDREW HALLIDAY.
Every-Day Papers.

BY LADY DUFFUS HARDY
Paul Wynter's Sacrifice.

BY THOMAS HARDY.
Under the Greenwood Tree.

BY JULIAN HAWTHORNE.

Garth.	Sebastian Str
Ellice Quentin.	Dust.
Prince Saroni's Wife.	

BY SIR ARTHUR HELPS.
Ivan de Biron.

BY TOM HOOD.
A Golden Heart.

BY MRS. GEORGE HOOPER
The House of Raby.

BY VICTOR HUGO.
The Hunchback of Notre Dam

CHEAP POPULAR NOVELS, *continued*—

BY MRS. ALFRED HUNT.
Thornicroft's Model.
The Leaden Casket.
Self-Condemned.

BY JEAN INGELOW.
Fated to be Free.

BY HARRIETT JAY.
The Dark Colleen.
The Queen of Connaught.

BY HENRY KINGSLEY.
Oakshott Castle. | Number Seventeen

BY E. LYNN LINTON.
Patricia Kemball.
The Atonement of Leam Dundas.
The World Well Lost.
Under which Lord?
With a Silken Thread.
The Rebel of the Family.
"My Love!"

BY HENRY W. LUCY.
Gideon Fleyce.

BY JUSTIN McCARTHY, M.P.
Dear Lady Disdain.
The Waterdale Neighbours.
My Enemy's Daughter.
A Fair Saxon.
Linley Rochford.
Miss Misanthrope.
Donna Quixote.
The Comet of a Season.

BY GEORGE MACDONALD.
Paul Faber, Surgeon.
Thomas Wingfold, Curate.

BY MRS. MACDONELL.
Quaker Cousins.

BY KATHARINE S. MACQUOID.
The Evil Eye. | Lost Rose.

BY W. H. MALLOCK.
The New Republic.

BY FLORENCE MARRYAT.
Open! Sesame! | A Little Stepson.
A Harvest of Wild | Fighting the Air.
Oats. | Written in Fire.

BY J. MASTERMAN.
Half-a-dozen Daughters.

BY JEAN MIDDLEMASS.
Touch and Go. | Mr. Dorillon.

CHEAP POPULAR NOVELS, *continued*—

BY D. CHRISTIE MURRAY.
A Life's Atonement.
A Model Father.
Joseph's Coat.
Coals of Fire.
By the Gate of the Sea.

BY MRS. OLIPHANT.
Whiteladies.

BY MRS. ROBERT O'REILLY.
Phœbe's Fortunes.

BY OUIDA.
Held in Bondage. | Two Little Wooden Shoes.
Strathmore. | Signa.
Chandos. | In a Winter City.
Under Two Flags. | Ariadne.
Idalia. | Friendship.
Cecil Castle- | Moths.
maine. | Pipistrello.
Tricotrin. | A Village Com-
Puck. | mune.
Folle Farine. | Bimbi.
A Dog of Flanders. | In Maremma.
Pascarel. |

BY MARGARET AGNES PAUL.
Gentle and Simple.

BY JAMES PAYN.
Lost Sir Massing- | Like Father, Like
berd. | Son.
A Perfect Trea- | A Marine Resi-
sure. | dence.
Bentinck's Tutor. | Married Beneath
Murphy's Master. | Him.
A County Family. | Mirk Abbey.
At Her Mercy. | Not Wooed, but
A Woman's Ven- | Won.
geance. | £200 Reward.
Cecil's Tryst. | Less Black than
Clyffards of Clyffe | We're Painted.
The Family Scape- | By Proxy.
grace. | Under One Roof.
Foster Brothers. | High Spirits.
Found Dead. | Carlyon's Year.
Best of Husbands | A Confidential
Walter's Word. | Agent.
Halves. | Some Private
Fallen Fortunes. | Views.
What He Cost Her | From Exile.
Humorous Stories | A Grape from a
Gwendoline's Har- | Thorn.
vest. | For Cash Only.

BY EDGAR A. POE.
The Myst of M rie Ro at

CHEAP POPULAR NOVELS, *continued—*

BY E. C. PRICE.
Valentina.

BY CHARLES READE.
It is Never Too Late to Mend.
Hard Cash.
Peg Woffington.
Christie Johnstone.
Griffith Gaunt.
Put Yourself in His Place.
The Double Marriage.
Love Me Little, Love Me Long.
Foul Play.
The Cloister and the Hearth.
The Course of True Love.
Autobiography of a Thief.
A Terrible Temptation.
The Wandering Heir.
A Simpleton.
A Woman-Hater.
Readiana.

BY MRS. J. H. RIDDELL.
Her Mother's Darling.
Prince of Wales's Garden Party.

BY F. W. ROBINSON.
Women are Strange.

BY BAYLE ST. JOHN
A Levantine Family.

BY GEORGE AUGUSTUS SALA.
Gaslight and Daylight.

BY JOHN SAUNDERS.
Bound to the Wheel.
One Against the World.
Guy Waterman.
The Lion in the Path.
Two Dreamers.

BY ARTHUR SKETCHLEY.
A Match in the Dark.

BY T. W. SPEIGHT.
The Mysteries of Heron Dyke.

BY R. A. STERNDALE.
The Afghan Knife.

BY R. LOUIS STEVENSON.
New Arabian Nights.

BY BERTHA THOMAS.
Cressida. | Proud Maisie.
The Violin-Player.

CHEAP POPULAR NOVELS, *continued*

BY WALTER THORNBURY.
Tales for the Marines.

BY T. ADOLPHUS TROLLOPE
Diamond Cut Diamond.

BY ANTHONY TROLLOPE.
The Way We Live Now
The American Senator.
Frau Frohmann.
Marion Fay.
Kept in the Dark.

By FRANCES ELEANOR TROLLO
Like Ships upon the Sea.

BY MARK TWAIN.
Tom Sawyer.
An Idle Excursion.
A Pleasure Trip on the Contine
of Europe.
A Tramp Abroad.
The Stolen White Elephant.

BY SARAH TYTLER.
What She Came Through.
The Bride's Pass.

BY J. S. WINTER.
Cavalry Life. | Regimental Legen

BY LADY WOOD.
Sabina.

BY EDMUND YATES.
Castaway. | The Forlorn Hope
Land at Last.

ANONYMOUS.
Paul Ferroll.
Why Paul Ferroll Killed his Wife

Fcap. 8vo, picture covers, 1s. each.
Jeff Briggs's Love Story. By BR
  HARTE.
The Twins of Table Mountain.
  BRET HARTE.
Mrs. Gainsborough's Diamonds.
  JULIAN HAWTHORNE.
Kathleen Mavourneen. By Auth
  of "That Lass o' Lowrie's."
Lindsay's Luck. By the Author
  "That Lass o' Lowrie's."
Pretty Polly Pemberton. By t
  Author of "That Lass o' Lowrie's
Trooping with Crows. By M
  PIRKIS.
The Professor's Wife. By LEONA
  GRAHAM.
A Double Bond. By LINDA VILLA

Lightning Source UK Ltd.
Milton Keynes UK
UKHW020823291118
333183UK00011B/832/P